A HISTORY OF THE WORLD IN 500 PEOPLE

A HISTORY OF THE WORLD IN 500 PEOPLE

San Diego, California

Thunder Bay Press
An imprint of Printers Row Publishing Group
9717 Pacific Heights Blvd, San Diego, CA 92121
www.thunderbaybooks.com • mail@thunderbaybooks.com

Copyright © 2024 Quarto Publishing plc

All rights reserved. No part of this publication may be reproduced, distributed, or transmitted in any form or by any means, including photocopying, recording, or other electronic or mechanical methods, without the prior written permission of the publisher, except in the case of brief quotations embodied in critical reviews and certain other noncommercial uses permitted by copyright law.

Printers Row Publishing Group is a division of Readerlink Distribution Services, LLC.
Thunder Bay Press is a registered trademark of Readerlink Distribution Services, LLC.

Correspondence regarding the content of this book should be sent to Thunder Bay Press, Editorial Department, at the above address. All other inquiries should be addressed to The Bright Press at the address below.

Thunder Bay Press
Publisher: Peter Norton
Associate Publisher: Ana Parker
Editor: Dan Mansfield

Library of Congress Control Number: 2023948104

ISBN: 978-1-6672-0521-2

Conceived, designed, and produced by
The Bright Press, an imprint of the Quarto Group,
1 Triptych Place, London SE1 9SH,
United Kingdom
www.quarto.com

Publisher: James Evans
Editorial Directors: Isheeta Mustafi, Anna Southgate
Art Director: James Lawrence
Managing Editor: Jacqui Sayers
Senior Editor: Joanna Bentley
Project Editor: Julie Brooke
Design: Tony Seddon
Picture Research: Katie Greenwood

Printed in Malaysia

27 26 25 24 23 1 2 3 4 5

CONTENTS

Introduction 6

1 Ancient and Classical World **2700 BC–AD 500** 10

2 The Age of Chivalry and the Renaissance **500–1500** 88

3 Exploration and Revolution **1500–1799** 160

4 Industries and Empires **1800–1899** 224

5 Modern and Postmodern **1900–present** 302

Index 392

Picture Credits 400

INTRODUCTION

How do we make sense of history? Some may agree with Scottish essayist Thomas Carlyle, who wrote in 1841 that "The history of the world is but the biography of great men"—though we would want to adapt the phrase to the modern era by including women and changing "men" to "people." But others may feel that history is really driven by the spread of technologies such as weapons or factories, the birth and spread of philosophical ideas and religions, and class or race conflict.

As is clear from its title, this book has a biographical focus, but it also sets out to capture these other elements beyond the "great men" timeline, to write a history not only of people who conquered, or governed, or achieved great scientific breakthroughs, but also of those who responded to trauma and drove protest movements, who promoted peace, and worked for the emancipation of the downtrodden.

It seeks out different perspectives, attempting to incorporate the histories of Indigenous peoples in the Americas and Australasia, of Black Americans, and of Africa, Japan, China, Korea, India, and Afghanistan, for example, as well as Europe and European Americans and Australians. It includes women who were in power, and culturally or intellectually active, across the centuries who are sometimes overshadowed; interrogates the slave trade and the efforts to abolish it; as well as the history of civil rights, women's rights, the environmental movement, and the labor movement.

The 500 chosen individuals are in fourteen categories—royalty, religious leader, artist, political leader, philosopher, military leader, scientist, explorer, activist, industrialist, inventor, entertainer, athlete, and entrepreneur. The book is divided into five chronological chapters, with individuals ordered by date of birth.

The first, "Ancient and Classical World," travels from the dawn of history to the collapse of the Roman empire in the fifth century AD. In a period of major developments in philosophy, science, and culture, when the first societies emerge, most entries are **royals, religious leaders, philosophers, military leaders, scientists,** and **artists**. Familiar "great men" such as Homer, Plato, Aristotle, Alexander the Great, and Julius Caesar share space with women poets Enheduanna and Sappho, possibly lesser-known figures such as Chinese scholars Gongsun Long and Sima Qian, and rulers including King Ezana of the African kingdom of Axum and Theodora, powerful consort of Justinian I of Byzantium.

The next chapter, "The Age of Chivalry and the Renaissance," passes from the classical almost to the dawn of the modern world. The Prophet Muhammad establishes the world religion of Islam, while in Europe the nun St. Hildegard of Bingen, anchoress Julian of Norwich, and poet Marie de France make their

LEFT: Julius Caesar was a gifted military leader, whose ambition led him to become dictator of Rome.

INTRODUCTION **7**

voices heard, despite the din raised by Pope Urban II, who unleashes centuries of bloody conflict and brings the worlds of West and East into (ultimately fruitful) collision by calling the First Crusade. Meanwhile great figures of the Islamic world such as Muhammad ibn Mūsā al-Khwārizmī, Abu Rayhan al-Biruni, and Avicenna make an enduring mark. The category of **explorer** is used for the first time for Icelander Leif Erikson, the first European to reach North America. Elsewhere, queen Seondeok of Silla in Korea, Kublai Khan in China, and Sundiata Keita in Mali are in power—while Gebre Mesquel Lalibela, hearing of the capture of the holy city of Jerusalem by Saladin (Salad ad-Din Yusuf ibn Ayyub) during the crusades, builds a New Jerusalem in Ethiopia.

In the third chapter, "Exploration and Revolution," centuries of exploration and colonization foster greed and the creation of the slave trade. A new category of **activist** marks early efforts to fight back, from figures such as Gaspar Yanga and abolitionist Olaudah Equiano. Mary Wollstonecraft's *A Vindication of the Rights of Woman* marks the first green shoots of feminism. An age of revolts against authority sees not only the French Revolution and the establishment of the United States, but the slave rebellion under Toussaint Louverture that leads to the creation of Haiti.

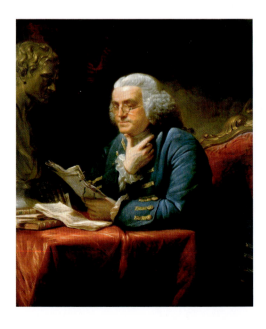

"There never was a good war or a bad peace."

Benjamin Franklin in a letter to
Sir Joseph Banks, 1783

RIGHT: As well as being one of the Founding Fathers of the United States, Benjamin Franklin was a writer, inventor, scientist, and publisher.

As the decades move forward we come to "Industries and Empires." Indigenous peoples fight back against their colonizers, with figures such as Vicente Guererro of Mexico, first Black president in the Americas, Tecumseh of the Shawnee, and John Ross and Sequoyah of the Cherokee. In the U.S., great women such as Sojourner Truth and Harriet Tubman are leaders of the struggle against slavery, and Elizabeth Cady Stanton works tirelessly to win women the right to vote. In a fast-changing society, new categories are needed: **industrialist** introduces steel magnate Andrew Carnegie and motor car pioneer Henry Ford, and **inventor**, Alexander Graham Bell, developer of the telephone, and Thomas Edison, creator of the phonograph (record player) and incandescent lightbulb.

The twentieth century sees the rise of a new industry, that of entertainment, and, in the chapter called "Modern and Postmodern," artists such as Alice Guy-Blaché, the first woman to direct a movie, and Fatma Begum, the first Indian woman movie director, share space with a new category of **entertainer**—figures including Hattie McDaniel, Elvis Presley, and Taylor Swift—and **athletes**, from Jesse Owens through Jackie Robinson and Muhammad Ali, to Michael Jordan and Serena Williams. The world is transformed by the invention of the internet, the personal computer, and online interaction through **entrepreneurs** and figures such as Tim Berners-Lee, Steve Jobs, Mark Zuckerberg, and Jack Ma. The rise of the environmental movement is driven by changemakers including Rachel Carson, Wangari Maathi, and Winona LaDuke, all the way through to Greta Thunberg, while the struggle for gay and transgender rights includes Alan Turing, Harvey Milk, and Sylvia Rivera. Major figures in the arts include Frida Kahlo, I. M. Pei, Bob Marley, and the great James Baldwin.

"People are trapped in history and history is trapped in them." So wrote Baldwin in his 1953 essay "Stranger in the Village." Our daily actions and decisions make history, and we are shaped by what has gone before—we all have the past within us, sometimes in the form of inherited or simply "accepted" attitudes or prejudices. *A History of the World in 500 People* seeks to present a rounded picture of our planet's past. There is an urgent need to address the history we share.

1

Ancient and Classical World
2700 BC–AD 500

1 ARTIST

IMHOTEP

Memphis (now Mit Rahina), Egypt
c. 2700–2600 BC

Statesman, priest, and astrologer who was later worshipped as a god of medicine.

A man of many and varied talents, Imhotep was chancellor to Djoser (ruled 2630–2611 BC) and high priest of the sun god Ra. He was also the royal architect, and built the 200-foot-tall, four-sided step pyramid of Djoser in the Saqqara necropolis (city of the dead) in the ancient Egyptian city of Memphis. This was a tomb for the pharaoh and monument to his memory—and is the world's oldest building of hewn stone that is still standing. An inscription on a statue of Djoser at Saqqara identifies Imhotep as leader of the seers or magicians, as well as chief of the sculptors or architects. He was a trained scribe, and noted as an author of wisdom texts (ethical writings). Imhotep was also associated with healing, and subsequently revered as a god of medicine and identified with the ancient Greek medicine god Asclepius. In the Greco-Roman period of ancient Egyptian history (332 BC–AD 395) the sick slept overnight at his temples at Memphis and on the island of Philae in the river Nile at Aswan, in the belief that he would send them guidance and healing in their dreams.

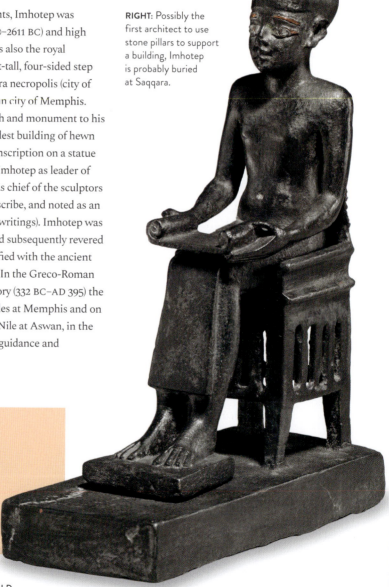

RIGHT: Possibly the first architect to use stone pillars to support a building, Imhotep is probably buried at Saqqara.

KNOWN FOR
- Being architect of the Saqqara step pyramid
- Becoming a god of medicine after being a physician
- Being the chief magician

2 ROYALTY

SARGON

Azupiranu, Mesopotamia (now Iraq)
r. 2334–2279 BC

Sargon rose from humble origins to become a great king in Mesopotamia. Tradition holds that he was found as a baby floating in a basket on the river and raised by a gardener, then became cupbearer to the king Ur-Zababa of Kish in ancient Sumer. After defeating Lugalzagesi of Uruk, he won victories over several Sumerian city-states, then expanded the empire into northern Syria, southern Anatolia, and Iran, where he even took control of the Elamites' capital of Susa. Archaeologists have never identified his capital, Akkad. He attributed his triumphs to the support of the goddess Ishtar.

3 RELIGIOUS LEADER

ENHEDUANNA

Mesopotamia (now Iraq)
c. 2300–2260 BC

Sumerian priestess of the moon god Nanna. She also wrote hymns and is the world's earliest author known by name.

The daughter of Sargon, ruler of Akkad, Enheduanna was appointed high priestess and wrote hymns, poems, and religious narratives. She is the earliest named author in history. Sargon entrusted his daughter with the position of high priestess in charge of worship of the moon god Nanna at Ur. She was viewed as a human form of Ningal, Nanna's wife, and thought to have been the author of a collection of temple hymns to Nanna as well as "Hymn to Inanna" and "The Exaltation of Inanna." After her, the role of high priestess was handed down in the royal family.

ABOVE: As high priestess, Enheduanna was ranked as highly as the king himself. Her writings are a forerunner of classical rhetoric.

> "She whips up wonder and chaos against all who disobey her, speeding carnage and inciting the ruinous floods, dressed in terrifying light."
>
> Enheduanna, "Hymn to Inanna," c. 2300 BC

4 ROYALTY

PEPI II NEFERKARE

Egypt
c. 2325–2150 BC

The son of Pepi I acceded to the throne at the age of six, following the death of his half-brother Merenre, and remarkably ruled for ninety-four years. He conducted military and trading expeditions to Nubia and Punt (Somalia), and issued decrees in support of the priests in Coptos (modern Qift) in Upper Egypt. Toward the end of his long reign, nomarchs (provincial governors) asserted their independence and the Sixth Dynasty—of which Pepi II was part—grew weak.

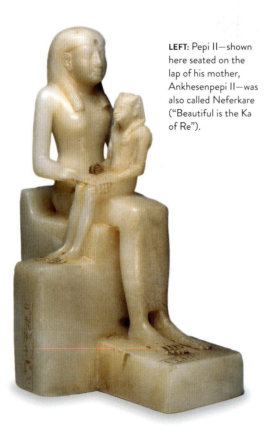

LEFT: Pepi II—shown here seated on the lap of his mother, Ankhesenpepi II—was also called Neferkare ("Beautiful is the Ka of Re").

5 RELIGIOUS LEADER

ABRAHAM

**Ur, Mesopotamia
(now Tell el-Muqayyar, Iraq)**
c. 2150–1975 BC

The founding father who established his people's special relationship with God.

Late in life, Abraham believed himself called by God to leave his home in Ur and settle in Canaan (Palestine and nearby) on the understanding that God had promised this land to his descendants and said they would become a great nation. Abraham's wife Sarah had been unable to have children, but now—despite Abraham being 100 years old—miraculously gave birth to a son, Isaac; Abraham also fathered a son, named Ishmael, with Sarah's maidservant Hagar. God then tested Abraham by demanding he offer Isaac as a ritual sacrifice; Abraham was prepared to obey but at the last moment an angel appeared and stopped him. Abraham is revered in Judaism as founder of the Jews' particular relationship with God and a prototype of virtuous behavior; in Islam as a prophet in the succession that runs from the first man, Adam, to the Prophet Muhammad; and in Christianity as a great patriarch, the father of believers. He was orginally called Abram, but God renamed him Abraham, which means "father of many."

RIGHT: Abraham, shown with Isaac, holds the weapon for the sacrifice of his son. For Christians, the event foreshadows God's sacrifice of Jesus.

6 ROYALTY

SOBEKNEFERU

Egypt
c. 1795–1756 BC

The last ruler of the Twelfth Dynasty was the first female pharaoh to rule as a woman. Unlike earlier possible female rulers such as Setibhor and Nitocris (Fifth and Sixth Dynasties), Sobekneferu did not try to have herself depicted as a man. She took the full royal title, and is represented in the complete monarchical regalia and in the same poses as male rulers.

7 ROYALTY

HAMMURABI

Babylon, Mesopotamia (now Iraq)
1792–c. 1750 BC

Hammurabi issued one of the first legal documents to emphasize the punishment of perpetrators rather than compensation of victims. It gave penalties for each crime. He said he received it from the Babylonian justice god, Shamash. The king also built an empire, defeating Elam and making the ruler of Assyria pay tribute.

8 RELIGIOUS LEADER

ZOROASTER

Airyanem Vaejah (now Iran)
c. 1575–1500 BC

This priest was the founder of a new religion and worshipped one god, Ahura Mazda.

A vision inspired Zoroaster to reject his native faith, in which many deities were revered, and proclaim a new religion based on worship of a single god, Ahura Mazda. Zoroaster rejected animal sacrifice, but kept rites of fire worship and wrote hymns collected in the *Gāthās* and the *Yasna Haptanghaiti*. The son of Pourusaspa, who was probably a nomad, Zoroaster likely began training as a priest aged seven, and left home at around twenty. In his vision, which he received aged thirty, he saw a bright being named Vohu Manah (Right Purpose) who taught him about Ahura Mazda (the Wise Lord). The purpose of humans was to align themselves with *asha* (truth/order) in the universe and resist *druj* (falsehood and deceit). Zoroaster converted a king named Vishtaspa and lived at the royal court, and the new faith, Zoroastrianism, became the state religion of Iran—especially under the Achaemenian Empire founded by Cyrus the Great in c. 550 BC—and is still followed by the Parsis today.

RIGHT: The religion Zoroaster founded was the world's first monotheistic faith and influenced Judaism, Christianity, and Islam.

HATSHEPSUT

Egypt
c. 1507–1458 BC

Female pharaoh Hatshepsut devoted her energies to temple building and expanding trade. She sent a celebrated expedition to Punt on the East African coast that brought back ebony, gold, animal skins, and baboons, as well as myrrh trees that were planted in the gardens at her temple in the Dayr al-Baḥri complex opposite Luxor.

BELOW: Hatshepsut married her half-brother Thutmose II. She was regent for her stepson Thutmose III, then took full control.

AMENHOTEP III

Egypt
r. 1390–1353 BC

Early in his reign, Amenhotep III issued commemorative medals in the form of scarab beetles to mark his hunting prowess. He built a magnificent mortuary temple in Thebes, with the famous Colossi of Memnon, and a temple in Nubia. His diplomatic exchanges, recorded in the Amarna Letters, included marriage negotiations with the Mitanni (in Syria), with Babylon, and with the Hittites.

ABOVE: Amenhotep III, shown with his mother Mutemwia, ruled at a time of great prosperity. His name means "[the god] Amun is satisfied."

11 ROYALTY

NEFERTITI

Thebes (now Luxor), Egypt
c. 1370–1330 BC

Queen who, with her husband Akhenaten, introduced the worship of a single god, the sun disc Aten.

Nefertiti and Akhenaten briefly changed the face of ancient Egyptian religious life, making the sun disc Aten the focus of worship and building a new religious center called Akhetaten (Tell el-Amarna). Aten was previously an aspect of the sun god Ra, but in his poem "Great Hymn to the Aten," Akhenaten declared Aten the creator of the world and giver of life. Later pharaohs Tutankhamun and Horemheb reversed this approach and reintroduced traditional worship. Nefertiti may originally have been a princess of the Mitanni Empire (northern Syria). She is celebrated as a paragon of beauty on account of the magnificent bust of her attributed to the sculptor Thutmose. Her name *nfr.t jj.tj* (which nowadays we give as Nefertiti) means "the beautiful one has come." With Akhenaten she had six daughters, two of whom became queens of Egypt. After her husband's death in 1336 BC she possibly ruled as pharaoh under the name Neferneferauten.

RIGHT: This world-famous bust of Nefertiti was discovered in the workshop of Akhenaten's official sculptor, Thutmose.

2700 BC–AD 500   19

12 RELIGIOUS LEADER

MOSES

Goshen, Egypt
1391–1271 BC

Inspirational leader who guided the Israelites out of slavery in Egypt toward the promised land.

Moses's Israelite mother Jochebed hid him in a basket on the river Nile, since Pharaoh had ordered a mass killing of infants. Found by Pharaoh's daughter, Moses was raised at the palace but had to flee after he killed an Egyptian who was beating a slave. On the slopes of Mount Sinai, Moses heard God's voice instructing him to return to Egypt, liberate the Israelites, and lead them to freedom. When Pharaoh refused to free the Israelites, God sent ten plagues on the country, culminating in the death of every firstborn son—the Israelites were instructed to mark their doors with a lamb's blood so God's angel of death would pass over them and let them live. Finally, Pharaoh told Moses and the Israelites to go, but then sent his army after them. Moses parted the Red Sea and, once the Israelites were safely across the waters, it flooded back, drowning their pursuers. The Israelites wandered in the desert for forty years. On Mount Sinai, Moses received the Ten Commandments from God. He died, aged 120, with the promised land within sight.

LEFT: Christians and Muslims celebrate Moses as a prophet. To Jews he is the great giver of laws, Moshe Rabbeinu (Moses, Our Teacher).

ABOVE RIGHT: Moses (left) leads the Israelites in a song of thanksgiving after God gave him the power to part the Red Sea.

KNOWN FOR
- Parting the Red Sea
- Receiving the Ten Commandments
- Possibly being the author of the Torah (the first five books of the Bible)

2700 BC–AD 500   21

13 ROYALTY

TUTANKHAMUN

Akhetaten (now Minya), Egypt
c. 1336–1327 BC

Tutankhamun became pharaoh aged eight or nine and died at eighteen or nineteen. In his short reign, he moved the capital back to Thebes from the new city of Akhetaten, and restored the traditional pantheon of gods after his father Akhenaten's brief religious revolution. Tutankhamun had a misshapen left foot and needed to walk with a cane—several were found in his tomb. The place of his tomb was forgotten, and it was never found by raiders. As a result, the full burial riches were not discovered until British archaeologist Howard Carter opened the tomb in 1922. They wowed all who saw them when they were exhibited.

RIGHT: Tutankhamun's golden funerary mask. He changed his name from Tutankhaten when he restored worship of the god Amun.

14 ROYALTY

RAMSES II

Egypt
c. 1303–1213 BC

Ramses fought the Battle of Kadesh against the Hittites in 1274 BC, the best-documented in the ancient world. It was inconclusive, and in 1269 BC he signed the first-known peace treaty, with the Hittite king Hattusili III. Ramses led military campaigns southward into Nubia, put down revolts in Syria, and reestablished Egyptian control in the eastern Mediterranean. He also built a new capital, Pi-Ramesses, in the Nile Delta, and several temples including the famous one at Abu Simbel (near the Egyptian border with Sudan).

ROYALTY

SOLOMON

Jerusalem, Judea (now Israel)
c. 1000 BC

This Israelite king built the First Temple in Jerusalem.

Solomon's mother Bathsheba, originally the wife of his father King David's general Uriah, worked with the prophet Nathan to have Solomon anointed as the successor to the throne ahead of his older half-brothers. Once king, Solomon eliminated all opposition and expanded the kingdom, using his heavy-hitting army with its powerful cavalry and chariots to win territory. He then established fortified royal cities to hold it, and created a great trading empire. In Jerusalem he built a city wall, a royal palace, and the First Temple on Mount Moriah—famous in its own right, and as the forerunner of Jerusalem's Second Temple, which was rebuilt in c. 515 BC and lasted until AD 70, when it was destroyed by the Romans. A story demonstrates Solomon's wisdom: When two women came to him, both claiming to be the mother of a baby, he suggested that the child be cut in two. One mother agreed, but the other said she would rather give up the baby. Solomon knew that the one who wanted to protect the baby must be the true mother and awarded the infant to her.

BELOW: In the classical world, King Solomon was celebrated as a magician and exorcist, and named on amulets and in seals.

16 ARTIST

HOMER

Ionia, Anatolia (now Izmir, Turkey)
b. *c.* 900 BC

Blind poet who wrote immortal epics.

The ancient Greeks celebrated Homer as the author of their great epic poems the *Iliad* and the *Odyssey*. These immortal poems were central to ancient Greek culture and education, and were a major influence on writers for centuries. Homer was said to be a blind, wandering poet who lived on the Greek island of Chios in the northern Aegean. Some of the stories about him were colorful—that he was the son of the river Meles and a nymph, Critheïs, and that he died on the island of Ios from despair after he was unable to answer a teasing riddle about lice set by some boys who were fishing.

BELOW: Blind, but open to the leadings of the Muse. Homer has been revered down the ages—the Italian poet Dante called him "poet sovereign."

17 ROYALTY

DAVID

Bethlehem, Judah (now Israel)
c. 1040–970 BC

David was a shepherd and harpist-poet who famously killed the giant Philistine warrior Goliath with a stone and sling. He brought the tribes of Israel together under one monarch, established the Judaean royal dynasty, made Jerusalem the capital, and brought the Ark of the Covenant into the city. In Judaism he is the ideal king and forerunner of the Messiah. He is celebrated as a poet and is credited as the author of the Bible's book of Psalms.

19 PHILOSOPHER

ANAXIMANDER

Miletus, Anatolia (now Balat, Turkey)
c. 610–546 BC

A Greek philosopher from Miletus in Ionia, Anatolia, Anaximander was a pioneering astronomer, physicist, and geographer who created one of the first world maps. He argued that the *apeiron* (the limitless or infinite) was the source and ultimate reality of all things in the cosmos. He was the pupil of Thales and may have taught Pythagoras.

18 ROYALTY

QUEEN OF SHEBA

Axum (now Ethiopia) or Saba (now Yemen)
975 BC

The Queen of Sheba, probably the Arabian kingdom of Saba, made a famous visit to the court of King Solomon in Jerusalem, bringing exotic spices, gold, and fabulous jewels in a great caravan. Biblical accounts say she came to test the king's wisdom, which was famed far and wide, and the royal pair became lovers and had a child. In Islamic tradition she is Bilqis, while Ethiopians call her Makeda and say that her kingdom was in Ethiopia—and her son by Solomon, Menelik, was the ancestor of the royal family that ruled to the time of Haile Selassie I (deposed in AD 1974).

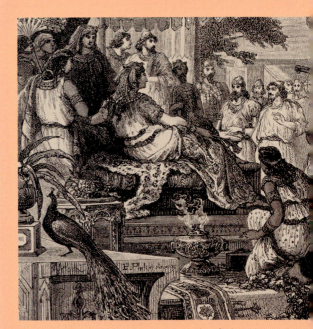

ABOVE: The Queen of Sheba is sometimes identified as the bride in the mystical "Song of Songs" in the Bible.

20　ROYALTY

NEBUCHADNEZZAR II

Babylon, Mesopotamia (now Iraq)
c. 630–561 BC

This Chaldean king destroyed the Jerusalem Temple and exiled the Jews.

Nebuchadnezzar was a brilliant general who expanded and consolidated the Neo-Babylonian (Chaldean) Empire his father and royal predecessor Nabopolassar had founded, conquering Palestine and Syria, and making the capital Babylon into a magnificent city celebrated throughout the ancient world. Before ascending the throne, he won a famous victory over Pharaoh Necho II at the Battle of Carchemish in 605 BC. As king, in 587 BC, he crushed the Kingdom of Judah, destroying the Temple and city of Jerusalem, and carrying its people off into captivity in Babylon, which is lamented in the Bible. The Jews called him "destroyer of nations." In Babylon he renovated the city's main processional way and built the beautiful Ishtar Gate in c. 575 BC. He also laid out the Hanging Gardens of Babylon, reputedly so that his wife Amytis, daughter of Astyages, king of the Medes, would be less homesick for her native land.

RIGHT: Nebuchadnezzar is shown conducting the siege of Jerusalem in a medieval edition of *The Antiquities of the Jews* by Roman-Jewish historian Josephus.

21 POLITICAL LEADER

SOLON

Athens, Greece
c. 630–560 BC

The Athenian poet, statesman, and lawmaker Solon ended rule by aristocrats in the city-state; introduced more humane legislation to replace the strict laws introduced by Draco; reformed the weights, measures, and coinage; and liberated citizens who had been enslaved for debt. He was celebrated as "Solon the lawmaker." After completing his reforms, he traveled abroad for ten years, to Egypt, where he was supposedly told the history of the lost civilization of Atlantis; to Cyprus; and to Lydia, where he gave the king, Croesus, the famous advice "Do not count a man happy until he is dead."

ABOVE: Solon. In one account, his brother Dropides was a direct ancestor of the philosopher Plato.

RIGHT: Sappho's poems are marked by their vividness and clear language. She remains an important influence on poets.

22 ARTIST

SAPPHO

Lesbos, Greece
c. 610–570 BC

Sappho was revered in the ancient world as one of its greatest poets and known as "the Tenth Muse." Her themes include the intimate education of young women in the arts of love and seduction in the *thiasos* (community) she led as a servant of Aphrodite, the Greek goddess of beauty and sexual love. Sappho is an icon of romantic and sexual love between women, and the word "lesbian" derives from the name of her home island of Lesbos. She was prolific, but of the 10,000 lines she wrote, only 650 lines—aside from *Ode to Aphrodite*, mostly fragments—survive. The poem calls on Aphrodite to help the poet make a desirable young woman warm to her. Tradition has it that, despairing on account of an unrequited love for the ferryman Phaon, Sappho threw herself to her death from cliffs on the island of Leucadia.

23 PHILOSOPHER

PYTHAGORAS

Samos, Greece
c. 570–490 BC

Mathematician and thinker who was a major influence on Plato, Aristotle, and all of Western philosophy.

Born in Samos, Greece, Pythagoras emigrated to Italy and founded a religious "brotherhood," or school, in Croton, where followers lived a communal lifestyle. Among his teachings was the "transmigration of souls"—that on death the human soul begins life again in a new body; the central importance of numbers in music and the observable world; and the contention that mathematical equations govern the movements of the planets, which create an inaudible music as they move.

"As soon as laws are necessary for men, they are no longer fit for freedom."

<small>Pythagoras, quoted in *Short Sayings of Great Men: With Historical and Explanatory Notes*, Samuel Arthur Bent, 1882</small>

LEFT: Pythagoras was reputedly the first person to call himself a "philosopher"—a lover of wisdom. Here he is depicted in *The School of Athens* by Raphael.

PHILOSOPHER

CONFUCIUS

Lu (now Shandong Province), China
551–479 BC

Thinker who is celebrated as the wisest Chinese sage and taught the importance of tradition and loyalty.

The self-educated Confucius rose from humble beginnings to become an admired teacher and serve as minister of works, and then minister of justice, in his native state of Lu (modern Shandong province). His teachings were collected in the *Analects* after his death, and he is also celebrated as the author or editor of revered Chinese texts such as the *Five Classics*, including the *I Ching* or *Book of Changes*, a divination manual. His rational approach emphasized the importance of humanity and personal virtue, of respect and loyalty in the family, and of venerating ancestors. He presented the family as a model of government.

"To study and not think is a waste. To think and not study is dangerous."

Confucius, *Analects*, c. 497 BC

LEFT: Confucius said he was a transmitter of ancient ways and established wisdom, and that he himself did not invent anything.

25 ROYALTY

CYRUS THE GREAT

Anshan, Persia (now Iran)
c. 585–529 BC

This king founded the Achaemenian Empire, and issued what may be the first statement of human rights.

Cyrus rose to greatness by defeating the Medes in 549 BC, becoming King of Persia the following year, and capturing Lydia c. 546 BC and Babylon in 539 BC. He established the largest empire the world had yet seen, which stretched from the Mediterranean in the west to the Indus Valley in the east. He was celebrated in the ancient world for his magnanimous government, and influenced Greek ideas of the ideal ruler. In 539 BC he also issued an edict authorizing and encouraging the return home of the people of Judah, ending the "Babylonian captivity" of the Jews described in the Bible. According to the biblical accounts, where he is celebrated as being anointed by God, he called for the rebuilding of the Temple in Jerusalem. The "Cyrus Cylinder," found in the ruins of Babylon in 1879, describes his willingness to restore religious shrines and allow the repatriation of people who had been deported by previous conquerors. In Iran, where the 2,500th anniversary of his founding of the monarchy was celebrated in 1971, the last shah, Mohammad Reza Pahlavi (deposed in the Iranian Revolution of 1979), celebrated the Cyrus Cylinder as the world's oldest declaration of human rights.

ABOVE RIGHT: In some accounts Cyrus the Great was killed fighting the Iranian Massagetae on the Jaxartes river (Syr Darya) in Central Asia.

KNOWN FOR
- Ending Jews' Babylonian captivity
- Being a just ruler
- Building an empire

DARIUS THE GREAT

Persia (now Iran)
r. c. 550–486 BC

"King of kings" who built the "great royal road" across the Achaemenian Empire.

Darius overthrew Bardiya, son of Cyrus, to seize the throne, and then expanded the empire to include Macedonia, Thrace, and land as far as the Indus Valley. But he twice failed to conquer Greece, and was famously defeated in the Battle of Marathon in 490 BC. He reorganized the empire in administrative provinces, each with a governing *satrap*, standardized weights and measures, and built the famous royal road running more than 1,500 miles from the imperial capital of Susa to Sardis and Smyrna. At Mount Behistun (western Iran) a clifftop inscription and relief carvings celebrate his exploits.

BELOW: A seated Darius receives homage. He is holding a staff and flower, symbols of royal authority.

27 MILITARY LEADER

SUNZI

Qi, China (now Shandong)
c. 545–496 BC

Sunzi (Sun Tzu) was reputedly a brilliant general from the state of Wu who shared his battlefield experience and strategic insights in the world's first military handbook. *The Art of War* emphasizes how vital it is for a general to have accurate intelligence of the size, movements, and deployment of the enemy, and urges flexibility in tactics and strategy. It was used by Mao Zedong and Chinese communists in their fight against the Japanese and the Chinese nationalists, and has remained popular to the present day.

28 PHILOSOPHER

LAOZI

Chu (now Hubei), China
6th century BC

Philosopher who founded Taoism.

Author of the *Tao Te Ching* and founder of the religious philosophy of Taoism, Laozi (Lao Tzu) possibly worked as librarian of sacred writings at the Zhou royal court. Legends tell that his mother conceived him after gazing on a falling star, was pregnant with him for seventy-two years, and he was born with the gray beard and long earlobes that signified a wise man. He was a contemporary of Confucius. He had many disciples, though he never actually opened a school. He had a son, Zong, who became a warrior, and Laozi showed him to respectfully bury his dead enemies rather than leave them out to be eaten by vultures. One tradition states that he set out to be a hermit in old age, but the city guard would not let him pass until he had written down his acquired wisdom—and the result was the *Tao Te Ching*. Taoism, which teaches that humans thrive if they align themselves with the Way (Tao) of the universe, probably influenced Buddhism.

ABOVE: The name Laozi is an honorific title meaning "Old Master." According to tradition, Laozi's birth name was Li Er.

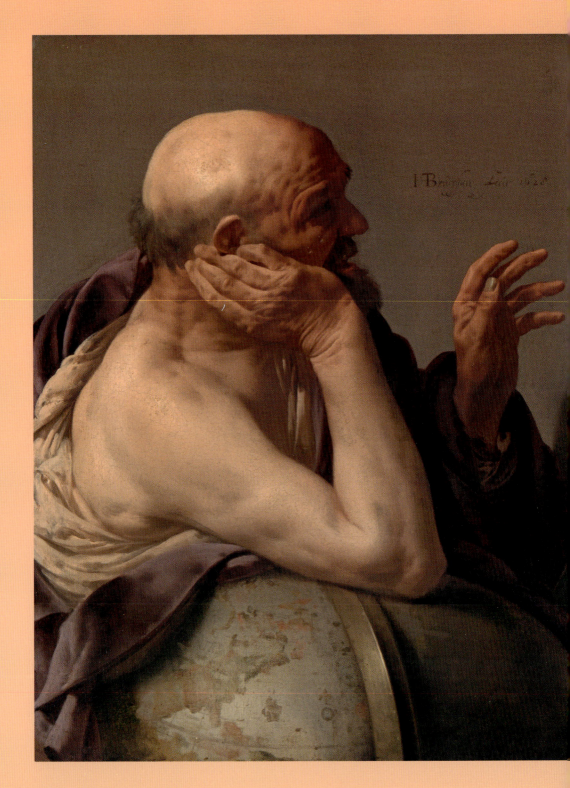

29 PHILOSOPHER

HERACLITUS

Ephesus, Anatolia (now Selçuk, Turkey)
c. 540–480 BC

Greek philosopher who argued that the world is in flux—constantly changing.

Heraclitus's most famous statements are "everything flows" and "no man ever steps in the same river twice"—the second time a person steps in the river, the waters that wet their feet before have moved on and the river cannot be said to be the same; what's more, the individual changes from moment to moment. Born into an aristocratic family in the Anatolian city of Ephesus, then part of the Persian Empire, he taught that fire is the fundamental element of the cosmos, and that opposites connect and define one another—dry and wet, hot and cold, waking and sleeping. The tension between opposites maintains order, and there is a hidden connection between apparently divergent things. Heraclitus was a melancholic figure, and is known as "the weeping philosopher" in contrast to the more cheerful figure of Democritus, who was called "the laughing philosopher." His only written work is lost, but around 100 fragments survive in quotations by other philosophers.

LEFT: This 1628 portrait by Dutch artist Hendrick ter Brugghen captures the melancholy outlook of Heraclitus—the "weeping philosopher."

30 ARTIST

AESCHYLUS

Eleusis, Greece
525–456 BC

Aeschylus was a soldier, and was wounded at the Battle of Marathon in 490 BC before achieving fame as a dramatist. He entered the annual Great Dionysia playwriting festival from 499, and first won in 484. He went on to write around sixty plays, but only seven survive—including the *Oresteia* trilogy (*Agamemnon*, *The Libation Bearers*, and *The Eumenides*), *Seven Against Thebes*, and *Prometheus Bound*.

31 ARTIST

PINDAR

Cynoscephalae (now Thessaly), Greece
c. 518–438 BC

Pindar wrote seventeen volumes of lyrics and is renowned as ancient Greece's greatest lyric poet. Four books of *Triumphal Odes* survive, celebrating victories in the Olympian, Pythian, Nemean, and Isthmian athletic games. One tradition about his life is that he was stung in the mouth by a bee as a child, and this enabled him to write verses as sweet as honey. He died in Argos, Greece.

32 ROYALTY

XERXES

Achaemenid Empire, Persia (now Iran)
c. 518–465 BC

King Xerxes led a failed invasion of Greece. He built a bridge of 700 ships across the Hellespont to reach the country, and rebuilt it when it was destroyed in a storm. His 360,000-strong army took a week to cross the bridge. He was seeking revenge following the defeat of his father Darius the Great at the Battle of Marathon. Xerxes's army won the Battle of Thermopylae and ransacked Athens, but his navy was destroyed at the Battle of Salamis and, after he returned to Persia, his troops were beaten at the Battle of Plataea. He put down revolts in Egypt and Babylon, and undertook building works at Persepolis.

33 POLITICAL LEADER

PERICLES

Athens, Greece
c. 495–429 BC

Greek general Pericles nurtured democracy in the golden age of the city-state of Athens and built an empire. The son of a wealthy family, he fostered the democratic reforms introduced by Ephialtes, which limited the power of the aristocracy by introducing the *ecclesia* popular assembly, law courts, and council. He oversaw the building of the Parthenon temple and other buildings on the Acropolis in Athens, and was famed for his public speaking.

LEFT: Pericles. His funeral oration for Athenian soldiers in 431 BC is compared to President Abraham Lincoln's Gettysburg Address of 1863.

34 ARTIST

SOPHOCLES

Hippeios Colonus (now Kolonus), Greece
c. 496–406 BC

A dramatist, Sophocles won the Athenian dramatic competition twenty-four times.

Sophocles was a major figure in the public life of Athens, serving as a general and treasurer as well as being one of the city-state's three great tragic dramatists—with Aeschylus and Euripides. While Aeschylus was the first to introduce a second actor on stage, Sophocles introduced a third, so reducing the importance of the chorus that comments on the action, though at the same time he increased the chorus size. He won his first victory in the dramatic festival in 468 BC, over Aeschylus, and went on to be a dominant figure in the competitions for almost fifty years. He wrote 123 dramas, of which seven tragedies survive—*Ajax*, *Antigone*, *The Women of Trachis*, *Oedipus the King*, *Philoctetes*, *Electra*, and *Oedipus at Colonus*. He was the son of Sophillus, a wealthy maker of armor, and was born in Hippeios Colonus in Attica (the region in Greece that includes Athens). In 480 he led the *paean* (chant of praise) following the Greeks' victory over the Persian navy at Salamis. He is thought to have been homosexual and lived to the age of ninety, dying—according to one story—after he tried to recite a long phrase from *Antigone* without drawing breath.

ABOVE RIGHT: As well as excelling in drama, Sophocles was made a general in 441 BC and served in the Athenian campaign against Samos.

"Blessed is Sophocles, who lived a long life, was a man both joyful and talented, and the author of many excellent tragedies; and he ended his life well without suffering any misfortune."

From *The Muses*, a eulogy to Sophocles, 406 BC

KNOWN FOR

- Being one of three great Athenian tragedians—with Aeschylus and Euripides
- Winning twenty-four dramatic competitions in Athens, compared to Aeschylus's thirteen and Euripides's four
- Being the first to introduce a third character on stage

35 RELIGIOUS LEADER/PHILOSOPHER

BUDDHA

Lumbini (now Nepal)
c. 490–410 BC

This philosopher-prince renounced royal life to seek enlightenment and to teach his followers how to escape suffering.

Gautama Siddharta was born a prince of the Shakya clan in Lumbini and, marrying at age sixteen, spent the first part of his life in isolation and comfort in the palace compound. But when he first left the palace aged twenty-nine with his charioteer, he was shocked by what he saw—an old man, a sick person, a dead body, and an ascetic monk. He realized that life was short and no one could escape unhappiness. He left the palace to become a wandering monk, determined to keep seeking until he found a way to explain human suffering and how to avoid it. When he was thirty-five he sat down under a bodhi tree (a type of fig) and declared he would not move again until he had seen the truth. After forty-nine days, he became enlightened. He had awakened from the dream of everyday existence to see what he understood to be the truth. From this time on he became known as "the Buddha," a Sanskrit term meaning "awakened person." He taught what he had learned for forty years, and founded a monastic order of nuns and monks. He explained that desire is the cause of suffering. Everything is changing but we want to hold on to things that cannot last, including other people and possessions. We need to train our minds to be detached. *Nirvana*—the secret of peace—is the blowing out of desire like the snuffing of a candle.

"Our life is shaped by our thoughts. What we think we become. More than those who despise you, more than your foes, a mind untrained does greater harm. More than mother, more than father, more than family, a well-trained mind brings greater good."

Buddha, *The Dhammapada*

KNOWN FOR

- Founding the religious-philosophical system of Buddhism
- Teaching people how to be free from suffering
- Developing the concept of *nirvana* ("extinguishing" self-will and separateness)
- Establishing one of the first communities of monks and nuns

RIGHT: The Buddha's eightfold path encourages right view, intention, speech, conduct, livelihood, effort, mindfulness, and *samadhi* (a stage of meditation).

36 ARTIST

EURIPIDES

Salamis Island, Greece
c. 484–406 BC

Greek playwright Euripides made enemies with his tragedies that challenged religious convention. He wrote about ninety plays, but won the Athenian playwriting competition only four times. His plays contain more realistic—sometimes strikingly modern—dialogue than those of his contemporaries, and depict a world of meaningless human suffering that the gods observe with indifference. Nineteen survive, including *Medea*, *Electra*, *The Trojan Women*, and *The Bacchae*.

37 ARTIST

HERODOTUS

Halicarnassus, Greece (now Turkey)
c. 484–430 BC

The man the Roman writer Cicero called "the father of history" wrote the first historical narrative, an account of Greece's war with Persia, in *c.* 430 BC. He traveled through much of the Persian Empire, and his book is a major source of information about the geography, culture, and customs of the ancient world in the fifth century BC.

ABOVE RIGHT: With Sophocles and Aeschylus, Euripides was the third of the three great Athenian tragedians.

RIGHT: Herodotus was criticized by Thucydides for including legends in his history, but Herodotus said he had written what he was told on his travels.

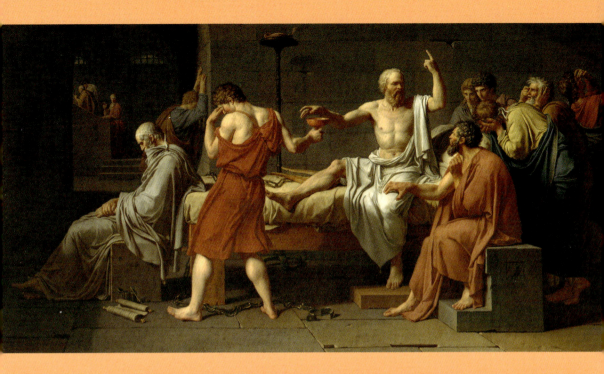

38 PHILOSOPHER

SOCRATES

Alopece, Athens, Greece
c. 470–399 BC

Philosopher who argued for the importance of self-inquiry and ethical conduct.

The son of a stoneworker and a midwife, Socrates fought with distinction in the Peloponnesian War with Sparta. In Athens he was a familiar and controversial figure, known for his unattractive appearance, washing infrequently, and having a single threadbare robe. He was moderate in his drinking, eating, and sex life—at a time when it was common for older men to seek liaisons with their younger counterparts; he avoided this because, his pupil Plato said, he preferred to educate their minds. He taught philosophy using question and answer—a technique known as "Socratic dialogue." He argued that, to be wise, a person first needed to accept how little they knew, and that ethical behavior was the most important thing. In 399 he was found guilty of impiety and corrupting youth and sentenced to death. He poisoned himself by drinking hemlock.

ABOVE: Socrates's dramatic suicide, by drinking hemlock, as imagined by the French painter Jacques Louis David.

39 PHILOSOPHER

MOZI

Lu (now Shandong Province), China
c. 470–391 BC

Philosopher who taught that all are equal, and that power and position should be distributed based on merit.

Mozi was originally a follower of Confucius, but he felt Confucianism was too ritualistic and placed too much emphasis on ancestors, the family, and the clan. He developed a teaching of universal, impartial love—arguing that people should not care for their relatives more than others, but develop an unconditional love for humankind. Mozi came from a relatively humble background and did not receive much love or attention from his parents. He was a skilled carpenter and expert on fortifications, rose to become a minister, and ran a school for people seeking to become officials. Mozi argued that, rather than rely on rituals, people should seek to know themselves and be authentic. He argued against offensive war and for a simple life in which people harmed no one. His teachings were collected in a book called the *Mozi* and attracted many followers. Mohism was an important religious-philosophical movement for centuries, but died out in the second century BC.

KNOWN FOR

- Founding the religious movement Mohism
- Teaching that people should harm no one and lead a simple life
- Promoting meritocracy

40 SCIENTIST

HIPPOCRATES OF COS

Cos (now Kos), Greece
c. 460–375 BC

The "Father of Medicine," who established the importance of clinical observation and categorized diseases.

Hippocrates learned medicine from his grandfather and father and, according to Plato (in his work *Phaedrus*), believed that doctors needed complete understanding of the body to practice medicine. He taught medicine throughout his life, traveling as far as Thrace, and is credited with establishing it as a distinct area of study and practice. Tradition has it that he created the Hippocratic Oath for doctors, the world's oldest code of medical ethics. Around sixty medical works that he reputedly wrote survive, but historians think his name was attached to the writings of others.

"I swear by Apollo ... and by all the gods and goddesses ... I will not cause harm or do injustice [to my patients] ... I will not give a poison to anyone ... In all houses, I will go in to aid to the sick and I will not engage in deliberate wrongdoing..."

From the oldest surviving version of the Hippocratic Oath, c. AD 275

ABOVE: Hippocrates taught that a shortage or excess of one of the humors or bodily fluids (blood, phlegm, yellow bile, black bile) was a sign of illness.

41 EXPLORER

HANNO OF CARTHAGE

Carthage (now Tunisia)
c. 450–400 BC

Hanno the Navigator was an aristocratic official who explored and colonized the west coast of Africa, according to some reaching as far south as Gabon. He set out with sixty ships, supposedly carrying 30,000 people, and sailed through the Pillars of Hercules (the promontories at the entrance to the Strait of Gibraltar) to found six cities, including Thymiaterium and Acra (Mehdya and Agadir, Morocco). Roman author Pliny the Elder claimed that Hanno sailed right around Africa and reached Arabia.

ABOVE: According to Plato, Aristophanes's attack on Sophocles in *The Clouds* contributed to the philosopher's downfall and death.

42 ARTIST

ARISTOPHANES

Athens, Greece
c. 450–388 BC

Comic playwright who pulled no punches in hard-hitting social satire.

Aristophanes poked public fun at figures including the populist leader Cleon, the philosopher Socrates, and the tragedian Euripides, and even made the god Dionysus—the patron of the festival in which his plays appeared—a ridiculous figure in *The Frogs*. He burst onto the scene, scoring a success when he was just eighteen. His plays are the only surviving examples of the "Old Comedy" in Athens, using mime, burlesque, and obscenity. He wrote around forty plays, of which eleven survive, including *The Wasps*, *The Clouds*, and his masterpiece *The Birds*. Contemporaries considered him to be the greatest living comic dramatist.

PHILOSOPHER

PLATO

Athens, Greece
c. 428–348 BC

This Greek philosopher founded the Western world's first university.

Born into an aristocratic family, Plato was a student of the philosopher Socrates. Profoundly distressed by his teacher's trial, condemnation, and suicide, Plato decided not to enter public life and left Athens for Megara, then spent twelve years traveling—during which he wrote a series of *Dialogues* from which we learn almost everything we know about Socrates. Back in Athens in the 380s, he founded the Academy—the prototype of modern universities—as a place of research and study; the philosopher Aristotle was one of his pupils. A key teaching was that the ever-changing world experienced through the senses is a copy of the real world of "forms" that people know through reason and their souls. His teachings, known as Platonism and revived in the third century AD as Neoplatonism by Plotinus, had a huge influence on early Christian theologians, then through the Renaissance and philosophy right to the present.

> "A penalty of refusing to take part in politics is that you end up being governed by lesser people."
>
> Plato, *Republic*, 375 BC

LEFT: According to tradition, Plato's real name was Aristocles. He was renamed Plato ("broad") because of his expansive forehead (indicating intelligence) and physical shape.

44 PHILOSOPHER

ARISTOTLE

Stagira, Greece (now Central Macedonia)
384–322 BC

This towering philosopher invented the study of logic and excelled in sciences, psychology, and the arts.

A student of Plato's Academy, Aristotle became tutor of the young Alexander the Great in Macedon then, in 335 BC, founded his own school, the Lyceum, in Athens. He was known for walking up and down while teaching, and his followers became known as the "peripatetics." He wrote the first treatises on logic, and had a major and enduring influence for 2,000 years through his groundbreaking work in zoology, physics, chemistry, botany, ethics, political theory, and literary theory among others. His books include *On the Soul*, *Politics*, *Nicomachean Ethics*, *Poetics*, *Rhetoric,* and the *Organon*. He left Athens in 322 and died that year in Chalcis on the Greek island of Euboea.

> "It is the mark of an educated mind to be able to entertain a thought without accepting it."
>
> Aristotle, *Nicomachean Ethics*, 350 BC

ABOVE: Aristotle and Plato engage in debate at the Lyceum in the painting *The School of Athens* (c. 1509) by Raphael.

45 POLITICAL LEADER

DEMOSTHENES

Athens, Greece
384–322 BC

Demosthenes was the finest of all ancient Greek orators. He delivered a magnificent speech (the "First Philippic") in 351 BC, urging Athens to go to war with Philip of Macedon. Then, after this conflict ended in defeat at Chaeronea (in 338), he superbly defended himself against criticism by the pro-peace faction led by a rival, Aeschines, in his greatest speech of all ("On the Crown"). But Demosthenes was later convicted of embezzlement; he was imprisoned, fled, sentenced to death, and took poison. He was studied in ancient Rome and celebrated for his eloquence through the Middle Ages and Renaissance.

ABOVE: Demosthenes was frail and did not have the normal Greek physical education; he trained in oratory instead.

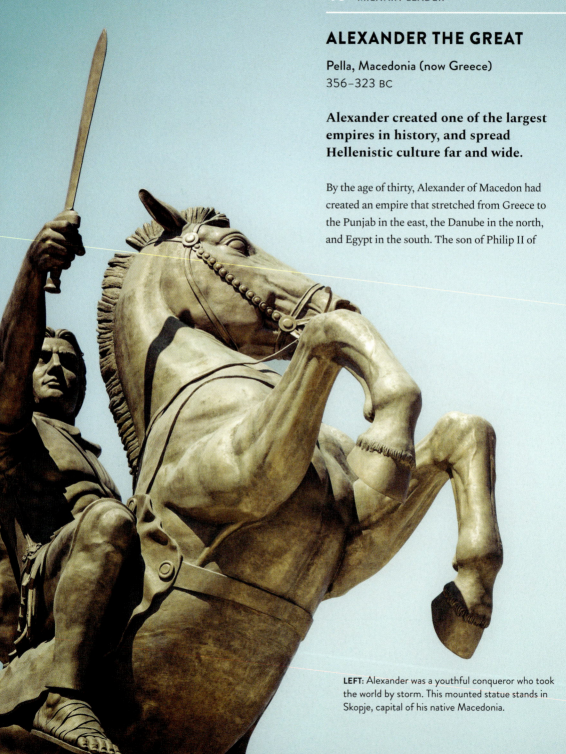

46 MILITARY LEADER

ALEXANDER THE GREAT

Pella, Macedonia (now Greece)
356–323 BC

Alexander created one of the largest empires in history, and spread Hellenistic culture far and wide.

By the age of thirty, Alexander of Macedon had created an empire that stretched from Greece to the Punjab in the east, the Danube in the north, and Egypt in the south. The son of Philip II of

LEFT: Alexander was a youthful conqueror who took the world by storm. This mounted statue stands in Skopje, capital of his native Macedonia.

Macedon, Alexander was tutored by Aristotle from the age of thirteen to sixteen, and acceded to the throne aged twenty. He enforced unity on the Greek states, and then led a swift conquest of the powerful Achaemenian Empire, defeating its ruler, Darius III, at Issus in 333 BC and Gaugamela in 331. By this stage he had been crowned pharaoh of Egypt in 332 and founded the city of Alexandria. He defeated the Scythians at the Battle of Jaxartes in 329 and invaded India in 326, defeating a local king, Porus, at the Battle of the Hydaspes that year. When his troops revolted, he retreated to Persia, and died in Babylon aged just thirty-two, possibly from poisoning, after drinking a great deal of wine. One of the greatest ever generals, he was never defeated in battle. Even in his lifetime he was the subject of tall tales that exaggerated his exploits. He was later the hero of a legend that endured for centuries—the Alexander romance.

"A tomb now suffices him for whom the whole world was not sufficient."

Epitaph on Alexander the Great's tombstone

KNOWN FOR
- Creating one of the biggest empires in history by the age of thirty
- Never being defeated in battle

47 SCIENTIST

GAN DE

Qi (now Shandong), China
c. 400–340 BC

Chinese astrologer and astronomer Gan De, also called "Lord Gan," made one of the first star catalogs in history and, in 365 BC, was possibly the first person to describe one of the moons of Jupiter—likely Ganymede or Callisto. Unfortunately, all his written works have been lost.

48 PHILOSOPHER

GONGSUN LONG

Zhao, China (now Hebei)
c. 325–250 BC

Gongsun Long was a leading light of the School of Names, a group of philosophers who studied words and their meanings. He famously argued that "a white horse is not a horse"—its whiteness, rather than its status as a horse, defines it. His notable work on logic, the *Gongsunlongzi*, survives in part.

49 SCIENTIST

EUCLID

Greece
c. 320–270 BC

Mathematician in Alexandria who wrote the classic geometry handbook *Elements*.

The man known as "the father of geometry" established a school of mathematics in Alexandria, and wrote the thirteen-volume *Elements*, which was the most celebrated mathematical book in the classical world and is still highly regarded and used today. He worked in Alexandria at the time of Ptolemy I Soter, one of Alexander the Great's generals, who became ruler of Egypt and founded the Ptolemaic dynasty. Ptolemy famously asked Euclid if there was an easier way to understand mathematics than by studying his voluminous works, and Euclid said, "There is no royal road to geometry." In the *Elements* he gathered the ideas and theories of earlier mathematicians, including Eudoxus of Cnidus, Hippocrates of Chios, Thales Miletus, and Theaetetus. Euclid may have studied at Plato's Academy and taught at the Museum, the great educational institute Ptolemy founded in Alexandria. He also wrote the books *Optics*, *Data*, and *Phaenomena*.

RIGHT: The author of the *Elements* is possibly the most influential mathematician in the history of the discipline.

POLITICAL LEADER

ASHOKA

Hassan, India
c. 304–232 BC

Third emperor of the Maurya Empire was a convert to Buddhism.

In *c.* 260 BC Ashoka led the bloody conquest of Kalinga on India's eastern coast, and afterward turned against violence. While tolerating other religions, he propagated the teachings of Buddhism through edicts carved on rocks and pillars. He is celebrated as the ideal Buddhist ruler. The national emblem of India is based on the Lion Capital of Ashoka, a column bearing four life-size lions that he erected at Sarnath to mark the site of the Buddha's first sermon.

ABOVE: Ashoka commissioned a magnificent monument to the Buddha at Sanchi, birthplace of his wife Devi and the location of their wedding.

51 PHILOSOPHER

ARISTARCHUS OF SAMOS

Samos, Greece
c. 310–220 BC

Aristarchus argued that the Sun is the center of the universe, and that the Earth rotates on its axis and revolves around the Sun once a year. He produced an estimate of the sizes of the Moon and the Sun and their relative distances from Earth—calculating that the Sun was eighteen times farther from Earth than the Moon, when in reality it is 400 times farther away. He also determined that the other planets also rotate around the Sun, and believed that the stars are other suns, only much farther away. Aristarchus's ideas inspired Polish astronomer Nicolaus Copernicus in the sixteenth century AD.

ABOVE: Aristarchus was taught by Strato of Lampsacus, third head of the Peripatetic School founded by Aristotle in Athens.

52 SCIENTIST

ARCHIMEDES OF SYRACUSE

Syracuse, Italy
c. 287–212 BC

The inventor of a "screw" for raising water was a great mathematician.

The son of an astronomer, Archimedes invented siege and siege-raising equipment, as well as the "Archimedes screw," a revolving, screw-shaped blade within a cylinder used to raise water. He is also known for the Archimedes' principle—a body in liquid is subject to an upward force equal to the weight of fluid it displaces. Hiero II of Syracuse asked Archimedes to determine whether a craftsman had cheated on a commission to make a gold crown by mixing silver with the gold supplied; Archimedes realized he could determine the density of the crown by dividing its mass by the amount of water it displaced. He had the insight while in the bath and was so excited that he ran through the streets naked shouting "Eureka! Eureka!" ("I have found it!"). The craftsman had cheated. He made many mathematical breakthroughs, including an approximation of pi (the ratio of a circle's circumference to diameter) that was the best available for more than 1,000 years.

RIGHT: The naked mathematician prepares to leap from his bath and run through the streets, after having the *Eureka!* insight that led to the Archimedes' principle.

53 SCIENTIST

ERATOSTHENES

Greek colony of Cyrene
(now Shahhat, Libya)
c. 276–195 BC

Eratosthenes was the head of the Library in Alexandria. As well as calculating the Earth's circumference to only 1.5 percent less than the true length, he made the first projection map to use parallels and meridians. In mathematics he invented the sieve of Eratosthenes, a method for identifying prime numbers; in history he developed the idea of chronology, and dated events back to the Siege of Troy (1183 BC); and in astronomy he invented the armillary sphere.

54 ROYALTY

QUIN SHIN HUANG

Handan, China
c. 259–210 BC

The first emperor of a unified China, Quin Shin Huang invented the title *huangdi* (emperor), which would be used by his successors for 2,000 years. Originally King Zheng of the state of Qin, he eliminated rival states, creating an empire and establishing an enduring imperial bureaucracy. When challenged, he executed scholars and burned books. He was buried in a mausoleum measuring 20 square miles alongside an army of 8,000 life-size troops and horses made from terracotta.

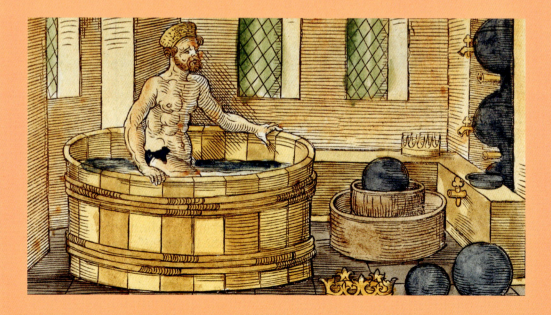

55 MILITARY LEADER

HANNIBAL

Carthage (now Tunisia)
247–183 BC

One of the greatest generals of the ancient world crossed the Alps with war elephants to attack the Romans.

The Carthaginian war leader Hannibal was the son of General Hamilcar Barca, and his father made him swear eternal enmity to Rome. Hannibal commanded armies in Spain during the First Punic War (264–241 BC), between the North African and Mediterranean empire of Carthage and the Roman Republic. Then, in 219, he attacked Rome's ally Saguntum, provoking the Second Punic War. Crossing the Pyrenees, he defeated the Gauls in southern France, and then inspired his army to achieve the seemingly impossible feat of crossing the Alps, in fifteen days with at least thirty-seven war elephants.

In Italy, he marched on Rome and defeated the Romans at Lake Trasimene in 217 and Cannae in 216. He remained in southern Italy until 203, when he returned to Carthage and was defeated in the Battle of Zama by the Roman general Scipio Africanus. After the war he became *sufet* (community leader) in Carthage, but went into exile when his reforms provoked opposition. He was a military advisor to Antiochus III at the Selucid court, and then in the Kingdom of Bithnia (in what is now Turkey). He took his own life by poison after being betrayed and to avoid capture by the Romans.

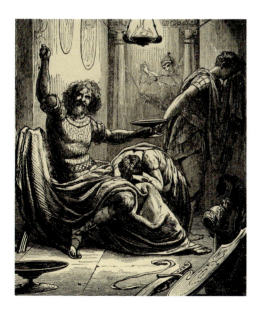

OPPOSITE: Hannibal directs his army on its famous mountain crossing. Greek historian Polybius said he crossed at the highest pass—historians think it was probably the Col de la Traversette.

LEFT: Hannibal's aides fail to dissuade the despairing leader from his desperate decision to take his own life.

> **KNOWN FOR**
> - Being one of the greatest generals of the ancient world
> - Crossing the Alps with his army and war elephants
> - His undying opposition to Rome

2700 BC–AD 500 **55**

56 ARTIST

TERENCE (PUBLIUS TERENTIUS AFER)

Carthage (now Tunisia)
c. 195–159 BC

Former slave who shone as a Roman comic dramatist.

Terence was brought to Rome by the senator Terentius Lucanus, who provided for his education and then freed him because he was so impressed by the young man's abilities. The use of Afer in his name may indicate that he was a Berber from Libya. He wrote and put on six plays that were preserved in the Middle Ages, partly because monks and nuns used them to learn Latin. They were highly regarded during the Renaissance, and an influence on William Shakespeare and the French dramatist Molière. They were *The Girl from Andros* (166 BC), *The Mother in Law* (165 BC), *The Self-Tormentor* (163 BC), *The Eunuch* (161 BC), *Phormio* (161 BC), and *The Brothers* (160 BC). His work was promoted by the actor Lucius Ambivius Turpio. As was customary at the time, the plays were based on Greek models, notably those by Menander. He may have died in a shipwreck.

> "I am a man, and judge nothing that is human alien to me."
>
> Terence, *The Self-Tormentor*, 163 BC

57 ARTIST

SIMA QIAN

Xiayang (now Hancheng), China
c. 145–87 BC

The first major Chinese historian wrote the *Shiji* (*Historical Accounts*), the most significant account of Chinese history down to the second century BC. He succeeded his father Sima Tan as astronomer-historian at the Han court in 108 BC, and began the *Shiji* in c. 105, when he took part in a reform of the Chinese calendar.

58 MILITARY LEADER

MITHRIDATES THE GREAT

Sinop, Turkey
c. 135–63 BC

As the king of Pontus in Anatolia, Mithridates was a formidable opponent of Rome, fighting three wars between 88 and 63 BC. When he was finally defeated by the Roman general Pompey at the Battle of the Lycus in 66 BC, he escaped and endured for another three years before finally taking refuge in the city of Panticapaeum (now Kerch, Crimea), where he took his own life.

59 MILITARY LEADER

SPARTACUS

Thrace (now Bulgaria)
c. 109–71 BC

Escaped slave and former gladiator who led a heroic but ultimately doomed rebellion against Rome.

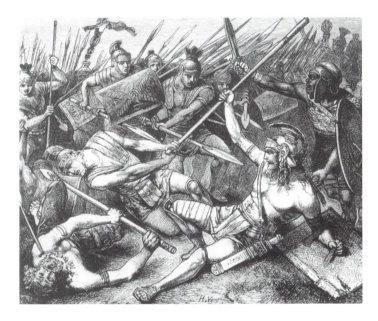

LEFT: Despite defeat by Crassus's indomitable legions, Spartacus endured as a symbol of heroic resistance against tyranny.

KNOWN FOR

- Leading the Third Servile War of slaves against Rome
- Being an inspiration for later political thinkers

Spartacus was probably born into a nomadic tribe in what is now Bulgaria. After serving in the Roman army, he became a bandit, and was then captured and sold into slavery. He was in training to be a *murmillo* gladiator when, with several fellow slaves, he made a dramatic escape from a training school near Capua in 73 BC. They defeated the soldiers sent to round them up, raided the local area, and finally retreated to a camp on Mount Vesuvius. When they trounced a militia group sent to besiege them, the success attracted huge numbers of other slaves, shepherds, and herdsmen to their cause until they had at least 70,000 at the camp. In 72 BC Spartacus defeated two consular legions sent against him, but the following year, after a failed attempt to escape to Sicily, the slave army suffered a crushing defeat at the hands of eight legions under Marcus Licinius Crassus. Spartacus was reported to have died in the battle, but his body was never found. To make an example of the rebels, Crassus crucified 6,000 of them along the Appian Way between Capua and Rome. Despite its failure, the revolt was an inspiration to later generations. The French philosopher Voltaire called it "the only just war in history."

60 POLITICAL LEADER

CICERO (MARCUS TULLIUS CICERO)

Arpino, Italy
106–43 BC

Roman statesman and greatest orator of his era.

Marcus Tullius Cicero tried to defend the principles behind the Roman Republic in a time of civil war that resulted in its collapse and the establishment of the Roman Empire. Elected consul in 63 BC, he prevented Catiline's uprising and made four celebrated speeches ("In Catilinum") against him. Cicero wrote his major works on philosophy and rhetoric from 46 to 44 BC while in retirement. Returning to public life, he made fourteen speeches ("Philippics") against Mark Antony in 43 BC. He was executed when Mark Antony, Marcus Lepidus, and Octavian joined forces in the Second Triumvirate.

ABOVE AND RIGHT: Man of letters. More than 900 letters and 58 speeches of Cicero's survive. He also wrote poetry and books on philosophy and rhetoric.

MILITARY LEADER

JULIUS CAESAR

Rome, Italy
100–44 BC

General who conquered Gaul and became a dictator in Rome before being assassinated.

Gaius Julius Caesar had a central role in the end of the Roman Republic and the beginnings of the Roman Empire. From 58 to 50 BC he displayed his immense gifts as a general in conquering Gaul (France) and invaded Britain twice (55 and 54 BC). Then, in 49 BC, Caesar defied orders from the Senate to relinquish military command, returning to Italy and precipitating the Roman civil war. He defeated his rival Pompey, then pursued him to Egypt, where he became the lover of Cleopatra. In 44 BC he was named "dictator for life" in Rome, but was assassinated on the Ides of March (the middle day) that year by the conspirators Brutus and Cassius.

*"I came,
    I saw,
        I conquered."*

Julius Caesar, in a letter to the Roman Senate about his swift victory over Pharnaces II, King of Pontus, in 47 BC

RIGHT: Caesar's decision to go over the Rubicon river and march on Rome in 49 BC was a decisive moment in world history.

62 PHILOSOPHER

LUCRETIUS (TITUS LUCRETIUS CARUS)

Pompeii, Italy
c. 99–55 BC

The Roman philosopher-poet Lucretius wrote the poem *De rerum natura* (*On the Nature of Things*) to explain the philosophy of Epicureanism, developed by the Greek philosopher Epicurus in *c.* 300 BC, to a Roman audience. Epicureanism argues against superstition and interventions by the gods, who were indifferent to humans and their doings, and proposes that people should aim to achieve a modest form of pleasure characterized by freedom from fear and pain. The poem was a major influence on the Roman poets Virgil and Horace.

63 ARTIST

VIRGIL (PUBLIUS VERGILIUS MARO)

Cisalpine Gaul (now northern Italy)
70–19 BC

Virgil's *Aeneid* describes the exploits of the Trojan warrior Aeneas, who comes to Italy after the fall of Troy (described in Homer's *Iliad*) and is the forefather of the Roman race. The emperor Augustus commissioned him to write it. The twelve-book epic poem, though unfinished when Virgil died, was a major influence on Western literature, and the Italian poet Dante Alighieri made Virgil his guide through Hell and Purgatory in the fourteenth-century masterpiece *The Divine Comedy*. Virgil also wrote the *Eclogues* and the *Georgics* (about pastoral and agricultural life). He was the son of a well-to-do farmer and had a good education.

ABOVE: Lucretius created the three-age classification (Stone Age, Bronze Age, and Iron Age).

ABOVE: A third-century mosaic depicts the national Roman poet Virgil with his muses, pondering poetic inspiration.

CLEOPATRA

Alexandria, Egypt
69–30 BC

Famously beautiful queen of Ptolemaic Egypt who was the lover of Romans Julius Caesar and Mark Antony.

A descendant of Alexander the Great's general Ptolemy I Soter, Cleopatra was the last ruler of the Ptolemaic Kingdom of Egypt that he founded. After her death the country became a province in the Roman Empire. She was initially co-ruler with her brother Ptolemy XIII, then, after becoming the lover of the Roman general Julius Caesar when he came to Egypt in pursuit of his rival Pompey, their army defeated and killed Ptolemy XIII at the Battle of the Nile in 67 BC. She and Caesar had a son, Caesarion, and she visited Rome and stayed in Caesar's villa. Another brother succeeded as Ptolemy XIV, but she ordered his assassination in 44 BC, the same year Caesar was killed in Rome, and she declared Caesarion her co-ruler as Ptolemy XV. In the next round of the Roman civil wars, she backed the Second Triumvirate of Octavian, Mark Antony, and Marcus Aemilius Lepidus, and married Mark Antony. Octavian later declared war, invaded Egypt, and defeated Mark Antony and Cleopatra's forces at the Battle of Actium. She took her own life—by allowing herself to be bitten by an asp.

RIGHT: Cleopatra's native language was the form of Greek used in the Hellenistic period, but she was the sole Ptolemaic ruler who learned Egyptian.

KNOWN FOR

- Being a great beauty
- Having love affairs with Roman generals Julius Caesar and Mark Antony
- Statecraft—making impressive deals safeguarding her kingdom and children
- Her suicide—bitten by an asp

65   ROYALTY

HYEOKGEOSE OF SILLA

Korea
69 BC–AD 4

Park Hyeokgeose founded Silla, one of the three kingdoms of Korea, in 56 BC. He reputedly married Lady Aryeong, and the pair were revered for improving harvests. In 32 BC he built a palace in Geumseong (modern Gyeongju). He reigned for sixty-one years and is claimed as the ancestor of the Park clans of Korea.

66   POLITICAL LEADER

AUGUSTUS CAESAR

Rome, Italy
63 BC–AD 14

Originally called Octavian, the great-nephew and adopted son of Julius Caesar defeated his rivals Lepidus and Mark Antony, becoming initially *princeps* (first citizen), then the first emperor of Rome as Caesar Augustus. He was a great patron of the arts, and consolidated the territory of the empire. On his death he was made a god.

ABOVE: Augustus gave his name to the Pax Augusta, a period of peace and prosperity throughout the Roman Empire.

67 MILITARY LEADER

AGRIPPA (MARCUS VIPSANIUS AGRIPPA)

Italy
c. 63–12 BC

Ally and deputy of Augustus who proved to be a brilliant general and architect.

Agrippa was of modest birth, but rose to become right-hand man to an emperor. He encountered the future Emperor Augustus, Octavian, in Illyria at the time of Julius Caesar's assassination in 44 BC. He returned to Rome with Octavian and was tribune of the plebs, prefect of Rome, governor of Transalpine Gaul, and consul, before proving himself a brilliant general in Octavian's cause, defeating Pompey at Mylae and Naulochus, and then taking command of Octavian's fleet in the defeat of Mark Antony and Cleopatra at the Battle of Actium in 31 BC. Octavian, now Emperor Augustus, set about improving Rome, and Agrippa was a brilliant architect who renovated aqueducts and built baths and gardens, as well as designing the Pantheon temple. Agrippa married Augustus's daughter Julia, and was the grandfather of Emperor Caligula and great-grandfather of Emperor Nero. When he died in 12 BC, Augustus gave him a grand funeral and mourned for more than a month.

RIGHT: This relief of Agrippa inspecting the Acqua Vergine aqueduct is part of the Trevi Fountain in Rome.

68 ARTIST

OVID (PUBLIUS OVIDIUS NASO)

Sulmona, Italy
43 BC – AD 17

Born into the equestrian (knightly) class, Publius Ovidius Naso trained in rhetoric with a view to becoming a lawyer, but withdrew from public life to be a poet. In addition to his masterpiece *Metamorphoses*, which describes stories in which physical transformations take place and was a major influence on Renaissance writers, he wrote *The Art of Love*, *Calendar*, and *Epistles of the Heroines*, as well as a lost play, *Medea*. In AD 8 he was banished for reasons unknown by Emperor Augustus to Tomis (now Romania), on the Black Sea, where—despite many appeals to return—he remained until he died.

69 ROYALTY

CHUMO THE HOLY

Buyeo, northern Manchuria (now China)
c. 58–19 BC

In c. 37 BC Chumo the Holy founded the Kingdom of Goguryeo, the name of which is the origin of the modern name of Korea. According to legend, he was born from an egg that could not be cracked. After his death, he was worshipped for hundreds of years.

BELOW: Ovid's *Metamorphoses* described how the sun god Apollo's son Phaeton failed to control the solar chariot and fell to his death.

70 RELIGIOUS LEADER

MARY, MOTHER OF JESUS

Jerusalem, Judea (now Israel)
c. 20 BC–AD 40

The young mother of Jesus of Nazareth who is revered in the Christian tradition.

Mary was betrothed to be married when she was visited by a supernatural being, the Angel Gabriel, who told her she would conceive a baby by the spirit of God and give birth while still a virgin. She was initially incredulous but accepted, saying, "I am the handmaid of the Lord. Let it be done unto me according to your word." Obedience to the will of God is one of her revered qualities. Her betrothed, Joseph, went ahead with the marriage after a dream vision of an angel. The couple traveled to Bethlehem for an official census and, unable to find accommodation, Mary gave birth in a stable. Mary and Joseph had the baby circumcised, named him Jesus (meaning "the Lord is salvation"), and presented him at the Temple in Jerusalem. Then, after another warning in a dream, they fled to Egypt to escape the cull of Jewish male babies ordered by King Herod. Mary raised Jesus in Nazareth. She is not much mentioned in accounts of Jesus's life, but she was present at his crucifixion. According to tradition, on her death she was bodily lifted into heaven. In Islam Mary is honored as the greatest woman in history, and she is the only woman named in the Quran.

KNOWN FOR

- Being the mother of Jesus of Nazareth
- Miracle of virgin birth
- In Christian tradition, being lifted bodily into heaven

ABOVE: Mary receives an angelic visitor and is told she has been chosen to bear God's child, in a painting by Florentine artist Masolino da Panicale.

"My soul glorifies the Lord and my spirit rejoices in God my Savior, for he has been mindful of the humble state of his servant. From now on all generations will call me blessed."

The Bible, New International Version, Luke 1:46

2700 BC–AD 500 **65**

71 RELIGIOUS LEADER

JESUS OF NAZARETH

Bethlehem, Judea (now Israel)
c. 6 BC–AD 30

Jewish teacher who was crucified and hailed by followers as the son of God.

The birth of the man revered by Christians as the son of God was surrounded by extraordinary events. His mother Mary conceived him by the Holy Spirit of God and gave birth while a virgin, angels appeared to shepherds in the field when he was born, and magi (wise men) "from the East" traveled to bring offerings to the baby. The traditional accounts hold that he began his teaching mission aged around thirty, after being baptized by John the Baptist. Becoming a wandering teacher, he called twelve men to be his disciples and taught through instructive stories, or parables. Tradition has it that he also performed miracles, including raising a man, Lazarus, from the dead, and turning water into wine at a wedding. His teachings threatened the Jewish religious establishment, which engineered his handing over to the Roman authorities and crucifixion aged thirty-three in Jerusalem. But he then rose from the dead and appeared to some of his disciples before ascending to heaven. In Islamic tradition Jesus is honored as the penultimate prophet before Muhammad, and he is said to have been raised bodily into heaven rather than crucified.

KNOWN FOR

- Being seen by Christians as the son of God
- Founding the global faith of Christianity
- Being a gifted teacher and teller of parables (instructional stories)

RIGHT: In Christian tradition, Jesus's crucifixion redeemed a world stained by Adam and Eve's sin.

72 ROYALTY

ONJO OF BAEKJE

Korea
c. 4 BC–AD 64

Onjo founded Baekje—with Goguryeo and Silla one of the "Three Kingdoms of Korea"—in the late first century BC. In one tradition, Onjo was the third son of Chumo the Holy, founder of Goguryeo, and left home to found his own kingdom. He was a great general who won a string of victories against rival powers, notably the Mahan and Jinhan, expanding his kingdom. He founded a capital where Seoul now stands. On his death he was succeeded by his son Daru.

73 RELIGIOUS LEADER

ST. PAUL

Tarsus, Cilicia (now Turkey)
c. 4 BC–AD 64

Important figure in the early Church who founded many Christian communities.

The man originally known as Saul of Tarsus trained as a rabbi and was a Pharisee who persecuted early Christians until, in c. AD 34, he reputedly had a dramatic encounter with the risen Jesus Christ while traveling from Jerusalem to Damascus and became a convert. He led many missions and became known for carrying the faith to the Gentiles (non-Jews). The thirteen letters he wrote to Christian communities are collected in the Bible. During a visit to Jerusalem, Jews angry at his behavior caused a disturbance, and he was imprisoned for two years. One tradition holds that he was executed by Emperor Nero.

ABOVE: St. Paul is often depicted with a sword. In his letter to the Ephesians (6:17), he wrote "take the . . . sword of the Spirit, which is the word of God."

*"If I speak in the tongues of men and
 of angels, but have not love, I am
 only a resounding gong or a
 clanging cymbal.
If I have the gift of prophecy and can
 fathom all mysteries and all
 knowledge, and if I have a faith
 that can move mountains,
 but have not love, I am nothing.
If I give all I possess to the poor and
 surrender my body to the flames,
 but have not love, I gain nothing."*

Paul's First Letter to the Corinthians

74 PHILOSOPHER

SENECA THE YOUNGER

Córdoba, Spain
c. 4 BC–AD 65

The Stoic philosopher and writer Seneca the Younger was tutor to Nero and a calming influence during the first part of the emperor's reign. But over time he had less influence and, accused of involvement in a conspiracy to kill Nero, was made to take his own life. His tragic plays, such as *Medea* and *Thyestes*, were an influence on Renaissance writers such as John Webster and William Shakespeare. He also wrote a series of *Moral Letters* to Lucilius Junior, procurator of Sicily.

75 ARTIST

JOHN OF PATMOS

Bethsaida, Galilee (now Golan Heights, Syria)
c. AD 1–90

John of Patmos was the author of the Book of Revelation in the Bible. He was exiled to the island of Patmos, possibly by Emperor Domitian (r. AD 81–96). He may have been John the Apostle, one of Jesus's twelve disciples. Some readers believe the apocalyptic visions of the book describe events destined to take place at the predicted Second Coming of Christ.

BELOW: John has a vision of the Virgin Mary and infant Christ as he writes the Book of Revelation in this painting by German artist Hans Baldung, c. 1511.

RELIGIOUS LEADER

ST. PETER

Bethsaida, Galilee (now Golan Heights, Syria)
c. AD 1–68

Apostle who provided leadership for the early Christian Church.

Peter was originally called Simon, a fisherman like his brother Andrew, when Jesus called them to become "fishers of men." According to biblical accounts, when he identified Jesus as the Messiah, the long-promised savior of the Jews, Jesus renamed him Peter (derived from the word for rock) and declared, "On this rock I will build my church." He is famous for an all-too-human failure of nerves: when Jesus was arrested before being crucified, Peter denied knowing him three times. Nonetheless, he became a centrally important leader in the early church, and is said to have been the first bishop in both Antioch and Rome—Peter is celebrated as the first pope in a succession that stretches to the present day. He was crucified in the persecution of Christians unleashed by Emperor Nero—insisting on being hung upside down since he believed he was not worthy to be executed in the same way as Jesus.

> "And I say also unto thee, That thou art Peter, and upon this rock I will build my church; and the gates of hell shall not prevail against it.
> And I will give unto thee the keys of the kingdom of heaven: and whatsoever thou shalt bind on earth shall be bound in heaven: and whatsoever thou shalt loose on earth shall be loosed in heaven."
>
> The Bible, Matthew 16:18–19

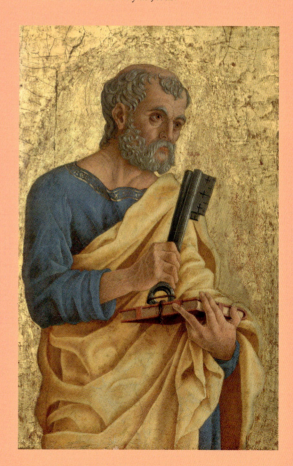

RIGHT: Peter is traditionally shown in yellow and blue, holding a key—Jesus said to him, "I will give you the keys to the kingdom of heaven."

77 POLITICAL LEADER

CALIGULA (GAIUS CAESAR AUGUSTUS GERMANICUS)

Antio (now Anzio), Italy
12–41

Emperor whose short reign descended into self-aggrandizing madness and excess.

Celebrated claims about Caligula include that he wanted to appoint his horse Incitatus to the important political position of consul, to have a statue of himself raised for worship in the Jerusalem Temple, and that when there were no more prisoners at some Roman games he commanded his guards to force members of the crowd into the arena to be consumed by wild animals. There are also allegations that he was self-obsessed; committed incest with his sisters Agrippina the Younger, Drusilla, and Livilla, and sold them to other men for sex; had affairs with men, including his sister Julia's husband Marcus Lepidus; and ordered the killing of people on a whim. We should take these stories with a grain of salt because in Rome opponents alleged extravagant behavior to discredit a person. Caligula was the son of Emperor Augustus's granddaughter Agrippina the Elder and the general Germanicus. "Caligula" (little boot) was a nickname given to him by soldiers when the family accompanied Germanicus on campaigns in Germany. Caligula succeeded Emperor Tiberius in 37. Initially he behaved with moderation, but after seven months he became severely ill and went mad. He became cruel and erratic, executed enemies and supporters, spent vast sums, erected many statues of himself in Rome, and began to present himself as a god. He ended up confiscating private estates to raise money. In 40 he led the army to the coast of the English Channel, supposedly in preparation to invade Britain, but then commanded them to gather seashells. Back in Rome, he was assassinated by his own Praetorian Guard in 41.

ABOVE: Caligula may have had epilepsy from childhood; it is possible that an attack in 37 resulted in paranoid and psychopathic behavior for the rest of his life.

KNOWN FOR
- Exhibiting sadistic and capricious behavior
- Claiming he was a god
- Bringing the army fully under control of the emperor
- Building two Roman aqueducts

BOUDICCA

Camulodunum (now Colchester), England
c. 30–61

British queen who led tribes in a violent revolt against Roman rule.

Boudicca led the Celtic Iceni tribe of Norfolk (eastern England) in a dramatic revolt against the Romans when she was humiliated following the death of her husband Prasutagus. After Rome conquered southern England in 43, Prasutagus remained in power as a client king, but when he died the Romans seized his land, stripped and whipped Boudicca, and raped her daughters. They say "revenge is a dish best served cold"; she waited until the governor Suetonius Paulinus was away, then led the Iceni and local allies on a rampage in which they put Camulodunum (modern Colchester, the capital of Roman Britain), Verulanium (modern St. Albans), and the marketplace in Londinium (modern London) to the torch. The historian Tacitus reports that they killed 70,000 Romans and Roman allies. However, on Suetonius's return he defeated Boudicca's army in the Battle of Watling Street in 61. Boudicca probably took poison to avoid capture. Her story was rediscovered in the Renaissance era and she became a symbol of British pride and national defiance, especially in the nineteenth century, when Queen Victoria's consort Prince Albert commissioned sculptor Thomas Thornycroft to make a celebrated statue of the queen and her daughters in a chariot that stands in central London.

LEFT: Thornycroft's stirring bronze statue of Boudicca in her chariot stands near the Houses of Parliament in London.

79 POLITICAL LEADER

NERO (NERO CLAUDIUS CAESAR AUGUSTUS GERMANICUS)

Antio (now Anzio), Italy
37–68

Roman emperor who persecuted early Christians and was blamed for the Great Fire of Rome.

Nero was adopted by Emperor Claudius aged thirteen, and succeeded him in 54. Initially he ruled successfully, following the advice of the philosopher Seneca, his mother Agrippina the Younger, and Praetorian Prefect Sextus Afranius Burrus. But after he had Agrippina murdered in 59, and the others' influence fell away, Nero indulged his love of musical performance, acting, and chariot racing. The historian Suetonius writes that in 64 Nero started what became the Great Fire of Rome, which destroyed large parts of the city, in order to clear ground for a palace. Tacitus reports that Nero attacked early Christians with cruelty and vigor, attempting to pin the blame on them and burning them alive. He may have been the initial inspiration for the Antichrist of Christian tradition. A revolt against Nero resulted in his being declared a public enemy by the Roman Senate, and he committed suicide.

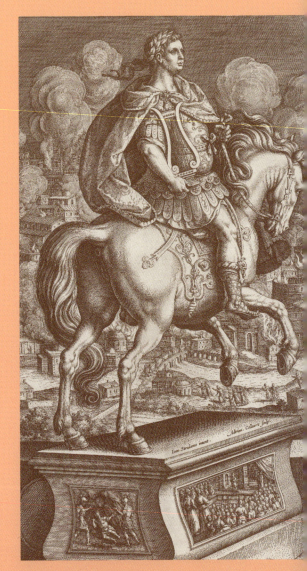

RIGHT: Tradition has it that Nero fiddled (played the lyre) while Rome burned. This may be true, but the story that he started the fire is probably not.

80 ARTIST

PLUTARCH

Chaeronea, Greece
46–119

The Greek author Plutarch was educated in Athens, and lectured on philosophy in Rome. His *Parallel Lives* presented biographies of twenty-three pairs of Greek and Roman figures. He also collected ethical and literary essays and speeches in the *Moralia*. *Parallel Lives* was translated into English by Sir Thomas North in 1579, and was the source for William Shakespeare's Roman history plays.

81 POLITICAL LEADER

TRAJAN
(CAESAR NERVA TRAIANUS)

Italica (now Santiponce), Spain
c. 53–117

Under Emperor Trajan (r. 98–117) the Roman Empire expanded to its largest extent. He was a popular emperor who cut taxes and provided welfare support for the poor. In Rome he built an aqueduct, public baths, and a new forum containing the celebrated 115-foot-tall Trajan's Column, which commemorates his campaigns in Dacia (Romania).

BELOW: Detail from the 620-foot-long carved frieze that winds around Trajan's Column in Rome.

TACITUS (GAIUS CORNELIUS TACITUS)

Gallia Narbonensis (now Occitane, France)
56–120

Tacitus studied rhetoric, and was a celebrated orator as well the author of the *Histories* and *Annals*, which detail events from the death of Emperor Augustus in 14 to that of Domitian in 96. Only parts of each work survive. He wrote in a lively, concise Latin that was a great influence on other authors, and his work provides important details on the early persecution of Christians. He made the earliest reference outside the Bible to the crucifixion of Jesus. He also wrote a biography of his father-in-law Agricola, who was governor of the Roman province of Britain in *c.* 77–83, and a book on oratory.

RIGHT: Tacitus was a friend of lawyer and author Pliny the Younger, and most of what we know of his life comes from Pliny's writings.

83 SCIENTIST

CAI LUN

Leiyang, China
62–121

Han dynasty official who invented paper, using bark to replace silk.

Cai Lun, an official under Emperor Hedi of the Eastern Han dynasty (r. 88–c. 105), invented paper as a cheaper and better alternative to the silk, cloth, wooden strips, or bamboo previously used for writing on. He entered palace service as a eunuch in around 75, and rose to become chief eunuch at Hedi's court. He was appointed to be in charge of the manufacture of tools and weapons at the palace workshop, and it was here that he had the idea for making paper in c. 105. His paper was made from tree bark, hemp, fishing nets, and old pieces of cloth, as well as bamboo. The ingredients were boiled to a pulp, mixed with water, then sieved and left to dry. Cai Lun's apprentice Zuo Bo later improved the process. He was appointed to oversee the production of a new edition of the *Five Classics*. In China he became a deity and was worshipped as the god of paper manufacture.

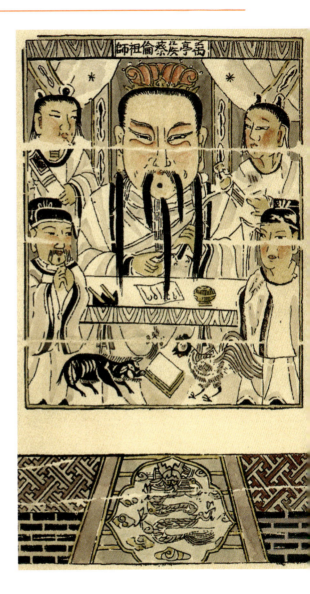

RIGHT: Cai Lun's invention, as improved by Zuo Bo, changed the course of history. Papermaking remains a major enterprise in his birthplace of Leiyang.

> "Cai Lun then initiated the idea of making paper from the bark of trees, hemp, old rags, and fishing nets. He submitted the process to the emperor in the first year of Yuanxing and received praise for his ability. From this time, paper has been in use everywhere and is universally called the 'paper of Lord Cai.'"
>
> *Hou Hanshu*, one of the Twenty-Four Histories of the Han dynasty

84 SCIENTIST

ZHANG HENG

Xi'e (now Henan and Hubei), China
78–139

Chinese polymath Zhang Heng invented the first seismoscope, which could detect an earthquake 300 miles away. He also developed a water-powered armillary sphere for demonstrating the positions of astronomical bodies, and created a star catalog containing 2,500 stars. In mathematics he made advances in the approximation of pi.

ABOVE: Zhang Heng was an accomplished poet, and also studied the Moon and the Sun.

85 SCIENTIST

PTOLEMY (CLAUDIUS PTOLEMAEUS)

Alexandria, Egypt
c. 100–170

Egyptian-born geographer and astronomer Ptolemy wrote two masterpieces. *The Guide to Geography* estimated the size of the Earth and listed locations by latitude and longitude. His *Almagest* on the stars and planets established an Earth-centered view of the universe that held until Nicolaus Copernicus corrected it in the early sixteenth century. In both these works he was indebted to the Greek astronomer Hipparchus (c. 190–120 BC). He also wrote an important treatise on astrology, usually called the *Tetrabiblos* (*Four Books*). He worked in the Great Library of Alexandria.

> "I know that I am mortal by nature, and ephemeral; but when I trace at my pleasure the windings to and fro of the heavenly bodies I no longer touch the earth with my feet: I stand in the presence of Zeus himself and take my fill of ambrosia."
>
> Ptolemy, *Almagest*, 150

RIGHT: Ptolemy holds an armillary sphere depicting the movements of the stars, Sun, and Moon.

86 POLITICAL LEADER

MARCUS AURELIUS
(MARCUS AURELIUS ANTONINUS)

Rome, Italy
121–180

In challenging times, this emperor wrote an influential notebook of Stoic philosophical musings.

Emperor Marcus Aurelius was the adopted son of Emperor Antoninus Pius and ruled alongside him from 147. Then, on Antoninus's death in 161, he chose to share power with his adopted brother Lucius Aurelius Verus. The empire was facing military challenges on many fronts, including Britain, Germany, and the East. Aurelius personally commanded the army on the Danube frontier for ten years. In Rome, the Column of Marcus Aurelius and a famous 14-foot-tall equestrian statue of the emperor celebrated his military victories. The Antonine Plague—probably smallpox brought back by legionnaires from the East—swept the empire in 165–180, killing 5–10 million people. In Aurelius's *Meditations*—a series of personal writings—he emphasizes how important it is to be rational and clear-headed, pointing out a person is often hurt by their reaction to events rather than the events themselves.

ABOVE RIGHT: Marcus Aurelius, considered to be the last of the five good emperors (after Nerva, Trajan, Hadrian, and Antoninus Pius), is depicted pardoning defeated enemies.

87 SCIENTIST

GALEN

Pergamon, Greece (now Bergama, Turkey)
129–216

The Greek physician Galen influenced medical practice until the seventeeth century. He argued that there are three body systems (brain and nerves, heart and artery, and liver and veins) and four humors, or fluids (black bile, yellow bile, blood, and phlegm), that need to be kept in balance. Around 150 of his approximately 300 works survive.

88 POLITICAL LEADER

SEPTIMIUS SEVERUS
(LUCIUS SEPTIMIUS SEVERUS)

Leptis Magna, Carthage (now Al-Khums, Libya)
145–211

African-born Roman emperor who saw off rivals, boosted the army, and campaigned in Britain.

Septimius Severus seized power in 193—the remarkable "Year of the Five Emperors." After the assassination of Commodus on the last day of 192, Pertinax was named emperor but was killed by the Praetorian Guard after three months. Didius Julianus was able to purchase the title from the guard, but was killed on June 1. The Senate declared Severus emperor but he had to defeat a rival, Pescennius Niger, and while at war he allowed Clodius Albinus (the fifth of the five emperors) to be co-ruler. In 194 Severus defeated Niger in Syria, then overcame Albinus in France in 197. That same year he defeated the Parthians and added Mesopotamia (Iraq) to the empire. He introduced military reforms, increasing pay and allowing soldiers to marry, and the power of the Senate declined. In 208 he led an army to Britain, strengthened Hadrian's Wall, reoccupied the Antonine Wall, and attempted an invasion of Caledonia (Scotland), but he fell ill and died at Eboracum (York).

RIGHT: Traditionally, Severus was remembered for persecuting Christians, but many historians dispute this. Tertullian says he saved Christians from attack.

89 MILITARY LEADER

CAO CAO

Qiao (now Bozhou), China
155–220

A great general and grand chancellor of the Eastern Han dynasty, Cao Cao was the power behind the throne of puppet ruler Emperor Xian. In a chaotic period, he imposed public order and rebuilt the economy. Also celebrated as a calligrapher and writer, he published the first known commentary on Sunzi's *The Art of War*. Popular narratives cast him as a scheming villain. He was instrumental in the creation of the state of Cao Wei and is remembered as "Emperor Wu of Wei."

90 MILITARY LEADER

GUAN YU

Xie (now Yuncheng), China
160–219

Guan Yu was, with Zhang Fei, a famously loyal general in the service of the warlord Liu Bei, and later was worshipped as the god of war Guandi. He helped Liu Bei establish the state of Shu Han. Tradition has it that Liu Bei intervened in a violent quarrel between Guan Yu and Zhang Fei and the three became inseperable.

BELOW: Guan Yu's loyalty and bravery were celebrated for centuries, and shrines to him are widely found in China today.

91 RELIGIOUS LEADER

MANI

Ctesiphon, Mesopotamia (now Baghdad, Iraq)
216–274

This prophet's new faith focused on a fight between the light and the darkness.

The Iranian prophet Mani founded the new faith of Manichaeism. The religion, which still exists in China, was the main rival to Christianity for a time but from the rule of Emperor Diocletian onward, its followers were persecuted and it was eliminated from the Roman Empire. Manichaeism is a dualistic faith, teaching that there is an eternal struggle between a spiritual world of light and goodness, and the material world associated with wickedness and darkness. Mani had two visions, aged twelve and twenty-four, of his own "heavenly twin," and was driven to spread the new faith. He traveled to India, where he converted followers. Subsequently the Persian ruler Shāpur I, while he did not convert from Zoroastrianism, allowed Mani to preach Manichaeism. But when Bahram I became king in 273, he imprisoned Mani and he died in jail. His ideas may have influenced the Christian theologian Augustine of Hippo.

BELOW: Spiritual light, material darkness. An eighth- or ninth-century mural from Goachang in Xinjiang, China, depicts three priests of the Manichean religion.

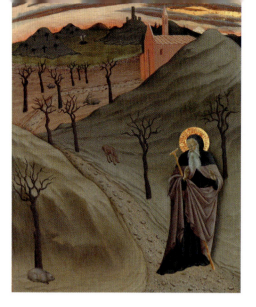

92 RELIGIOUS LEADER

ST. ANTHONY

Koma, Egypt
251–356

Born to wealthy landowners, Anthony sold his land and possessions following the death of his parents when he was twenty. He lived a strict ascetic lifestyle, eating only bread with salt and water then, after about fifteen years, retreated into the desert and lived entirely alone in a disused Roman fort. Fellow hermits began to settle nearby, and asked him to lead them. Around 305 he began to instruct and organize them—which led to his being known as the "Father of all monks." Subsequently, he withdrew again into total isolation in the desert, although he visited Christians in Alexandria when they were suffering persecution under Emperor Diocletian.

ABOVE: In the wilderness: this saint is called Anthony the Great or Anthony of the Desert to distinguish him from others of the same name.

93 POLITICAL LEADER

CONSTANTINE THE GREAT

Naissius (now Serbia)
c. 280–337

The first Roman emperor to accept Christianity also moved the capital of the empire to the east.

The son of Flavius Constantius, one of the co-emperors under the tetrarchy system established by Diocletian, Constantine was acclaimed emperor by the army on his father's death at Eboracum (York) during a British campaign. He defeated rival Maxentius in the Battle of Milvian Bridge in 312, after having a vision of the Christian cross and the message "In this sign you shall conquer." He converted to Christianity and, in 313, with co-emperor Licinius, issued the Edict of Milan, which decreed that Christians should not be persecuted in the empire. In 324 he defeated Licinius and became sole emperor. That year he moved the imperial capital eastward, renaming the ancient Greek city of Byzantium, Constantinople. (It was renamed Istanbul in 1930.) In 325 Constantine called the First Council of Nicaea, which debated Christian doctrine and issued the statement of belief known as the Nicene Creed. He ordered the building of the Church of the Holy Sepulchre, one of the holiest sites in Christianity, on the site of Jesus's tomb in Jerusalem.

RIGHT: Constantine is shown carrying the city of Constantinople in this celebrated mosaic from the former church, now mosque, of Hagia Sophia, Istanbul.

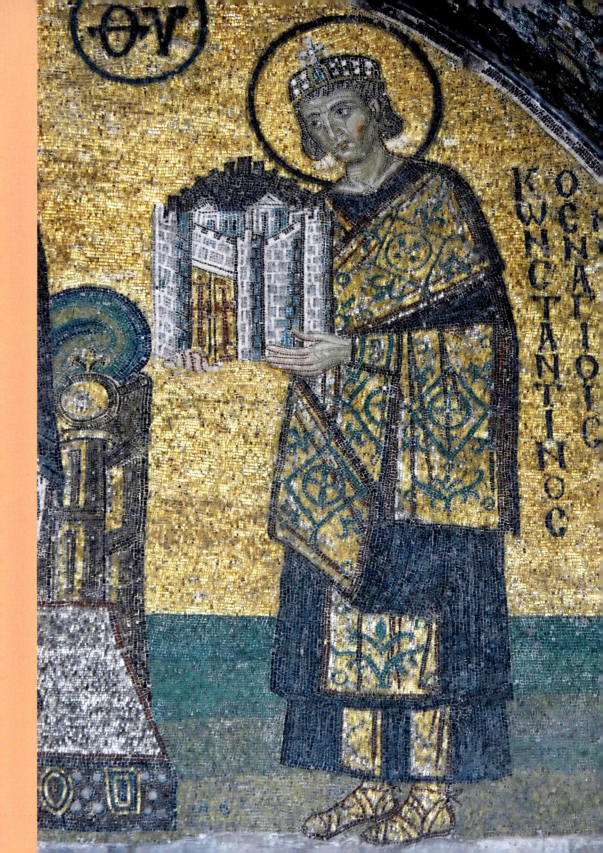

94 ROYALTY

EZANA OF AXUM

Aksum, Axum (now Ethiopia and Eritrea)
c. 303–350

King of Axum who converted to Christianity and conquered Kush.

Ezana was the first king of the African Kingdom of Axum to convert to Christianity. He was converted by his childhood tutor Frumentius, a freed slave who is celebrated as "the Father of Peace" and "Apostle to Ethiopia." Ezana acceded to the throne as a child on the death of his father Ousanas, with his mother Sofya as regent. Ezana conquered the Kingdom of Kush (northern Sudan/southern Egypt) in 350, taking and sacking the city of Meroë. His religious conversion and conquests are recorded on the Ezana Stone, a column inscribed in three languages: Greek, the Arabian language of Sabaean, and the ancient Ethiopian Semitic language of Ge'ez. Ezana also issued coins bearing the Christian cross and the inscription "May it gratify the people," some of which have been found in India, indicating that the kingdom had a far-reaching trade network. King lists for the country name Abreha and Asbeha as the rulers when Christianity was introduced, and these may have been the baptismal names taken by Ezana and his brother Saizan.

LEFT: Brothers Ezana and Saizan in a mural from a c. 1100 church built in their honor in Tigray, Ethiopia.

95 MILITARY LEADER

ALARIC

Peuce, Scythia Minor (now Romania)
c. 370–410

Alaric, chief of the Visigoths, led the sack of Rome in August 410, which signaled the start of the end for the Western Roman Empire. It was the first time the city had been captured by a foreign force in 800 years. Earlier, in 395, his men sacked the port of Athens, and pillaged Greek cities including Argos and Sparta. The attack in 410 was the third year running he had besieged Rome. Afterward, Alaric gave up on a plan to invade North Africa, and died as the Visigoth army was marching northward through Italy.

96 MILITARY LEADER

ATTILA THE HUN

Pannonia, Transdanubia (now Hungary)
c. 406–453

The widely feared ruler of the Huns, who repeatedly attacked the Eastern and Western Roman Empires, became known as "the scourge of God." He crossed the Danube on raids in 441 and 443, destroying Belgrade and Sofia, and in 447 invaded the Balkans and Greece, exacting a demanding tribute from the Eastern Roman Empire. In 451, he invaded Gaul but was defeated in the Battle of the Catalaunian Plains. A year later, he invaded and ransacked northern Italy but did not attack Rome, driven back by plague and famine-induced starvation. He died on his wedding night, possibly killed by his bride. After his death he became a hero of Germanic legend.

97 RELIGIOUS LEADER

POPE LEO I

Tuscany, Italy
c. 400–461

The first pope to be called "the Great," Leo made an important statement, or tome, explicating that as the son of God, Jesus had two natures, human and divine, distinct but not separate, and this was accepted by the Council of Chalcedon in 451. Leo is also said to have persuaded Attila the Hun, who had invaded northern Italy and sacked Aquileia, to turn back and spare Rome—although plague in his army may also have influenced Attila.

LEFT: Leo I established that each pope draws his authority from St. Peter—to whom Christ gave command over the Church.

98 SCIENTIST

ZU CHONGZI

Jiankang (now Nanjing), China
429–500

The Chinese mathematician and astronomer calculated pi to between 3.1415926 and 3.1415917, a level of accuracy that was not bettered for 800 years. He introduced a new calendar, the Daming calendar, and accurately calculated the length of a year on Earth and on the planet Jupiter.

THEODORA OF BYZANTIUM

Crete or Syria
c. 500–548

This empress, consort of Justinian I, was one of the most powerful women in Byzantine history.

Theodora was the daughter of a bear trainer and a dancer. She reputedly worked in a brothel and on stage in a sexually explicit representation of the Greek myth of Leda and the Swan, traveled to North Africa, and lived for a while in Alexandria. Back in Constantinople, when Justinian wanted to marry her, the law had to be changed to allow someone of senatorial rank to wed an actress. Theodora was crowned empress on Justinian's accession to the throne in 527, two years after they were married. Thereafter she played a central role, attending state councils, sharing in his deliberations, and wielding a significant influence over him. In January 532, when riots broke out in Constantinople, Justinian was preparing to flee but Theodora spoke out in council and persuaded him to show bravery and remain. After the riots, Justinian and Theodora built the supremely beautiful Church of Holy Wisdom (Hagia Sophia) as part of their rebuilding of the city. Theodora died aged forty-eight, probably from breast cancer, and was buried in the Church of the Holy Apostles in Constantinople.

BELOW: A mosaic in the Basilica of San Vitale, Ravenna, represents Theodora and her attendants. She is a saint in the Eastern and Oriental Orthodox Churches.

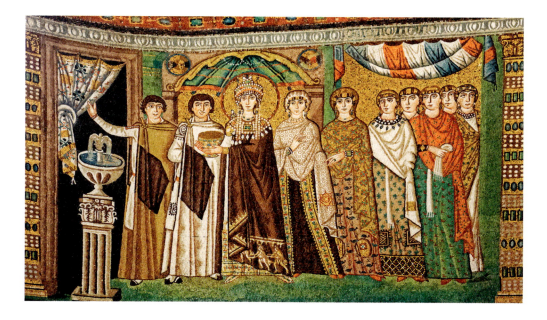

2

The Age of Chivalry and the Renaissance
500–1500

100 RELIGIOUS LEADER

PROPHET MUHAMMAD

Mecca, Arabia (now Saudi Arabia)
570–632

Prophet who founded the world religion of Islam, based on submission to the one god, Allah.

The Prophet Muhammad received the revelations that inspired the birth of Islam during a mystical encounter with the Angel Jiba'il (Gabriel in the Judeo-Christian tradition) in a mountain cave near Mecca, in 610. His message was that there is no god except Allah, and that all people should live in submission to him. He began preaching in 613 and made converts in Mecca, then in 619 had another profound religious experience—the *Mir'aj*, a night journey to Jerusalem and heaven. In 622 he led his followers from Mecca to settle in Yathrib, an event celebrated as the *Hijra* (migration). He established a religious and social community of Muslims there, and the city was renamed Medina ("the City of the Prophet"). The event marks the start of the Islamic calendar. He had conquered Mecca and all of Arabia by 631, and the following year made the first pilgrimage to Mecca—the *hajj* performed each year by millions of Muslims. At this time, he received the final revelation of the Quran, the holy book of Islam. However, the same year he fell ill and died on June 8. His followers carried the new faith he had founded across the world through *jihad* ("full exertion" or "holy war").

101 POLITICAL LEADER

SHOTOKU TAISHI

Yamato, Japan
574–622

Prince who is revered as a Buddhist saint and the protector of Japan and the Imperial Family.

The second son of Emperor Yomei, Shotoku became regent and crown prince under the rule of his aunt, Empress Suiko (r. 593–628). He reestablished diplomatic relations with China, resuming the sending of envoys and bringing Chinese clerks, craft workers, and artists to Japan. He initiated the use of the Chinese calendar and instituted many government reforms along Chinese lines, while promoting Confucianism and Buddhism over Japan's native Shinto faith—although he was always respectful of Shinto traditions. Shotoku erected several Buddhist temples, including Shitenno-ji in Osaka, and the celebrated Horyu Temple in Ikaruga, Nara—one of the world's oldest still-standing wooden structures.

"Everyone has their own task. When wise men hold office, praise can be heard. If corrupt men take power, disasters and misrule follow."

The Constitution of Prince Shotoko, 604

102 RELIGIOUS LEADER

POPE GREGORY I

Rome, Italy
540–604

Gregory the Great (r. 590–604) was the first monk to become pope. He had studied rhetoric, music, law, history, and mathematics. He wrote *Pastoral Rule*, a guide for rulers; a book of saints' lives called *Dialogues*; and *Magna Moralia*, a thirty-five-book treatise on the biblical book of Job; as well as more than sixty homilies (short sermons). Inspired by the sight of "Angles" (English youths) for sale in Rome as slaves (reputedly he was moved to say, "They're not Angles, they're angels"), he sent a mission to England under Augustine, prior of the Benedictine monastery of St. Andrew that Gregory had founded in the city.

ABOVE: Shotoku Taishi aged sixteen. He wrote the first Japanese history, which was modeled on Chinese exemplars.

ABOVE: Divine inspiration—the Holy Spirit, in the form of a dove, dictates to Pope Gregory, who is seated at his writing desk.

103 ROYALTY

SEONDEOK OF SILLA

Korea
c. 606–647

Seondeok came to the throne of the Kingdom of Silla when her father Jinpyeong (r. 579–632) died without a male heir. With the general Kim Yu-sin and diplomat Kim Chunchu, she consolidated Silla's preeminence over the rival Korean kingdoms of Koguryeo and Paekche. Her reign saw the building of the Cheomsongdae tower, East Asia's oldest astronomical observatory.

104 ROYALTY

PAKAL THE GREAT

B'aakal, Mexico
603–683

Mayan king who is famous for his long reign and magnificent architectural legacy in Palenque.

King Pakal, ruler of the Mayan city-state of Palenque in southern Mexico, reigned for sixty-eight years from July 27, 615, making him the longest-reigning monarch in the Americas, and the fifth-longest in world history. He came to the throne as a child, being next in succession after his grandfather Janaab Pakal (died 612), and he succeeded aged twelve in 615; his mother Lady Sak K'uk' served as regent for the first three years and may have remained the power behind the throne until her death in 640. Pakal (whose name means "Shield") built up Palenque to become the dominant city-state in the region, and made alliances with Tikal, Pomoná, and Tortuguero. He erected some of the most enduring of all Mayan architecture, greatly expanding the Palace of Palenque. His supremacy can be judged from his burial: he was laid to rest wearing a mask of jade, obsidian, and shells, in a red-painted stone sarcophagus in a superb funerary crypt beneath the city's imposing Temple of the Inscriptions.

"This is a name linked with war."

Guillermo Bernal of the National Autonomous University of Mexico on deciphering the name on Pakal's tomb as "The House of the Nine Sharpened Spears," 2015

RIGHT: A carving of Pakal at Palenque. During his reign the city-state was at war with Toniná, and one of Pakal's sons, Kan Xul, was captured.

105 ROYALTY

KAYA MAGAN CISSÉ

Africa
b. 670

In *c.* 700, the king of Wagadou, Kaya Magan Cissé, founded the Cissé Tounkara dynasty, whose monarchs ruled the Ghana Empire in the century that followed. The empire, situated in what is now western Mali and southwestern Mauritania, lasted to 1100, and became wealthy from trans-Saharan trade in gold, salt, and slaves. It took its name from the royal title *ghana*.

106 ROYALTY

K'AK TILIW CHAN YOPAAT (CAUAC SKY)

Quiriguá (now Izabal, Guatemala)
c. 690–785

This king of the Mayan city-state of Quiriguá defeated the rival city of Copán (now Honduras) in 738. Copán's ruler, Uaxaclajuun Ub'aah K'awiil (sometimes called "Eighteen Rabbit"), was taken prisoner and beheaded. Formerly a vassal of Copán, Quiriguá grew rich on trade from the Caribbean. Its stonemasons raised stelae (carved uprights) and zoomorphs (carvings representing humans as animals) to glorify the king.

107 ARTIST

ZHANG XU

Suzhou, China
c. 725–775

Chinese poet and calligrapher who is celebrated for his energetic style.

Zhang Xu was one of a group of Tang dynasty artists—including Li Bai and He Zhizhang—known as the "Eight Immortals of the Wine Vessel." He was famous for throwing off his cap when drunk, and then using his hair to create calligraphic designs while shouting and striding about; on sobering up, he would be astonished by the quality of the work he made under the influence of alcohol, but he could never re-create it in the cold light of morning. He was an expert in regular and cursive scripts, especially the variant called *kuangcao* (wild cursive script), and so good at the latter that he was called "the Divine cursive writer." His work was wild, forceful, and highly varied. Surviving masterpieces include *Shiwuri Tie* and *Gushie Sitie*. Some identify Zhang Xu and his younger fellow artist Huaisu, another big drinker, as the greatest calligraphers in Chinese history—under the name "crazy Zhang and drunk Su."

> *"Zhang Xu requires three full glasses to perform his art but then his brush makes magical mists bloom on silk."*
>
> Du Fu, *The Eight Immortals of the Wine Cup*, 712–770

RIGHT: Zhang Xu's trademark spontaneous, free-flowing script can be appreciated in this page from his work *Four Poems*.

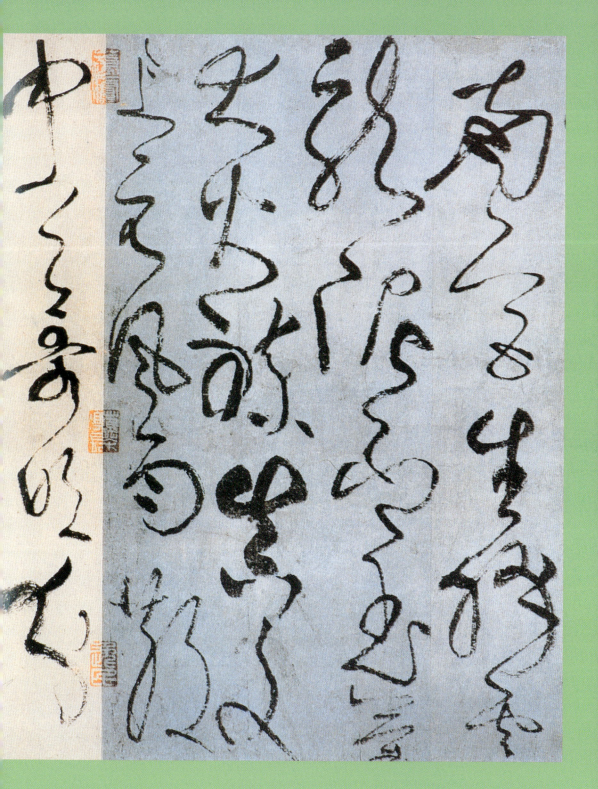

108 ROYALTY

CHARLEMAGNE

Liège, Francia (now Belgium)
c. 747–814

King of the Franks who established a great empire in Europe and is revered as an ideal ruler.

When he was crowned Emperor of the Romans by Pope Leo III on Christmas Day in the year 800, Charlemagne revived the Western Roman Empire that had collapsed in the fifth century. After becoming King of the Franks in 771 on the death of his brother and co-ruler Carloman, he conquered the Saxons, Lombards, and Avars, and won favor as the pope's protector. At his court in Aachen (now Germany), he oversaw a great flowering of learning and artistic activity—the Carolingian Renaissance.

LEFT: The Frankish king is crowned first Holy Roman Emperor—as imagined by Raphael in 1516–1517.

109 RELIGIOUS LEADER

KUKAI

Zentsu-ji (now Kagawa), Japan
774–835

Poet and teacher who brought tantric Buddhism to Japan.

Kukai—known after his death as Kobo Daishi (Great Master Who Spread the Dharma)—founded the Shingon school of Buddhism. Raised in a wealthy family, he studied Confucianism and reputedly, at the age of just seventeen, wrote a book, *Essential Parts of the Three Traditions*, which argued that Buddhism was superior to Confucian and Taoist teachings. Traveling to China in 804, he became a disciple of Hui-kuo (known as Keika in Japan) and a master of Chinese esoteric Buddhism (a strand of Vajrayana, the tradition that foregrounds Tantra and secret mantra). On returning to Japan two years later, Kukai won imperial backing to teach this tradition under the name Shingon. He built a monastery on Mount Koya that became a great religious-philosophical center, and established the popularity of Shingon in Japan. His masterpiece was the *Ten Stages in Consciousness*, which classified Confucian, Taoist, and Buddhist teachings, and declared that Shingon was the highest expression of them all. He was also a renowned poet and calligrapher.

KNOWN FOR
- Being a Japanese Buddhist saint
- Founding the Shingon Tantric school of Buddhism
- Promoting public education in Japan

"The affection for science ... that friendliness and condescension God displays to the learned ... has encouraged me to compose a short work on calculating by al-jabr (restoring) and al-muqabala (comparing), confining it to what is easiest and most useful in arithmetic."

Muhammad Ibn Mūsā al-Khwārizmī, quoted in *History of Mathematics*, David Eugene Smith (1923)

110 SCIENTIST

MUHAMMAD IBN MŪSĀ AL-KHWĀRIZMĪ

Khwarazm, Persia (now part of Turkmenistan and Uzbekistan)
c. 780–850

Persian polymath who passed ancient mathematical theories to the West.

Through the work of Muhammad ibn Mūsā al-Khwārizmī, the way numbers (Hindu-Arabic numerals) are written and algebra is used were introduced to European mathematics. His books, which incorporated material from ancient Babylonian, Hebrew, and Hindu mathematics, were translated into Latin in the twelfth century. The words *algebra* and *algorithm* come from his name. He worked at the House of Wisdom, a great library and academy in Baghdad, run by the Abbasid caliphs, under Caliph al-Ma'mun.

Al-Khwarizmi also wrote a celebrated *Geography*, which listed places by their coordinates, worked on determining the Earth's circumference, and issued influential astronomical tables.

ABOVE: Monument to the great polymath in al-Khwārizmī's birthplace, now known as Khiva (Uzbekistan).

111 RELIGIOUS LEADER

POPE LEO III

Rome, Italy
750–816

Leo III, pope from 795 to 816, consolidated the papacy's relationship with the Franks. In 799 he escaped a violent attack by Pascalis, nephew of the previous pope, Hadrian I, by seeking the protection of Charlemagne, the great king of the Franks. The following year Charlemagne visited Rome and Leo crowned him on Christmas Day in St. Peter's Basilica. Charlemagne is generally viewed as the first Holy Roman Emperor, and, according to one account, Leo prostrated himself before Charlemagne and kissed the ground in the act of homage due to an emperor.

ABOVE: Alfred's biographer, Bishop Asser of Sherborne, said he was a just man, a great warrior, and filled with learning.

112 ROYALTY

ALFRED THE GREAT

Wantage, England
849–899

King Alfred of Wessex translated Latin texts into English and set out to spread learning and literacy in his kingdom. The composition of the *Anglo-Saxon Chronicle* (a national history) began in his reign. He constructed forts, established a navy, reorganized the army, and repeatedly defied the invading Danes, winning a major victory at the Battle of Edington in 878. Alfred may have been emulating Charlemagne and the Frankish king's Carolingian Renaissance when he promoted literacy and learning in Wessex.

113 SCIENTIST

AL-YAQUBI

Baghdad, Persia (now Iraq)
c. 850–897

Historian and geographer al-Yaqubi wrote the world chronicle *Tarikh ibn Wadih* (*Ibn Wadih's History*) and the celebrated geography *Kitab al-buldan* (*Book of Lands*). Born in Baghdad, he lived in Armenia and Khorasan, then voyaged to India and northern Africa; he died in Egypt. The chronicle covers world history before the advent of Islam in part one, and Islamic history to 872 in part two.

114 ARTIST

FERDOWSI (ABŪ AL-QASEM MANṢŪR)

Tus, Persia (now Iran)
c. 935–1020

Poet who wrote the *Book of Kings*, the national epic of Iran.

Celebrated as one of the greatest authors in world history, Ferdowsi wrote the *Book of Kings* between 977 and 1010. The 60,000-couplet work is one of the longest epic poems created by a single author. According to twelfth-century Persian poet Nezami-ye 'Aruzi, Ferdowsi was a landowner and began writing the poem to generate a dowry for his daughter. He based his epic on earlier works, including a prose history of Persian kings, and a 1,000-verse account written by Daqiqi. In 1010 he traveled to court to present the poem to Sultan Mahmud of Ghazna, but was disappointed by the paltry reward given him—which he reputedly split between a bath attendant, a beer-seller, and the slave who had delivered it. He then went to Mazandaran where, at the court of local king Sepahbad Shahreyar, he wrote a scathing satire on Mahmud. Ferdowsi died and was buried in his garden near the city of Tus; the mausoleum later built over the grave is a national shrine.

> "Kayumars was first to occupy the throne of Persia, and was governor of all the world. He made his home in the mountains, and dressed himself and his people in the skins of tigers."
>
> Ferdowsi, *Book of Kings*, c. 977–1010

LEFT: A page from Ferdowsi's epic history—the battle between Bahram Chubina and Sava Shah—in the *Book of Kings*.

500–1500   101

EXPLORER

LEIF ERIKSON

Iceland
c. 970–1025

Norse explorer who was probably the first European to land in North America.

Leif Erikson was the son of Erik the Red, who founded the first Norse settlement in Greenland, and Thjodhild. The Icelandic sagas report that Erikson established a settlement in Vinland; this was possibly at L'Anse aux Meadows in Newfoundland, Canada, where the remains of a Norse settlement of that date have been found.

LEFT: The sagas report that Leif landed in Vinland after being blown off course when sailing from Norway to Greenland to convert its settlers to Christianity.

ABU RAYHAN AL-BIRUNI

Khwarazm, Khorasan (now Uzbekistan)
973–c. 1050

The world's first anthropologist who made a study of eleventh-century India.

The extravagantly gifted al-Biruni excelled as a mathematician, astronomer, linguist, geographer, and historian. He was initially supported by the princes of his native Khwarazm in central Asia, but fled a civil war there. He took refuge at the court of the Samanid rulers, and then at Gurgan, close to the Caspian Sea, where he met the scientist Avicenna. He was later forced into the service of Sultan Mahmud of Ghazna. While he was in India with the sultan on a campaign, al-Biruni wrote his celebrated work on India, which describes the country's customs, culture, literature, religion, and science. Al-Biruni also wrote a more general anthropological study, *The Chronology of Ancient Nations*, and pioneered the field of comparative religion, detailing the ways and beliefs of Zoroastrianism, Judaism, Hinduism, Christianity, Buddhism, and Islam. His position was that Islam was superior to its rival faiths. In total he produced 146 works, including many on mathematics, astronomy and calendars, astrology, and geography.

> "... acquiring knowledge is delightful, and unlike any pleasures to be taken in other pastimes."
>
> Abu Rayhan al-Biruni

RIGHT: A page from al-Biruni's *Chronology of Ancient Nations* shows him gathering information on his travels. He said that pursuing knowledge for its own sake was what distinguishes humans from animals.

117 SCIENTIST

AVICENNA (IBN SINA)

Afshona, Persia (now Uzbekistan)
980–1037

Philosopher, astronomer, and physician who wrote a medical encyclopedia.

The Persian polymath Avicenna wrote *Al-Qānūn fi al-ṭibb* (*The Canon of Medicine*), which was used as a textbook in universities until 1650. He served as physician and vizier (administrator) to a number of sultans. He was also a major philosopher, and his treatment of Neoplatonism and the works of Aristotle influenced medieval European Scholastic philosophers such as Albertus Magnus and Thomas Aquinas. *Kitab al-Shifa* (*The Book of Healing*) was a remarkable blending of mathematics, astronomy, music, psychology, physics, logic, and metaphysics.

118 ROYALTY

GHANA BASSI

Ghana
1010–1062

Ghana Bassi defended the Ghana Empire against attacks from the Berber Muslim Almoravids of Morocco. Bassi came to the throne aged thirty in 1040, at the end of his father Farbas Ousmane's sixty-year reign. According to one account, he refused to convert to Islam, which angered the Berber Muslim dynasty of the Almoravids (in Morocco), and they launched an invasion in 1050. Bassi was succeeded on his death in 1062 by his son Farbas Tunka Menin, who—reputedly at the head of a 200,000-strong Ghanaian army—led forceful military resistance to the Almoravid attacks.

"*One of the greatest thinkers and medical scholars in history . . . the most famous scientist of Islam and one of the most famous of all races, places, and times.*"

George Sarton, *The History of Science*, 1975

LEFT: The opening decoration and invocation to Allah from a sixteenth-century manuscript of Avicenna's *Canon of Medicine*.

119 RELIGIOUS LEADER

POPE GREGORY VII

Sovana, Italy
c. 1020–1085

Reforming pope who clashed with Holy Roman Emperor Henry IV.

Gregory VII twice excommunicated Henry IV, and ended his papal reign in exile with a rival pope, Clement III, installed in Rome by Henry—Gregory had apparently been beaten in a major clash between the papacy and the Holy Roman Empire. Nevertheless, he is remembered as a major reforming pope who gave his name to the Gregorian Reform, the program of improvements begun by Leo IX. The conflict with Henry, known as the Investiture Controversy, was over the right to appoint bishops and abbots and invest them with the symbols of their position: Gregory felt that this was the prerogative of the pope rather than a secular ruler. The first time he was excommunicated, Henry traveled to see Gregory, who was staying at the Castle of Canossa with the Countess Matilda of Tuscany and, denied entry, reputedly waited three days in the snow wearing a hair shirt before kneeling before the pope to beg forgiveness and being readmitted to the church. The second time Henry marched on Rome and installed Archbishop Wilbert of Ravenna as pope. Gregory took refuge in the Castel Sant'Angelo and then went into exile in Salerno.

KNOWN FOR

- Carrying out "Gregorian Reform" in church
- The Investiture Controversy
- Henry IV's penance at Canossa

ABOVE: Gregory held that the pope had authority over all secular rulers and answered only to God.

120 ROYALTY

WILLIAM THE CONQUEROR

Falaise, France
c. 1028–1087

William, Duke of Normandy, invaded and conquered England in 1066, winning the Battle of Hastings against King Harold II. He built the forbidding Tower of London and distributed lands to his Norman lords to keep the peace, pacifying England's borders with invasions of Scotland (1072) and Wales (1081). He ordered the Domesday Survey of his English possessions in 1086, and left the throne to his son William Rufus on his death.

ABOVE: William at his coronation. He spent the second half of his reign in France, fighting French king Philip I, and died there after falling from his horse.

121 MILITARY LEADER

EL CID
(RODRIGO DIAZ DE VIVAR)

Vivar, Spain
c. 1043–1099

Castilian knight Rodrigo Diaz de Vivar, better known as El Cid, fought valiantly for both Christian and Muslim armies, and became a national hero and the subject of the Spanish epic poem *El Canta de mio Cid* (*The Song of My Lord*). His byname derives from the Arabic *al-sid* (lord). He took control of Valencia from its Moorish rulers in 1094, and on his death his wife Jimena Diaz remained as ruler until the kingdom was recaptured in 1102.

ABOVE: According to legend, after his death Jimena Diaz sent El Cid's corpse into battle on horseback and won a victory against Moors besieging Valencia.

POPE URBAN II

Lagery, France
c. 1035–1099

Pope who called for the First Crusade and sent Christian armies to the Holy Land.

On November 27, 1095, Pope Urban II issued a stirring call to arms, asking the knights of Europe to defend Jerusalem, the city of Christ's death, from Arabs and Turks. He promised remission of sins as the reward for taking part; the crowd shouted "God wills it! God wills it!" and Bishop Adhemar of Puy stepped forward to be appointed leader of the First Crusade. With this, Urban launched centuries of bloody conflict between Christians and Muslims, unleashing the crusading era that dramatically changed relations between East and West. Earlier that year, in an attempt to repair relations with the Church in the East, he had asked Byzantine Emperor Alexius I to send delegates to the Council of Piacenza, and there he heard tales of the threat to sacred sites in the East posed by the Seljuk Turks. He called for the First Crusade at the Council of Clermont in France. He died in Rome a fortnight after its armies took Jerusalem on July 15, 1099.

> "From you she [the city of Jerusalem] calls for help . . . Embark on this journey for the remission of your sins, in confidence you will attain undying glory of God's kingdom."
>
> Pope Urban II, Clermont, France, November 27, 1095

BELOW: Urban arrives at Clermont and preaches the fateful sermon. From the fourteenth-century *Roman de Godefroi de Bouillon*.

123 ARTIST

ST. HILDEGARD OF BINGEN

Bermersheim vor der Höhe,
West Franconia (now Germany)
1098–1179

Mystic, poet, composer, and saint who was one of the most important women in the medieval church.

Benedictine abbess Hildegard of Bingen was a genius. As well as composing otherworldly sacred music and recording mystic visions, she was a poet, natural scientist, and medic—excelling in all fields. She had her first visions when young, embarked on life as a nun aged fifteen, and became prioress in 1136. *Scivias* (*Know the Ways*, 1141–1152) was written with the help of a monk provided by the Church for the purpose, and records her apocalyptic-prophetic visions. She set her own poems to music in the *Symphonia armoniae celestium revelationum*, and also wrote what some identify as the first morality play, the *Ordo Virtutum* (*Play of the Virtues*). She compiled works on natural history and medicine, and reportedly worked miracles. She also traveled across Germany, preaching to the faithful. Her soaring sacred melodies are highly praised and much studied in the modern era, and her life celebrated by the Church: she was canonized as a saint by Pope Benedict XVI in 2012.

> "For her, the entire creation is a symphony of the Holy Spirit who is in himself joy and jubilation."
>
> Pope Benedict XVI, September 8, 2010

RIGHT: Hildegard transmits a vision from on high to her secretary, the monk Volmar. Her assistant, Richardis von Stade, is also with her.

124 SCIENTIST

MUHAMMAD AL-IDRISI

Sabtah, Morocco (now Ceuta, Spanish North Africa)
1100–1165

Arab geographer al-Idrisi wrote a key work of medieval geography, the *Kitab nuzhat al-mushtaq* (*Diversion for One Longing to Travel to Distant Lands*), and in 1154 created one of the most detailed medieval maps, the *Tabula Rogeriana*, for the Norman king Roger II of Sicily, at whose court he served. Al-Idrisi combined knowledge of Islamic merchants and Norman adventurers to create the map, which depicted Eurasia and northern Africa.

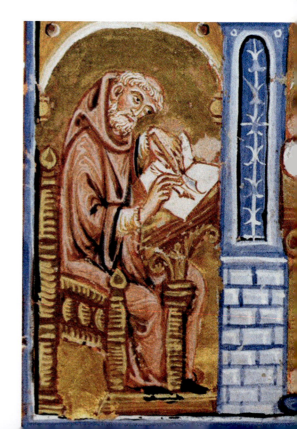

108 THE AGE OF CHIVALRY AND THE RENAISSANCE

ABOVE: The *Tabula Rogeriana* was produced by al-Idrisi with scholars at the court of Roger II of Sicily. The map shows south at the top.

125   ROYALTY

TSARAKI

Kano (now Nigeria)
c. 1110–1194

Tradition has it that the Hausa city-state of Kano (in what is now northern Nigeria) was founded in 999 by Bagauda, one of the grandsons of Bayajida, who is celebrated as the father of the Hausa people. Tsaraki was its ruler from 1136 to 1194 and completed the construction of a wall around the city in *c.* 1150. The wall had been begun by his father and predecessor Gijimasu. According to the Kano Chronicle, Tsaraki raided Karaie, and won the submission of the people of Badari. Military shields were first used during his reign.

126 MILITARY LEADER

SALADIN (SALAH AD-DIN YUSUF IBN AYYUB)

Tikrit, Persia (now Iraq)
c. 1137–1193

Brilliant general who was a redoubtable foe to Christians in the Holy Land.

Salah ad-Din Yusuf ibn Ayyub—known as Saladin ("Righteousness of the Faith")—founded the Sunni Muslim Ayyubid Empire. He captured Jerusalem from Christian settlers in 1187. A brilliant and refined man, in his youth he was a great polo player, well-versed in the genealogies of Arabian horses. He was also a widely revered general. He succeeded his uncle, Skirkuh, as vizier of Egypt, and took power in Damascus following the death of Nur ad-Din. He faced the armies of the Third Crusade, led by Richard I of England, in 1189–1192, and the encounters of these two generals were celebrated in chivalric literature. He died in Damascus shortly after the crusade.

"So many about me of high rank have put aside mercy as a weakness."

Saladin

127 ARTIST

MARIE DE FRANCE

France
c. 1140–1215

First female French poet who delighted the English royal court.

Marie de France is the first known female French poet. Her name is taken from a line in one of her poems: *"My name is Marie, and I am from France."* We do not know where she lived and worked, but her poems were popular in England at the court of Henry II and his wife Eleanor of Aquitaine. She may have been Marie, Abbess of Shaftesbury, who was Henry II's half-sister. She wrote the *Lais of Marie de France*, a collection of twelve verse narratives about love and chivalry, in Anglo-Norman. These were an important influence on medieval romance writers. She also translated *Aesop's Fables*, moral stories ascribed to the

110 THE AGE OF CHIVALRY AND THE RENAISSANCE

KNOWN FOR

- Being the first known female French poet
- Influencing *trouvère*—courtly love poems
- Translating *Aesop's Fables*

ancient Greek slave Aesop (620–564 BC), from Middle English to Anglo-Norman. The fables were dedicated to "Count William," probably William Longsword, Earl of Salisbury, an illegitimate son of Henry II, and the *Lais* were dedicated to a "noble king," thought to be Henry II himself, or possibly his son Henry the Young King.

BELOW: Marie was a major influence on courtly love poets. Here she is depicted in a thirteenth-century French illuminated manuscript.

128 RELIGIOUS LEADER

POPE GREGORY IX

Piacenza, Italy
c. 1170–1241

Pope Gregory IX established the papal inquisition to counter heresy in 1227. Many of the first judges he appointed were Dominican and Franciscan friars. Later, Pope Innocent IV empowered the inquisitors to use torture on resistant heretics. Gregory was a stern but highly spiritual individual and friend of Francis of Assisi. He was already eighty when elected pope, and reigned for fourteen years, from 1227 to 1241.

ABOVE: As pope, Gregory canonized both Francis of Assisi and Dominic Guzman, founder of the Dominican movement.

129 ROYALTY

RICHARD I

Oxford, England
1157–1199

Richard I was the foremost English warrior-king, celebrated as *Coeur de Lion* (Lionheart) for his battlefield exploits during the Third Crusade (1190–1192) and in Europe. In the Holy Lands, he made a truce with the Muslim sultan Saladin, who kept Jerusalem but allowed Christian pilgrims access to it. Returning to Europe, Richard died in France campaigning against King Philip II.

LEFT: Richard's tomb in Fontrevault Abbey, France. He reestablished the basis for a crusader kingdom in the Holy Land.

130 RELIGIOUS LEADER

POPE INNOCENT III

Gavignano, Italy
c. 1160–1216

The most powerful pope of the Middle Ages reasserted papal authority, called the Fourth and Fifth Crusades, backed the new monastic order of the Franciscans, and presided over the Fourth Lateran Council in 1215, which defined the way in which the bread and wine of Holy Communion becomes the body and blood of Christ. He died of malaria aged fifty-five.

LEFT: In a letter written in 1198, Pope Innocent III likened the papacy to the Sun and secular princes to the Moon—the Moon reflected the brightness of the Sun.

131 ROYALTY

GEBRE MESQEL LALIBELA

Bugna (now Ethiopia)
1162–1221

Blessed by bees, this emperor built a "New Jerusalem" in Ethiopia.

A member of the Zagwe dynasty, Gebre Mesqel Lalibela was emperor of Ethiopia from 1181 to 1221. He was given his name, which means "the bees recognize his sovereignty," after a swarm of honeybees surrounded him as an infant—his mother saw this as a sign that he would become emperor. Lalibela came to power in opposition to his brother Kedus Harbe, with the backing of the nobles. After having a vision of Jerusalem, and then hearing that the city had been captured by Saladin in 1187, he set out to build a new Jerusalem as his capital at Roha in Bugna, Ethiopia. A famous group of eleven rock-cut churches there reportedly took twenty-four years to build on his command—one account claims he built them himself with the help of angels. Toward the end of his reign, his nephew Na'akueto La'ab usurped the throne, but Lalibela reimposed his authority and was succeeded by his son Yetbarak.

> "King Lalibela . . . set out to construct in the twelfth century a 'New Jerusalem,' after Muslim conquests halted Christian pilgrimages to the Holy Land."
>
> UNESCO

ABOVE: Lalibela's capital Roha—renamed Lalibela—is a place of pilgrimage for Ethiopian Orthodox Christians. Its churches are a UNESCO World Heritage Site.

132 ROYALTY

MANCO CAPAC

Tamputoco (now Pumaurco), Peru
c. 1170–1230

Founder of Cusco who laid the foundations for the Inca Empire.

Manco Capac was the first ruler of the Inca and founder of their capital city, Cusco, in Peru. Born to nomads in Tamputoco, he led his family clan over the Altiplano to establish a settlement in the Cusco Valley, where they had to fight off attacks from local tribes. He was succeeded as ruler by his son Sinchi Roq'a. His body was mummified and kept in Cusco until the era of the ninth Inca ruler, Pachacuti (r. 1438–1472), who moved it to the Temple of the Sun on Isla del Sol in Lake Titicaca. In mythology, Manco Capac was a fire god sent to Earth by his father, the sun god Inti, and he emerged from a cave carrying a golden staff. He traveled to Cusco and set up a temple there in which people could worship his father. In another myth, he was a son of the creator god Viracocha, called Ayar Manco, who trapped his three brothers in stone and married his sister and his mother, the fertility goddess Mama Ocllo, before founding Cusco. They had a son named Sinchi Roca.

KNOWN FOR
- Being the first ruler of the Inca
- Being the founder of Cusco
- Being worshipped as god of fire and sun

133 MILITARY LEADER

GENGHIS KHAN (TEMUJIN)

Near Lake Baikal, Khentii Mountains, Mongolia
c. 1162–1227

Warrior-leader Genghis Khan founded the vast Mongol Empire. He was infamous for his ruthlessness, and in some accounts was responsible for 60 million deaths. Originally known as Temujin, he survived the death of his father when he was just nine, building alliances in his teens, and uniting the tribes of the Mongol steppe: in 1206 he was proclaimed Genghis Khan (Mighty Ruler). He overwhelmed northern China, the Qara Khitai Empire, and the Muslim Khwarezm Empire, and died on campaign in command of a territory that stretched from the Black Sea to the Pacific Ocean, and that was set to be made larger still by his descendants.

ABOVE: The Mongol army led by Genghis Khan was known for being organized, flexible, and highly disciplined. Khan also promoted religious tolerance.

134 RELIGIOUS LEADER

ST. FRANCIS OF ASSISI

Assisi, Italy
c. 1181–1226

Italian saint who founded the Franciscan monastic order.

Francis of Assisi sought to follow the example of Jesus, and saw the natural world as a reflection of God's glory. In his youth he served as a soldier, and was a prisoner of war before a vision convinced him to give away his wealth (he was the son of a cloth merchant), and embark on a life of poverty and religious devotion. Francis founded the Franciscan monastic order in 1209, its female branch the Poor Clares in 1212, and a lay order in 1221. In 1219 he traveled to Egypt during the Fifth Crusade to urge peace, and preached to Sultan al-Kamil.

"All praise to you, Oh Lord, in all that you have created,
And to begin with Brother Sun,
Who delivers the day; and light you give to us through him.
How glorious is he, how bright-shining in all his splendor!
Lord most high, he has your likeness."

St. Francis of Assisi, *The Canticle of Creation*, c. 1224

ABOVE: St. Francis was reputedly the first person to develop stigmata—wounds in the hands and side where Christ was injured when being crucified.

500–1500 **115**

135 ARTIST

RUMI (JALAL AL-DIN AL-RUMI)

Balkh (now Afghanistan)
1207–1273

Persian Sufi poet who was an influence on Islamic mysticism and literature.

Jalal al-Din al-Rumi was a religious instructor and follower of Sufism, a mystical strand of Islam, who turned to writing poetry after his spiritual teacher Shams-e Tabrizi disappeared—possibly murdered. Rumi's work teaches that by being loving and forgetting their individual needs, people can become one with Allah. He wrote while in religious ecstasy, and performed his poems while whirling in dance. On his death, Rumi's followers established the Mawlawiyyah Sufi religious order—often known in the West as the "whirling dervishes."

LEFT: Mawlawiyyah Sufi followers of Rumi—"whirling dervishes"—dance in religious ecstasy in a ceremony called *sema*. *Dervish* is a name for a Sufi initiate.

136 MILITARY LEADER

KUBLAI KHAN

Mongolia
1215–1294

Mongolian general who conquered China and founded the Yuan dynasty.

In 1279, Kublai Khan finished the conquest of China launched by his grandfather Genghis Khan in 1211, and became the first foreign emperor of the whole country. In the course of the conquest he appointed Confucian advisers, and in 1271 proclaimed the dynastic name of "Great Yuan," claiming succession from earlier Chinese rulers—so founding the Yuan dynasty that would rule until the rise of the Ming in 1368. Khan made Buddhism the state religion, and moved the winter capital to Khanbaliq (or Dadu) at the heart of what is now Beijing. He built an empire that stretched from the Caspian Sea to Korea, encouraged trade, and supported the arts, sciences, and education. Foreigners were welcomed at court, and Italian traveler Marco Polo served Khan as a diplomat. The magnificence of the summer court at Shangdu (also known as Xanadu) was described by Polo and widely celebrated—and inspired English Romantic poet Samuel Taylor Coleridge's poem *Kubla Khan*.

> "In Xanadu did Kubla Kahn
> A stately pleasure dome decree:
> Where Alph, the sacred river, ran
> Through caverns measureless
>   to man
> Down to a sunless sea."

Samuel Taylor Coleridge, *Kubla Khan*, 1797

LEFT: Celebrated by English Romantic poet Samuel Taylor Coleridge, Kublai Khan was himself a prolific poet, though very few of his poems survive.

137 ROYALTY

SUNDIATA KEITA

Dakadjalan (now Mali)
c. 1190–1255

"Lion of Mali" who founded a powerful trading empire in western Africa.

Sundiata Keita emerged from a persecuted, sickly childhood to establish a great empire. By tradition he was one of the twelve sons of Naré Maghann Konaté, ruler of the Malinké Kingdom of Kangaba, close to the border of Mali and Guinea. Sundiata could not walk well, and he and his mother were driven into exile by the bullying of relatives, including his paternal half-brother Dankaran Touman. He won the support of the king of Mema (a region of Mali) then, when a rival king named Sumanguru conquered Kangaba, Sundiata returned from exile and defeated him in the Battle of Kirina in c. 1235. He was the first Malinké king to take the name *Mali* (emperor). After the battle, leading nobles issued the Manden Charter, a constitution that emphasized the right to life, the importance of tolerance, equal rights for women and slaves, and the need for education—one of the world's first statements of human rights. It was not written down but handed down orally. In 1240, Sundiata took Kumbi, the capital of the West African empire of Ghana. He set about consolidating his power, sending his generals to take control of the southern Sahara and the Wangara goldfields, and established a new capital at Niani where the Niger and Sankarani rivers meet. Sundiata was the hero of the Malinké people's *Epic of Sundiata*, transmitted orally by griots (historian musician-poets).

ABOVE: The empire founded by Sundiata became powerful and wealthy. His great-nephew Mansa Musa would be famous for his great wealth.

KNOWN FOR

- Founding the Mali Empire
- Issuing the Manden Charter, an early statement of human rights
- Being the hero of the orally transmitted poem the *Epic of Sundiata*
- Being known as "Lion King of Mali"
- Possibly inspiring Disney's *The Lion King*

118 THE AGE OF CHIVALRY AND THE RENAISSANCE

138 EXPLORER

MARCO POLO

Venice, Italy
1254–1324

Venetian merchant who described the wonders of the East in a travel book he wrote while in jail.

As a young man, Marco Polo embarked on a trading journey to China with his merchant father Niccolo and uncle Maffeo, arriving at Mongol ruler Kublai Khan's court in *c.* 1274. They stayed in China for seventeen years, and Marco was sent by the khan on diplomatic missions across Southeast Asia. Returning to Europe via Persia and Constantinople, Marco and his relatives were captured by the state of Genoa, which was at war with Venice. While in jail, in *c.* 1300, Marco wrote the story of his adventures with the help of a jailed writer named Rustichello. It was the first detailed account of life in China published in Europe, and inspired many travelers, including Christopher Columbus.

ABOVE: Marco Polo and his companions explored many places along the Silk Road trade route in the course of their journeys.

139 ARTIST

DANTE ALIGHIERI

Florence, Italy
1265–1321

Italian poet who wrote one of Western literature's greatest works.

Dante's masterpiece *The Divine Comedy* depicts the passage of a man through hell, purgatory, and paradise—the three possible destinations for the souls of the deceased in Roman Catholic Christianity. He wrote the poem c. 1308–1321 in his native tongue as opposed to Latin, establishing Italian as a literary language. He contracted an arranged marriage with Gemma Donati and had three children, but his spiritual love for Beatrice Portinari, whom he met as a boy, was an enduring and powerful inspiration—he dedicated most of his poetry to her, praised her in *The New Life* (c. 1293), and made her the poet's guide to paradise in the *Comedy*. He was exiled from his native Florence in 1302 as part of political machinations in the city, and was never able to return. He was hailed as "the Supreme Poet," and was a major influence on later European writers, notably Bocaccio, Petrarch, Chaucer, Milton, and Tennyson.

"Before me things created were none, save things
Eternal, and eternal I endure.
All hope abandon ye who enter here."

Dante, words written at the entrance of hell, *The Divine Comedy*, c. 1308–1321

LEFT: Holding his great masterpiece, Dante wears a laurel to indicate his stature as "the Supreme Poet." His rejection of Latin in favor of the Tuscan dialect had a huge influence on literary history.

140 ROYALTY

KATO KIMERA

Bunyoro (now Ssese Islands, Lake Victoria) Uganda
c. 1265–1295

Kato Kimera was the first king, or *kabaka*, of the Kingdom of Buganda, which developed into one of East Africa's biggest and most powerful states. The king also took the name "Kintu" after that of the first man in the Buganda creation myth. He built a capital at Nnono, in Busujju County, where he was buried after his death aged just thirty.

141 ROYALTY

MANSA MUSA

Mali
c. 1298–1337

Under Mansa Musa (r. 1312–1337), the Mali Empire grew to its largest extent and Timbuktu was established as a great center of learning. Musa is sometimes said to have been the wealthiest person in history: he went on the *hajj* pilgrimage to Mecca in 1324 with a vast entourage and a huge supply of gold. Stopping in Cairo, Egypt, he made so many gifts of gold that he affected the value of the precious metal in the country.

BELOW: This detail from the world map known as the Catalan Atlas (1375) depicts Mansa Musa crowned and holding precious gold.

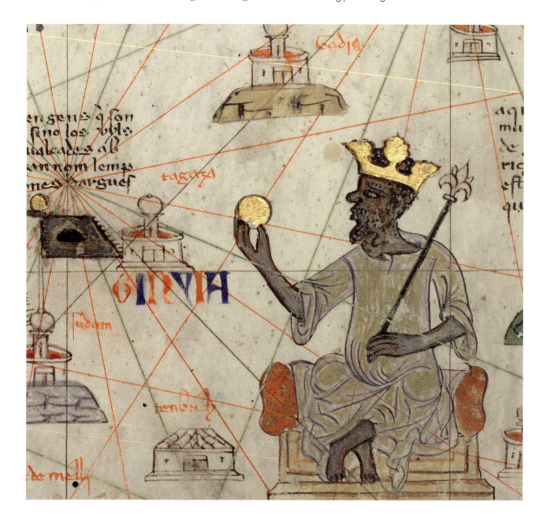

142 EXPLORER

IBN BATTUTA

Tangier, Marinid Sultanate (now Morocco)
1304–c. 1369

Berber Arab explorer who wrote one of history's most famous travel books.

Ibn Battuta covered 75,000 miles in twenty-seven years of wide-ranging travels across Asia, Europe, and Africa, before settling down to record what he had seen and experienced in his book *Rihlah* (*Travels*). Of Berber descent, Ibn Battuta trained as a *qadi* (Islamic judge), but dedicated himself to traveling after making the *hajj* pilgrimage to Mecca in 1325–1326. On the *hajj* he had a dream that was interpreted by a pious ascetic in Alexandria to mean he was destined to be a global traveler, and he determined to see as much of the world as he could, promising "never to walk the same road twice." He met Sufi mystics and leading Islamic scholars, traveling in trade caravans and along pilgrim routes, being welcomed by religious brotherhoods, and receiving financial support at local and imperial courts. In time, he acquired a retinue of attendants and had a harem of wives.

> "*It was my habit on my travels never, as far as possible, to retrace any route I had traveled over.*"
>
> Ibn Battuta, *Travels*, 1325–1354

RIGHT: On his first *hajj*, Ibn Battuta traveled through Egypt—then governed by the Mamluk Sultanate—and admired the country's ancient monuments.

ABOVE: Working for the government of Florence, Boccaccio was delegated to greet and host Petrarch on a 1350 visit. The two writers were friends thereafter.

143 ARTIST

GIOVANNI BOCCACCIO

Certaldo, Italy
1313–1375

Greatest prose author of the fourteenth century who wrote the bawdy *Decameron*.

Poet, scholar, and author Giovanni Boccaccio wrote his masterpiece *The Decameron*, a collection of 100 sometimes risqué prose stories, in 1348-1353. The tales are supposedly told by three men and seven women sheltering in a villa outside Florence to escape the Black Death (bubonic plague). Boccaccio came up with the idea after the plague epidemic of 1348. The work was a major influence on European literature, notably on Geoffrey Chaucer's *The Canterbury Tales* (1387–1400) and on Miguel de Cervantes, whose *Don Quixote*, published in two volumes in 1605 and 1615, is recognized as the first modern novel. Boccaccio was the son of a merchant, and tried banking and studied canon law before settling on poetry and writing. He was a friend and pupil of the poet Petrarch, and together they were early proponents of Renaissance humanism. Boccaccio also copied and promoted the work of Dante—and added the word "Divine" to the title of Dante's masterpiece, which was originally known as *The Comedy*. He, Dante, and Petrarch are celebrated as the "Three Crowns" of Italian literature.

KNOWN FOR
- Writing *The Decameron*
- Promoting the works of Dante
- Being an early humanist

144 ROYALTY

ALI YASI DAN TSAMIYA

Kano (now Nigeria)
c. 1325–1385

Ali Yasi Dan Tsamiya—also known as Yaji I—made the Kingdom of Kano (northern Nigeria) into an Islamic sultanate, establishing Islam as the official religion and stamping out resistance by followers of the local animist cult at the Battle of Santolo. During his reign (1349–1385), he conquered rival kingdoms in the area, laying the groundwork for the Kano Empire that flourished under Sultan Muhammad Kisoki (1509–1565).

145 SCIENTIST

IBN KHALDUN

Tunis, Tunisia
1332–1406

Arab historian who examined society and social change.

Ibn Khaldun wrote a history of Muslim North Africa, *Kitab al-Ibar*, and the *Muqaddimah* or "Introduction," an investigation of history-writing and social change. He was the greatest Arab historian of the premodern age. The *Muqaddimah*, published in 1377, pioneered cultural history, sociology, and demography (study of populations) in its probing of economics, and how and why societies cohere or change. The work influenced nineteenth-century Ottoman historians and modern Islamic thinkers, as well as twentieth-century Reaganomics (the neoliberal economic policies of United States president Ronald Reagan). Ibn Khaldun also served as a judge in Cairo from 1382, and in 1400 negotiated with the Mongol conqueror Timur the Lame when he besieged Damascus.

> "He has conceived and formulated a philosophy of history which is undoubtedly the greatest work of its kind that has ever yet been created by any mind in any time or place…"
>
> English historian Arnold Toynbee (1889–1975)

ABOVE: The enduring influence of Khaldun can be seen today: he is celebrated as the father of social sciences such as sociology, economics, and demographics.

146 ROYALTY

YI SONG-GYE

Yeongheung-gun, Korea
1335–1408

After defeating the last Koryo king, Yi Song-gye seized the throne and founded the Choson dynasty, which ruled Korea until 1910. A former Koryo general, he built a capital at Hanyang (modern Seoul), and made agriculture the focus of the economy. He also oversaw a program of land redistribution after ownership had been concentrated among the bureaucracy. He ensured that engagement with Japan was improved, and close relations were maintained with the Ming dynasty in China. He rejected Buddhism and revived Confucianism as the state religion. He ruled for six years but abdicated in 1398; he was succeeded by his son Taejong.

147 MILITARY LEADER

TIMUR THE LAME

Kesh, Transoxania (now Uzbekistan)
1336–1405

Islamic warlord who founded the Timurid Empire and dynasty.

Mongol-Turkic warlord Timur gained control of his native Transoxania (modern Uzbekistan) in the 1360s, and built an empire that stretched from the Mediterranean to Russia and India. With swift, brutal military campaigns he defeated all he encountered, including the Mamluks, the Ottomans, and the Delhi Sultanate in India, becoming the Islamic world's most powerful ruler. He also launched what became known as the Timurid Renaissance, backing the arts and making Samarkand a center of science and learning.

ABOVE: Power in reserve—Timur before battle. His descendants in the Timurid dynasty include Babur, who founded the Indian Mughal Empire.

148 ARTIST

GEOFFREY CHAUCER

London, England
c. 1341–1400

"Father of English literature" who wrote *The Canterbury Tales*.

> *"Full wise is he that can himselven knowe."*
>
> Geoffrey Chaucer, *The Canterbury Tales*,
> *The Monkes Tale*, 1387–1400

The son of an important wine merchant, Geoffrey Chaucer was a diplomat, courtier, and civil servant, as well as England's first great poet. Appointed a page to Elizabeth de Burgh, Countess of Ulster, and wife of King Edward III's son the Duke of Clarence, Chaucer became closely involved with the royal court and, in 1336, married Philippa Pan, a lady-in-waiting to Philippa of Hainault, King Edward III's queen. In 1359 he was captured and ransomed during the Siege of Reims in France in the Hundred Years' War (1337–1453). He was sent on several diplomatic missions. He wrote *The Canterbury Tales*, a long poem that uses the frame of a pilgrimage to the shrine of St. Thomas Becket at Canterbury to contain a group of varied stories, from 1387 to 1400. He established the English vernacular as the language for poetry rather than Latin or Anglo-Norman French.

ABOVE: Poet as pilgrim—a marginal illustration of Geoffrey Chaucer in the near-contemporary Ellesmere manuscript of *The Canterbury Tales*.

149 ARTIST

JULIAN OF NORWICH

Norfolk, England
1342–1416

English mystic and anchoress who had "revelations" of Jesus Christ.

Mother Julian of Norwich's mystical *Revelations of Divine Love* is the earliest surviving work in English by a woman. In 1373, aged around thirty and so ill she believed herself to be dying, Julian had sixteen visions of the Passion of Jesus Christ (the final events of his life, including his crucifixion), and soon after she recovered, she wrote them down; twenty to thirty years later she wrote a longer version of her *Revelations*. Julian was an anchoress (Christian recluse) who lived in a tiny cell at St. Julian's Church, Norwich. She became known as a source of spiritual wisdom and advice and, in 1413, mystic Margery Kempe traveled to Norwich to seek her counsel. Almost half the population of Norwich, second only to London as a commercial center in this period, had been killed by the Black Death from 1348 to 1350. It is possible that Julian lost her family in the plague and became an anchoress as a result.

> "... all shall be well, and all shall be well and all manner of things shall be well."
>
> Julian of Norwich

LEFT: Julian emphasized God's great love for his creation—"ere God made us he loved us; which love was never lacking nor ever shall be."

150 EXPLORER

ZHENG HE

Yunnan-fu, China
1371–1433

From 1405 onward, admiral and diplomat Zheng He commanded seven exploratory voyages that led to increased emigration from China to Southeast Asia. Zheng had been captured, castrated, and forced into the army when his native Yunnan was overrun by Ming dynasty forces in 1381. He sailed to Vietnam, Thailand, Java, India, and Sri Lanka on his first voyage; later journeys took him to the Arabian peninsula and eastern Africa.

151 ROYALTY

LUKENI LUA NIMI

Kongo (now Angola)
1380–1420

Lukeni lua Nimi founded the Kingdom of Kongo in west-central Africa, defeating a local ruler named Mwene Kabunga and establishing a capital at Mbanza Kongo in what is now northern Angola. His father Nimi a Nzima had established a solid power base by making a marriage alliance with princess Lukeni lua Nzanze of the neighboring Mbata kingdom. Lukeni lua Nimi led expansion southward. He was succeeded by his cousin Nanga of Kongo rather than his son Nkuwu a Ntinu, indicating that he probably died at a young age.

> "Then [Lukeni lua Nimi] gave the territory to his followers and relatives of his father and they generously imitated him ... and as time passed a great Kingdom was established."
>
> Italian missionary Giovanni Antonio Cavazzi (1621–1678)

LEFT: Zheng He's maritime journeys boosted trade and population movement in South and Southeast Asia.

152 POLITICAL LEADER

ITZCOATL

Tenochtitlan, Mexico (now Mexico City, Mexico)
1380–1440

Itzcoatl, the fourth king of the city-state of Tenochtitlan in the Valley of Mexico, defeated the dominant Tepanecs and, in 1428, established the Triple Alliance with Tetzcoco and Tlacopan—so founding the Aztec Empire that dominated the region until its conquest by Spanish invaders in 1519. He defeated Xochimilco, Mixquic, Cuitahiac, and Texompa, and took control of the floating gardens, or *chinampas*, in the lakes of Xochimilco and Chalco, south of Lake Texcoco. He developed Tenochtitlan, building a causeway, roads, and temples. He was succeeded by his nephew Motecuhzoma I, who consolidated the empire.

ABOVE: Itzcoatl is represented with a snake; his name means "Obsidian Serpent." The Aztecs believed the volcanic glass obsidian to be divinely provided.

153 ROYALTY

HENRY V

Monmouth, Wales
1386–1422

Famous English warrior king who took war to France.

King Henry V's victory in the Battle of Agincourt, northern France, entered English folklore. On October 25, 1415, an English army of 6,000 defeated a 20,000-strong French force against all odds. Playwright William Shakespeare immortalized the scene, giving Henry a stirring speech to his men. The king won a series of victories in France, capturing Caen and Rouen, and in 1420, under the Treaty of Troyes, married Catherine, daughter of French king Charles VI, was made French regent, and was recognized as heir to the French throne. He had proven himself a great warrior during a raucous youth in which, as a teenage Prince of Wales, he led the battle against Welsh rebel Owain Glyndwr, and was involved in ambushes, a midnight fight in a London tavern, and practical jokes at court. He famously put all his pranks behind him on becoming king—and even declared that none of his former friends could come within ten miles of him. Poised to unite the English and French thrones, he died at only thirty-five of dysentery contracted in the siege of Meaux, near Paris.

> *"Once more unto the breach, dear friends, once more . . . Cry 'God for Harry, England, and Saint George!'"*
>
> Henry V, William Shakespeare, c. 1599

KNOWN FOR
- Winning the Battle of Agincourt
- Becoming French regent and heir to throne
- Living a dissolute youth as Prince of Wales
- Early death ends very promising reign

ABOVE: Some historians say Henry V's successes in the Hundred Years' War fostered a sense of nationalism that laid the groundwork for England's rise as a great power.

154 ROYALTY

YESHAQ I

Ethiopia
c. 1390–1429

Yeshaq I, emperor of Ethiopia from 1414 to 1429, is celebrated in a poem that is one of the finest jewels of Ethiopian literature. He defeated Sa'ad ad-Din II and destroyed the Sunni Muslim Sultanate of Ifat in the historical province of Shewa. He also put down a revolt by Ethiopian Jews, and erected the church Debre Yeshaq to celebrate. He made the earliest known contact with Europe in this era, writing to Alfonso V of Aragon suggesting that a marriage between Peter of Aragon and Yeshaq's daughter would seal an alliance against Muslims—there is no record of Alfonso's response.

155 ROYALTY

SEJONG THE GREAT

Hansung (now Seoul), Korea
1397–1450

One of the greatest rulers in Korean history, King Sejong (r. 1419–1450) developed the Hangul phonetic writing system still used today, which greatly helped the spread of literacy in the country. He was privately a Buddhist, but took steps to limit the power of the faith since Korea officially honored Neo-Confucian ideas. He limited the permitted number of Buddhist temples and monks, and cut the number of permitted Buddhist orders from seven to two. He created an institute for scientific research

156 RELIGIOUS LEADER

POPE PIUS II

Corsignano (now Pienza), Italy
1405–1464

Pope who condemned the enslavement of newly baptized Africans—and published an erotic novel.

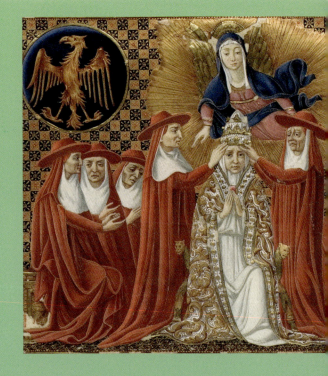

RIGHT: Pius II tried to lead a crusade against the Ottomans, but failed to inspire support. He died at Ancona, from where the crusade was due to leave.

RIGHT: Sejong also introduced a peasant relocation policy to settle the north of the country, and defeated Japanese pirates in the south.

"A wise ruler should never ignore minority opinions but should listen carefully to them."

King Sejong the Great

at his palace, and supported the inventor Jang Yeong-sil, who developed a rain gauge and improved designs for water clocks and sundials.

In an address to the ruler of the Canary Islands in 1462, Pius II (pope 1458–1464), declared that it was a "great crime" to enslave Africans who had been newly baptized in the Christian faith, and urged bishops to impose strict penalties on those who did this. He did not, however, condemn the slave trade as a whole. In other areas Pius II was a skilled diplomat and writer. Before becoming pope, in 1444 he wrote an erotic novel, *Historia de duobos amantibus* (*The Tale of Two Lovers*), which consists of letters between a married woman, Lucretia, and one of the Duke of Austria's men. It is an early example of an epistolary novel, structured around an exchange of letters between two characters. He also wrote a thirteen-book autobiography, *Commentaries*—the only autobiography to be written by a reigning pope. In his early life, Pius II took part in a failed diplomatic mission to persuade James I of Scotland to invade England, and was excommunicated when he served as secretary to the antipope Felix V. He failed in his main drive as pope—to call a crusade against the Ottoman Turks who had captured Constantinople in 1453.

157 SCIENTIST

JOHANNES GUTENBERG

Mainz, Holy Roman Empire (now Germany)
c. 1406–1468

German craftsman who developed the movable-type printing press.

Johannes Gutenberg's invention transformed Europe and the world, impacting the Renaissance and Reformation, and the development of humanism. He went far beyond earlier printing techniques from China and Korea, developing oil-based ink, a mold for casting type, and a wooden printing press similar to the ones used in bookbinding and paper manufacture. He worked as a goldsmith and gem-cutter, before turning to printing. He produced the first printed Bible (the forty-two-line Gutenberg Bible), an edition of the Vulgate Bible in Latin in 1455. He made about 180 copies printed on vellum.

LEFT: In 1999 Johannes Gutenberg was hailed as "the man of the millennium" because his invention had such major and far-reaching effect.

158 ROYALTY

PRINCE NYATSIMBA MUTOTA

Zimbabwe
c. 1410–1450

Prince from Great Zimbabwe who created the Shona kingdom of Mutapa.

Prince Nyatsimba Mutota founded the Kingdom of Mutapa (on the Zambezi River in what is now northern Zimbabwe) in the mid-fifteenth century. It grew rich trading local gold and ivory with Muslim merchants in eastern Africa and later the Portuguese, and was a thriving kingdom—if not an empire—for 200 years. The prince and other Shona-speaking Bantu came north from the Great Zimbabwe, the city founded in the eleventh century near Lake Mutirikwi in the southeast of the country, which was in decline by this period. In one account, he first traveled north alone to investigate the Zambezi River region, and found it to be rich in game and salt deposits, so returned to fetch his people. In another version, he went north because war had broken out with his brother or cousin, Prince Mukwati. Nyatsimba Mutota's son, Nyanhewe Matope, expanded the kingdom, defeating regional powers such as Manyika, Kiteve, and Madanda.

159 MILITARY LEADER

JOAN OF ARC

Domrémy-la-Pucelle, France
c. 1412–1431

The "Maid of Orleans" who inspired the French to a famous victory over English invaders.

Joan of Arc believed she was guided by saints in her mission to help the French crown prince Charles defeat the English and their Burgundian allies. Although she was later captured and executed, she inspired victories that set the stage for France's eventual victory over England in the Hundred Years' War (1337–1453). Born to a peasant family in northeast France, in 1429 Joan was inspired by St. Catherine of Alexandria, St. Margaret of Antioch, and St. Michael to seek an audience with Charles. Arriving dressed in men's clothes, she sufficiently impressed Charles to send her with reinforcements to Orleans, where the city was besieged by the English. The French were electrified by Joan's arrival, and forced the English to lift the siege; she later defeated them at Patay. Charles was crowned at Reims as King Charles VII of France, with Joan at his side. But after she failed in an attack on Paris, Joan was captured by the Burgundians, sold to the English, and tried for witchcraft and heresy in an ecclesiastical court. She initially recanted, but then reasserted that she had divine guidance, and was burned at the stake on May 30, 1431. Pope Calixtus III annulled her conviction in 1456, and she was declared a saint in 1920. She became an enduring icon for her religious faith, youthful fearlessness, and explosion of fifteenth-century gender restrictions.

> "All I have done is by Our Lord's command . . . I have done nothing in the world but by the order of God."
>
> Joan of Arc at her trial, 1431

KNOWN FOR
- Being the "Maid of Orleans" and leading the French to victory in 1429
- Believing she was inspired by God
- Being burned at the stake as a heretic by the English aged nineteen
- Being the patron saint of France

BELOW: Joan, dressed in full armor, arrives at the Chateau of Chinon for a meeting with Crown Prince Charles.

160 RELIGIOUS LEADER

POPE SIXTUS IV

Celle Ligure, Italy
1414–1484

Corrupt pope who left a magnificent legacy in Rome.

Pope Sixtus IV (pope 1471–1484) was responsible for the transformation of Rome into an elegant Renaissance city. He built the first bridge over the Tiber since the classical period—the Ponte Sisto, named in his honor—as well as laying out piazzas and wide streets, most famously the Via Sistina (later known as Borgo Sant'Angelo) from Castel Sant-Angelo to St. Peter's Basilica, and repairing the Acqua Vergine aqueduct. In addition to restoring around thirty churches, he built and began the decoration of the Sistine Chapel, although the revered ceiling by Michelangelo was commissioned by Pope Julius II. He revived the Roman Academy and tripled the size of the Vatican Library. But he was also a corrupt and venal figure who made two nephews cardinals (one reputedly his son by his own sister), appointed an eight-year-old boy Bishop of Lisbon, and was involved in a sordid, botched assassination plot against Lorenzo de'Medici in Florence Cathedral. In 1478 he created the notorious Spanish Inquisition to combat heresy, at the request of Ferdinand II and Isabella I of Spain.

LEFT: Sixtus IV had a mixed legacy—beautifying Rome but also disgracing the papacy through nepotism and corruption.

161 EXPLORER

ANTAO GONÇALVES

Travanca de Lagos, Portugal
1415–1501

In 1441, Portuguese explorer Antao Gonçalves was the first European to enslave Africans. He was on an exploratory expedition along the west coast of Africa, commanded by Nuno Tristao on behalf of Portuguese prince Henry the Navigator. His initial goal was to collect the skins of Mediterranean seals, but he captured Africans, including a nobleman by the name of Adahu in the Rio de Oro region (Western Sahara). The following year he returned and exchanged Adahu for slaves, gold dust, and ostrich eggs.

162 POLITICAL LEADER

PACHACUTI INCA YUPANQUI

Cusco, Inca Empire (now Peru)
c. 1418–1472

Warrior chief Pachacuti Inca Yupanqui built the Kingdom of Cusco into the Inca Empire. He developed the cult of the sun god Inti, and reputedly created the famous Inti Raymi celebration of the winter solstice and the Inca new year. The iconic 7,970-foot-high mountain-ridge citadel of Machu Picchu—probably called Huayna Picchu by contemporaries—was built for him in c. 1450.

163 ROYALTY

EWUARE THE GREAT

Benin, West Africa
c. 1420–1473

Ewuare—*oba* or king of Benin—came to power in a coup against his brother Uwaifiokun in 1440. He was originally named Ogun, and as a prince was sent into exile by another brother, Orobiru. Once king, he rebuilt the city, much of which had been destroyed in fighting during the coup, expanded the kingdom into a great empire, and developed the arts such as ivory and wood carving and the casting of bronze heads in Benin. Tradition has it that, after doing a good deed for a jungle spirit, Ewuare was given a magic bag that could never be filled and from which he could draw whatever he needed.

164 RELIGIOUS LEADER

RODRIGO BORGIA
(POPE ALEXANDER VI)

Xàtiva near Valencia, Spain
1431–1503

One of the most degenerate popes, Alexander VI (pope 1492–1503) had three daughters and six sons—including Juan (or Giovanni), Duke of Garcia, who was murdered in Rome in June 1497, probably by his brother Cesare, an event that briefly shocked the pope into piety. As Rodrigo Borgia he famously bought the key vote needed to be elected pope by bribing Cardinal Ascanio Sforza with four mules loaded with silver. But he was popular with the people of Rome, who cheered him and held a bullfight in the square in front of St. Peter's Basilica to celebrate his election.

BELOW: Alexander VI presents Jacopo Pesaro, commander of the papal fleet, to St. Peter. The painting celebrates a 1502 Venetian victory over the Ottomans.

"May the Lord array thee in the garment of salvation and surround thee with the cloak of happiness."

Words on the the mantle given by Pope Alexander VI to his son Cesare Borgia on March 29, 1499

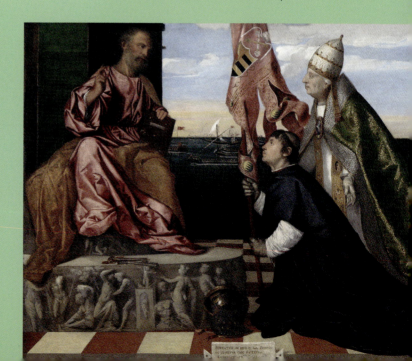

165 MILITARY LEADER

MEHMED THE CONQUEROR

Adrianople, Ottoman Empire (now Edirne, Turkey)
1432–1481

Sultan who was known as "the Father of Conquest" and took historic Constantinople.

In 1453 Ottoman sultan Mehmed II "the Conqueror" shook Europe by capturing Constantinople (modern Istanbul), which had been the capital of the Eastern Roman or Byzantine Empire for more than a millennium. He had prepared carefully for an assault on the city, gathering a navy of 320 vessels and an army of up to 200,000 troops, and building a fortress, Rumerlihisari, on the European side of the Bosporus to match an existing one on the Asian side and enforce control of the strait. The Ottomans took the city on May 29 after a fifty-seven-day siege. Mehmed claimed the title of Caesar of Rome, calling himself *Qayser-i Rum*. He also conquered Anatolia and much of southeast Europe. An Ottoman army even invaded Italy in 1480 and Pope Sixtus IV, fearing they meant to take Rome, tried to raise a crusade against him—but in the end the invasion led to a negotiated settlement. At home Mehmed rebuilt much of Constantinople. He ordered the transformation of the famous fourth-century church of Hagia Sophia into a mosque, and the building of the Fatih Mosque (1463–1470). He presided over a highly cultured court that promoted learning, and was a patron of many Renaissance artists, including Gentile Bellini, who painted his portrait in 1480.

ABOVE: Venetian artist Gentile Bellini painted his portrait of Mehmed II to celebrate a peace treaty between the Ottomans and Venice.

KNOWN FOR
- Capturing Constantinople
- Being a patron of the arts
- Conquering vast territories

166 RELIGIOUS LEADER

POPE INNOCENT VIII

Genoa, Italy
1432–1492

Pope Innocent VIII (pope 1484–1492) kept Prince Cem, a rival for the Ottoman sultanate, in captivity in Rome. He was rewarded by Sultan Bayezit II with the vast sum of 120,000 ducats—as well as the gift of a treasured relic, the Holy Lance that was used to pierce Christ's side on the cross. He issued a bull in 1484, backing German inquisitor Heinrich Kramer's witch hunts, and one in 1487 appointing Tomas de Torquemada—the man called "the hammer of heretics"—to be inquisitor general in Spain.

ABOVE: After Sixtus IV's extravagance, the papacy was in desperate need of money. As well as taking Ottoman funds, Innocent created ecclesiastical posts for sale.

167 ROYALTY

IVAN III

Moscow, Russia
1440–1505

In 1480, Grand Prince Ivan III "the Great" (r. 1462–1505) restored Russian independence when he drove off the Great Horde, the surviving rump of the Turkic-Mongol khanate the Golden Horde. He renovated the Kremlin, and was the first Russian ruler to call himself "tsar." His reign of forty-three years is the second-longest in Russian history after that of Ivan IV, his grandson.

ABOVE: After marrying Byzantine princess Sofia Paleologue, Ivan III made the double-headed eagle Russia's coat of arms.

168 SONNI ALI

Ali Kolon, West Africa
c. 1440–1492

West African ruler who founded the Songhai Empire that flourished until 1600.

Beginning from a small Niger valley kingdom centered on the trading city of Gao, Sonni Ali Ber (Sunni Ali or Sunni Ali Kulun) (r. c. 1464–1492) built a great power base on the ruins of the collapsing Mali Empire. He defeated the Fulani and Dogon peoples, and in 1468 captured the city of Timbuktu—an important trading post and famous center of scholarship—by driving out its rulers, the Tuareg desert nomads. He then moved against the city of Jenne (now Djenné), an ancient trading post in southern Mali, and finally took it in 1473 after a siege of many years. He could be a cruel and unpredictable ruler. In taking Timbuktu he sacked the city and slaughtered many of the people; historian Abd al-Rahman al-Sadi reported that he would order the summary execution of both allies and enemies. His kingdom included Muslims and followers of the traditional animistic Songhai religion, and he combined the two faiths, which may have turned Muslim historians against him.

> "He has advisers and when he wants to act for his own ends he summons them . . . and they acquiesce in his selfish goals."
>
> Muhammad al-Maghili (1425–1505), Berber scholar, on Sonni

169 TOPA INCA YAUPANQUI

Cusco, Inca Empire (now Peru)
c. 1441–1493

Yaupanqui commanded the army in the reign of his father Pachacuti, conquering what is now Ecuador and rebuilding Quito. Then, as Sapa Inca (emperor, r. 1471–1493), took Chimor (on the northern coast of Peru) and built a fortress, Saksaywaman, above Cusco. A sixteenth-century Spanish history recounts how Topa Inca led a ten-month exploratory voyage to islands in the Pacific—he may have visited the Galàpagos Islands and Easter Island.

ABOVE: Tupa Inca Yapuanqui was poisoned by one of his wives, Chuqui Ocllo, in a quarrel over which of his sons should succeed him.

POPE JULIUS II

Albisola Superiore, Italy
1443–1513

Pope who commissioned Raphael's and Michelangelo's masterpieces.

In ten years Julius II (pope 1503–1513) began the reconstruction of St. Peter's Basilica with leading architect Donato Bramante and commissioned not only Raphael's frescoes in the Vatican, but also Michelangelo's immortal ceiling painting in the Sistine Chapel. He was also the "warrior pope," who often wore full armor and fought alongside the papal troops. He defeated Venice in 1509, and put together a Holy League of Venice, England, Spain, Naples, and the Holy Roman Empire that drove the French out of Italy. In 1506 he established the Swiss Guard, who are still tasked with safeguarding the pope today.

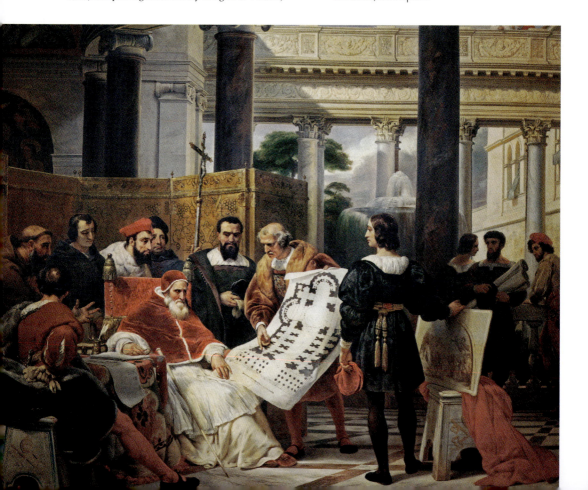

BELOW: Papal patron and immortal artists—Julius II inspects plans presented by Michelangelo, Donato Bramante, and Raphael.

171 EXPLORER

CHRISTOPHER COLUMBUS

Genoa, Italy
1451–1506

Genoese adventurer's voyages of discovery paved the way for European colonization of the Americas.

KNOWN FOR
- Being the navigator who explored the Americas
- Opening the way for European colonization
- Traditionally seen as being the first European to land in the New World, but Norse explorers were first

Christopher Columbus was a superb navigator and fearless explorer who made four transatlantic voyages to the Americas between 1492 and 1504. He was traditionally seen as the first European to land in the New World, and so its "discoverer," but Norse explorers under Leif Erikson are now known to have sailed to and settled in Vinland (Newfoundland) in the early eleventh century. In 1492–1493 Columbus was sponsored by Ferdinand II and Isabella I in Spain to find a route to Asia by sailing westward: he sighted land and went ashore on October 12, 1492 (probably on San Salvador Island in the Bahamas), then on October 28 landed in Cuba, and in December established a garrison in what is now Haiti, before returning to Spain in 1493. On his next trip, in 1493–1496, he established the first European settlement in the New World: La Isabela in the Dominican Republic; on his third voyage (1498–1500) he sailed to South America, landing in Venezuela and exploring the mouth of the Grande River. On his fourth and final trip (1502–1504), he explored the coasts of Honduras and Panama.

ABOVE: Columbus's voyages and the years of colonization and conquest they ushered in are sometimes identified as the beginning of the modern era.

172 ROYALTY

ISABELLA OF CASTILE

Madrigal de las Altas Torres, Spain
1451–1504

Queen Isabella I of Castile married King Ferdinand II of Aragon in 1469, and from 1479 the pair ruled jointly until her death, uniting the two major kingdoms of Spain. The Spanish Inquisition was created in 1478 to enforce orthodox Catholicism, and the *Reconquista* (Reconquest)—the driving of Muslims out of Spain—was completed in 1492 with the recapture of Granada. With Ferdinand, Isabella sponsored the 1492 voyage of Genoese navigator Christopher Columbus, which paved the way for the European colonization of the Americas.

ABOVE: Isabella in c. 1490. She and Ferdinand were also behind the Alhambra Decree of 1492, which ordered the expulsion of Jews from Spain.

173 ARTIST

LEONARDO DA VINCI

Vinci, Italy
1452–1519

Painter of the *Mona Lisa*, who was a superb engineer and scientist as well as an artist.

Leonardo painted two of the most famous works in the history of art—*The Last Supper*, a wall painting in the monastery of Santa Maria delle Grazie in Milan (1495–1498), and the *Mona Lisa* (c. 1503). He was a genius in every field he tried—painter, sculptor, scientist, engineer, architect, poet, musician. His parents, a landlord and a young peasant woman, were unmarried, but he was raised as a legitimate son on his father's estate and received a good education. From 1482 to 1499 he worked in Milan for Duke Ludovico Sforza as a painter, sculptor, and engineer. Later he worked for Cesare Borgia, the notorious son of Pope Alexander VI, as a military architect and engineer; and from 1516 lived in France in the service of King Francis I. His papers are filled with an extraordinary range of drawings and notes on mathematics, anatomy, botany, and landscapes, and include designs for cannons and guns, spiral staircases, submarines, flying machines, and parachutes.

LEFT: Leonardo began his career aged fourteen as an apprentice to the artist Andrea del Verrocchio, but soon overtook his master.

174 ROYALTY

AFONSO I OF KONGO

M'banza-Kongo, Kongo (now Angola)
1456–1543

Mvemba a Nzinga changed his name to Afonso in 1491 when he was baptized by Portuguese priests. He ruled as the first Christian king of Kongo from 1509 to 1543. When he fought his half-brother Mpamnzu a Kitimia for the crown, Afonso was supposedly backed by Christian angels—Mpanzu's much larger army fled on seeing a vision of St. James the Great and five heavenly horsemen. The event was celebrated in Kongo's coat of arms, which was in use until c. 1860.

175 ROYALTY

MONTEZUMA II

Tenochtitlan, Aztec Empire (now Mexico City, Mexico)
c. 1466–1520

Montezuma II ruled the Aztec Empire in its greatest glory for eighteen years from 1502, but met a messy end during the Spanish invasion led by conquistador Hernán Cortés in 1520. The Spanish account is that, having invited Cortés into Tenochtitlan, his capital, Montezuma was made a prisoner and then mortally injured in an assault by his own people. But he may have been strangled by the Spanish.

176 RELIGIOUS LEADER

POPE PAUL III

Canino, Italy
1468–1549

Paul III (pope 1534–1549) was the first pope of the Counter-Reformation, the Catholic Church's response to the Protestant Reformation launched by Martin Luther in 1517. Paul called the Council of Trent, which met from 1545 onward, and ushered in reform. Paul approved the creation of reforming orders, including the Society of Jesus (or Jesuits) and the Ursulines, a teaching order of nuns. He was a patron of Michelangelo and Titian—the latter painting several profound portraits of the pontiff; he encouraged learning, and the Polish astronomer Copernicus dedicated *De revolutionibus orbium coelestium* (*On the Revolutions of the Heavenly Spheres*) to Paul in 1543.

177 ARTIST

NICCOLÒ MACHIAVELLI

Florence, Italy
1469–1527

Author who advised leaders on how to hold on to power.

Niccolò Machiavelli was a diplomat for the republic of Florence before he wrote his famous treatise for rulers, *The Prince*, in 1513. He had been imprisoned for conspiracy following the Medicis' return to power in Florence, and he wrote the book, and dedicated it to Lorenzo de'Medici, in the hope of gaining favor—without success. He advises princes to use

178 EXPLORER

VASCO DA GAMA

Sines, Portugal
1469–1524

Portuguese explorer who was the first European to reach India by sea.

Vasco da Gama's discovery of the sea route to India opened the way for European colonialism along the route and in India. King John II of Portugal was determined to find a sea route for the spice trade from Asia. Departing from Lisbon on July 8, 1497, da Gama sailed a fleet of four ships around the Cape of Good Hope, up the African coast, and across the Indian Ocean, arriving at Calicut in southwest India on May 20, 1498. On the way he stopped in Mozambique, and Mombasa and Malindi in Kenya. The local Calicut monarch was not impressed with the gifts sent by John II, however, and the interview was not productive in terms of trade. But after a difficult return voyage, da Gama received a hero's welcome when he finally reached Lisbon on September 9, 1499. A second voyage, led by Pedro Alvares Cabral, established a Portuguese presence in Calicut, but a riot there ended in seventy Portuguese being killed. Da Gama returned there with a fleet of twenty ships in 1502–1503 and succeeded in enforcing Portugal's authority. He returned to Portugal, then in 1524 was made Portuguese viceroy, or governor, in India. But he died in Goa the same year.

RIGHT: *The Return of Vasco da Gama* depicted in a tapestry made c. 1500 for King Manuel I of Portugal. The bearded figure (right) with a spear is thought to be da Gama.

> "It is safer by far to be feared than to be loved."
>
> Niccolò Machiavelli, *The Prince* (1513)

cunning and force as necessary to maintain power, and from this work he became known to history as a diabolical cynic—the adjective "Machiavellian" describes ruthless political scheming. But he also wrote *Discourses on Livy*, which studies how republics should be constructed, and which is seen as a key influence on modern republicanism.

RIGHT: Machiavelli's career was more varied than is often remembered—he also wrote songs, poetry, and plays.

179 ARTIST

MICHELANGELO BUONARROTI

Caprese (now Caprese Michelangelo), Italy
1475–1564

Sistine Chapel artist who was the sculptor of *David* and an architect.

Michelangelo is celebrated above all for his magnificent frescoes of the creation of Adam and other scenes from Genesis (painted 1508–1512) and of the Last Judgment (1536–1541) in the Sistine Chapel in Rome. Known in his lifetime as *il divino* (the godlike one), he also excelled as a sculptor and architect, and was an accomplished poet. As a child he developed a feeling for marble when a nanny and her stonecutter husband cared for him in Settignano near Florence while his mother was ill. He was apprenticed to artist Domenico Ghirlandaio before winning commissions from Lorenzo de'Medici. He then traveled to Rome, where he sculpted the magnificent *Pietà* (1498), a representation of the crucified Christ in his mother's arms. His statue *David* (1501–1504) was commissioned for Florence Cathedral. He was one of a series of artists appointed architect of St. Peter's Basilica, and he also designed the Laurentian Library in Florence, pioneering what became known as the Mannerist style.

"It is beyond doubt a miracle that a formless block of stone could be reduced to a perfection that nature is scarcely capable of reaching in the flesh."

Italian painter Giorgio Vasari (1511-1574), on Michelangelo's *Pietà*

LEFT: An unfinished portrait of Michelangelo painted by his follower Daniele da Volterra in around 1545. The painting focuses on the artist's eyes and hand.

180 SCIENTIST

NICOLAUS COPERNICUS

Toruń, Prussia (now Poland)
1473–1543

Polish astronomer who determined that the Earth is not the center of the universe.

In his groundbreaking *De revolutionibus orbium coelestium* (On the Revolutions of the Heavenly Spheres) in 1543, Nicolaus Copernicus placed the Sun rather than the Earth at the center of the universe. He was also a physician, diplomat, cathedral canon, and mathematician who developed key concepts in economics, including the quantity theory of money (prices of services and goods depend on the quantity of money circulating).

ABOVE: Though foreshadowed by Aristarchus of Samos, Copernicus's revolutionary view of the cosmos was a transformative moment in scientific history.

181 EXPLORER

LUCAS VÁZQUEZ DE AYLLÓN

Toledo, Spain
c. 1480–1526

In 1526, Spanish adventurer Lucas Vázquez de Ayllón founded a settlement in the Spanish territory of La Florida (now the southeastern United States). The African slaves he brought along were probably the first to arrive in what is now the United States. When he died on October 18 that year, and the settlement at San Miguel de Gualdape (on the coast of Georgia and South Carolina) collapsed, the slaves escaped and settled among the Indigenous Americans.

183 ROYALTY

BABUR (ZAHIR AL-DIN MUHAMMAD)

Fergana Valley (now Andijan, Uzbekistan)
1483–1530

Babur (Persian for "Tiger") founded the Mughal Empire and dynasty in India. He was also a great poet and memoirist who wrote a celebrated autobiography, the *Babur-nameh*. Babur's dynasty takes its name from the Persian for "Mongol," since he was of Mongol origins—a descendant of both Genghis Khan and Timur. He took Kabul in 1504, then repeatedly tried to capture Delhi. He won major battles at Panipat in 1526 against Sultan Ibrahim Lodi of Delhi, and over Rana Sanga of the Rajput Confederacy at Khanua in 1527, to establish his position in northern India.

182 EXPLORER

FERDINAND MAGELLAN

Sabrosa, Portugal
1480–1521

Portuguese navigator who discovered the sea passage between the Atlantic and Pacific Oceans.

In 1521, Ferdinand Magellan discovered what is now called the Strait of Magellan—the sea passage connecting the Pacific and Atlantic

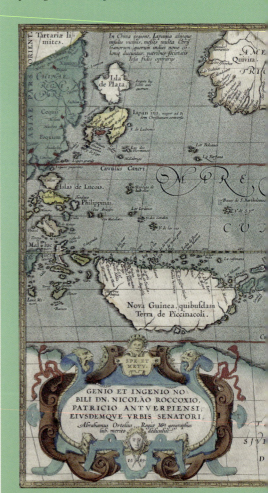

Oceans that separates Tierra del Fuego from mainland South America. This was an important time-saving route for shipping until the construction of the Panama Canal in 1914. Magellan was on a voyage backed by Charles I of Spain (later Holy Roman Emperor Charles V) to navigate westward around America to the Moluccas, or "Spice Islands," in Indonesia, and was the first European to sail from the Atlantic to Asia. Later in the same voyage, on April 27, 1521, Magellan was killed by Indigenous fighters led by a local chief named Lapulapu on Mactan Island, in what is now the Philippines. One of the ships continued back to Spain under the command of the Spanish navigator Juan Sebastián del Cano, arriving in 1522, completing the first circumnavigation of the world—and confirming that the world is round rather than flat. The name of the Pacific Ocean comes from Magellan's name for it, the *Mar Pacifico* (Peaceful Sea). It had previously been called the Southern Sea.

KNOWN FOR

- Discovering the Strait of Magellan
- Naming the Pacific Ocean
- Being the first European to sail from the Atlantic to Asia
- Taking part in the first circumnavigation of the world

LEFT: A map of the Pacific Ocean, from the first modern atlas, the *Theater of the World* by Abraham Ortelius, shows Magellan's ship, the *Victoria*—the first to circumnavigate the world.

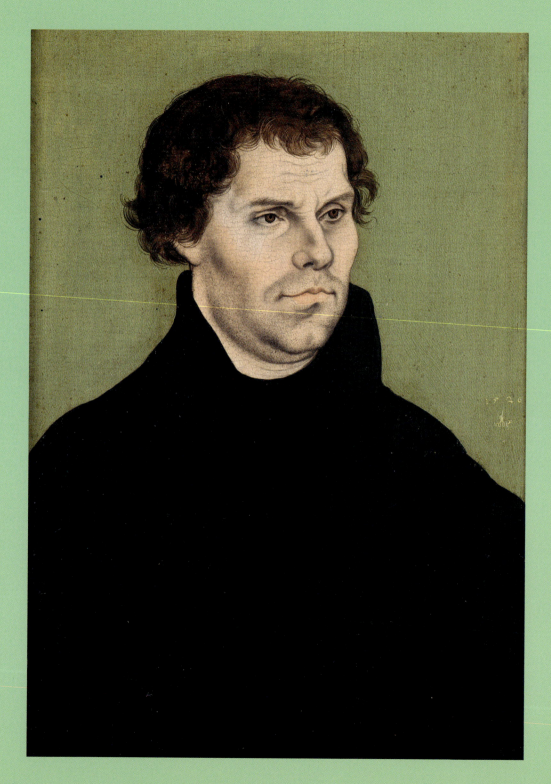

184 RELIGIOUS LEADER

MARTIN LUTHER

Eisleben, Germany
1483–1546

Priest whose attack on Church corruption was the spark for the Reformation.

Priest Martin Luther launched the Protestant Reformation in 1517, issuing his *Ninety-Five Theses*, which attacked the papacy's sale of indulgences (granting remission of the penalty for sins). When he defied Pope Leo X's call to recant, and called the pope an "antichrist sitting in the temple of God," Luther was excommunicated and then, in 1521, made an outlaw in the Edict of the Diet of Worms. In 1526 the Diet of Speyer declared that rulers should be free to decide whether to enforce the edict and, when in 1529 Holy Roman Emperor Charles V withdrew this decision, six Lutheran princes and fourteen German cities protested. Supporters of the Reformation became known as Protestants. Luther attacked the Church's teaching that people needed to do good works to be saved, arguing instead that people were saved by God's grace through faith alone. He made German translations of the New Testament in 1522 and the whole Bible in 1534.

LEFT: Luther married former nun Katharina von Bora in 1525, and while Catholic priests had to remain celibate it became customary for Protestant clergy to wed.

185 ARTIST

RAPHAEL (RAFAELLO SANZIO DA URBINO)

Urbino, Italy
1483–1520

With Leonardo and Michelangelo, one of the trinity of the greatest Renaissance artists.

Painter and architect Raphael did his finest work for the papacy—most famously his "School of Athens," depicting ancient Greek philosophers, at the Vatican (c. 1508–1511). He was also architect of St. Peter's Basilica after Bramante and was commissioned by Pope Leo X to design ten tapestries for the Sistine Chapel. He lived in Florence from 1504 to 1508, and spent his final twelve years in Rome. He painted no fewer than thirty-four Madonnas (portraits of the Virgin Mary, mother of Jesus).

ABOVE: Raphael's work is celebrated above all for the serene humanity of the figures he represents, which seems to celebrate their (and our) potential.

186 EXPLORER

HERNÁN CORTÉS

Medellín, Spain
1485–1547

Spanish conquistador (explorer-soldier) Hernán Cortés led the conquest of the Aztec Empire that won Mexico for the Spanish crown in 1519–1521. He was in Hispaniola (now Santo Domingo) from 1504, and Cuba from 1511 to 1519, before leading the attack. He made allies of Indigenous Mexicans including the Tlaxcalans, to fight the Aztecs, and following his victory was made governor of the new territory.

187 ARTIST

MIMAR SINAN (SINAN THE ARCHITECT)

Ağırnas, Turkey
c. 1488–1548

Chief Ottoman architect who designed historic mosques and hundreds of other buildings.

Mimar Sinan is best known for the Selim Mosque in Edirne, built for Sultan Selim II in 1569–1575, and the work Sinan himself viewed as his masterpiece. Its vast dome is supported on eight pillars and surrounded by the four tallest minarets in Turkey. He is also revered for the exquisite

188 ROYALTY

HENRY VIII

Greenwich, England
1491–1547

In a momentous reign of six queens, the king split with the pope and created the Church of England.

A king of vast appetites and imperious will, Henry VIII (r. 1509–1547) married six wives and split from the pope and the Roman Catholic Church, creating the Church of England with

RIGHT: Henry was an imposing figure. The words "His Majesty," traditionally associated with the Roman emperor, were first used of Henry in 1534.

RIGHT: Sinan's Sülemaniye Mosque in Istanbul was commissioned by Sultan Suleiman the Magnificent to commemorate his son Crown Prince Mehmed.

Sehzade Mosque (1543–1548), and the huge Süleymaniye Mosque (1550–1557) in Istanbul. In the course of four decades, from 1537, as principal Ottoman architect, Sinan was responsible for around 360 structures, including more than fifty schools, nineteen tombs, and thirty-four palaces.

himself as its head. Initially a devout Catholic, Henry was declared "Defender of the Faith" in 1521 for a pamphlet he wrote against Martin Luther. But when Pope Clement VII refused to annul Henry's marriage to Catherine of Aragon, on the grounds that Catherine had previously been the wife of Henry's brother Arthur (died 1502), the king—aided by Archbishop of Canterbury Thomas Cranmer and Chancellor Thomas Cromwell—defied papal authority and wed his mistress, Anne Boleyn, in 1533. The following year the Act of Succession annulled the marriage to Catherine and recognized Anne's daughter Elizabeth as heir, and the Act of Supremacy made Henry head of the Church of England. Henry tired of Anne and had her beheaded for adultery in 1536. The same year he married Jane Seymour, who died after giving birth to the future Edward VI in 1537. Next was a disastrous marriage to Anne of Cleves (1540) arranged by Cromwell, who was executed as a result. After another divorce, Henry married Catherine Howard (also 1540), who was also beheaded for adultery. His sixth wife, Catherine Parr (married 1543), outlived him.

KNOWN FOR
- Having six wives
- Creating the Church of England
- Executing Thomas Cromwell

189 ROYALTY

SULEIMAN

Trabzon, Turkey
1494–1566

The self-styled "master of the world" ruled over 115 million subjects.

Suleiman presided over the Ottoman Empire at the height of its extent and prestige. He led further expansion of Ottoman territory, capturing Belgrade and Rhodes, and even besieged Vienna in 1529, although he did not conquer it. He called himself "master of the world" and "ruler of the territories of Caesar and Alexander the Great," and in size his territory matched that of the Byzantine or East Roman Empire under Emperor Justinian I. He was known as "the Magnificent," and the splendor and glittering high culture of his court in the Topkapi Palace was celebrated everywhere. Suleiman was a skilled poet and goldsmith, and was patron of artistic societies called *Ehl-i Hiref* (Groups of the Skilled) that attracted artists and artisans from all over the empire. He was also a major patron of the greatest architect of the Islamic world, Mimar Sinan. Suleiman was also known as "the Lawgiver," as he reworked the law code first issued by Mehmed the Conqueror. Muslims see Suleiman as the successor to King Solomon, biblical paragon of wisdom, and as the perfect ruler. But he maintained the correct degree of humility, describing himself as "slave of Allah."

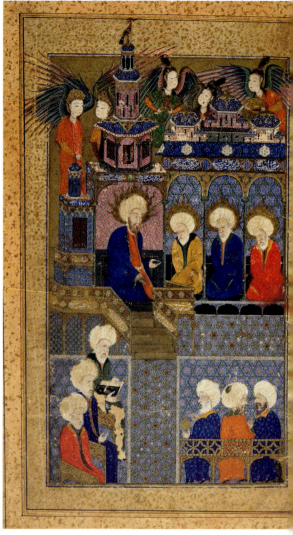

ABOVE: This manuscript page represents Suleiman as embodying and transmitting the wisdom of the great King Solomon.

KNOWN FOR
- Ruling the Ottoman Empire at its greatest extent
- Being the patron of architect Mimar Sinan
- Being celebrated by Muslims as the perfect ruler

190 EXPLORER

PEDRO DE MENDOZA

Guadix, Spain
1499–1537

Spanish explorer Pedro de Mendoza sailed from Spain in 1535 with the backing of Holy Roman Emperor Charles V, and founded Buenos Aires on February 2, 1536. He was made the first governor of Rio de la Plata in Argentina. The settlers had a difficult time, facing famine and repeated attacks by Indigenous fighters. Suffering from syphilis, Mendoza appointed Juan de Ayolas as his successor and embarked for Spain, but he died en route. Ayolas defeated the Indigenous groups and founded Asunción (in what is now Paraguay) in 1537.

191 ROYALTY

CHARLES V

Prinsenhof, Flanders (now Belgium)
1500–1558

King and Holy Roman Emperor who controlled vast territories.

Charles was Duke of Burgundy from 1506, King Charles I of Spain from 1516, and Holy Roman Emperor Charles V from 1519. With dominions across Europe and in the Americas, he presided over an empire "on which the sun never sets." He had no fixed capital and spent one-quarter of his long reign traveling. In Europe he engaged in a long struggle with Francis I of France while attempting to defend the Holy Roman Empire against the Protestant Reformation and the Ottoman Empire. Suffering from gout, Charles abdicated in 1556, making way for his son Philip II in Spain and the Netherlands, and brother Ferdinand I as Holy Roman Emperor.

"My life has been one long journey."

Charles V, in his final speech

ABOVE: Mounted majesty—the great Venetian artist Titian painted this impressive portrait of Charles V in 1548.

Exploration and Revolution
1500–1799

192 ROYALTY

ATAHUALPA

Inca Empire (now Peru)
c. 1502–1533

The last Inca emperor who was executed.

RIGHT: Atahualpa wears some of the gold that so enflamed the greed of the conquistadors.

Atahualpa was the thirteenth and final emperor of the Inca Empire. His rule ended when he was tricked, captured, and put to death by conquistador Francisco Pizarro. The previous year, Atahualpa had defeated his half-brother Huascar in a civil war following the death of their father Huayna Capac. Then, on November 15, 1532, Pizarro ambushed Atahualpa, capturing him and killing thousands of Inca troops. Atahualpa—aware that the Spaniards were dazzled by precious metals—offered to fill the room in which he was standing with gold, and another with silver, to secure his release. Pizarro accepted. Over the next two months the emperor's subjects gathered the most lavish ransom in history—jewelry, statues, and pieces of art that produced 24 tons of gold and silver when melted down. Kept in prison, Atahualpa reputedly became friendly with Pizarro and his captors and, according to one account, learned to play chess. But despite the ransom being met, he was executed. His initial sentence of being burned alive was commuted to death by strangulation when he converted to Christianity.

KNOWN FOR
- Being the last Inca emperor
- Being double-crossed by Francisco Pizarro
- Amassing a vast ransom of gold and silver

193   ROYALTY

ROXELANA

Rohatyn, Poland (now Ukraine)
c. 1505–1558

Also known as Hürrem Sultan, Roxelana was one of the most powerful women in Ottoman history. Captured in a slave raid, she became a concubine in the imperial harem and rose to become Sultan Suleiman the Magnificent's favorite, and then his legal wife. They had six children, including future sultan Selim II. She played an active role in imperial affairs, advising the sultan, writing diplomatic letters, and overseeing major architectural works, including the Haseki Sultan Complex in Constantinople. When Suleiman was away on campaign, they wrote poetry to one another.

ABOVE: Suleiman broke with tradition in marrying Roxelana, a woman from his harem rather than a noble-born lady.

194   RELIGIOUS LEADER

JOHN CALVIN

Noyon, Picardie, France
1509–1564

John Calvin was a central figure in the Protestant Reformation, founding the Calvinist tradition that emphasized predestination (the idea that all events in a human life have been willed by God, meaning there are limits on free will). He studied law and religion then, after breaking with the Catholic Church in 1530, fled to Basel in Switzerland in 1536 to escape the persecution of Protestants. While there he wrote *Institutes of the Christian Religion*. He moved to Geneva where, though expelled in 1538, he returned in 1541 and went on to establish Protestantism.

ABOVE: A learned and prolific man, Calvin stands surrounded by books, holding a copy of his *Institutes of the Christian Religion*.

ABOVE: Europe's first Black ruler? Alessandro de'Medici ruled Florence for seven years until he was assassinated.

195 POLITICAL LEADER

ALESSANDRO DE'MEDICI

Florence, Italy
1510–1537

Some identify Alessandro de'Medici as the first Black head of state in modern Western Europe. The first duke of the Florentine Republic (1532–1537), he was nicknamed *Il Moro* (the Moor) because of his dark complexion. He was the son of either Lorenzo di Piero de'Medici (grandson of art patron Lorenzo the Magnificent) or Giulio de'Medici (later Pope Clement VII). His mother was probably a Black servant, though some say she was a peasant from the Roman Campagna region. He was murdered in 1537 in a plot by his cousin Lorenzino de'Medici.

196 EXPLORER

JOHN HAWKINS

Plymouth, England
1532–1595

English naval commander and privateer John Hawkins pioneered English involvement in the Atlantic slave trade. In 1562–1563 he was the first English merchant to make money selling slaves from Africa to Spanish colonies in the Caribbean. On his return, Queen Elizabeth I granted him a coat of arms displaying an enslaved man. Later he was a vice-admiral in the Royal Navy during the defeat of the Spanish Armada in 1588, and became treasurer of the navy.

197 ROYALTY

ELIZABETH I

Greenwich, England
1533–1603

"Gloriana" led a confident England to triumphs at home and overseas.

Under Elizabeth I (r. 1558–1603), the last of the Tudor monarchs, England became a major global power, dominant on the high seas, active in the New World of the Americas, and the envy of the world in poetry, theater, music, and fine art. When poet Edmund Spenser dedicated his epic poem *The Faerie Queene* (1590–1596) to Elizabeth, he indicated that he meant the fairy monarch of the title, Gloriana, to represent "the most excellent and glorious person of our sovereign the Queen." Taking no foreign prince as consort, she ruled as the "Virgin Queen," married to her country. She was greatly loved. Her accession day, November 17, was a national holiday from the 1570s onward. During her reign, England foiled an attempted invasion by the Spanish Armada in 1588; established its first overseas colony, Virginia, in what is now North Carolina; and in Sir Francis Drake had a national hero who led overseas explorations and was the first Englishman to sail around the world. At home, poet-playwright William Shakespeare, composers Thomas Tallis and William Byrd, and artist Nicholas Hilliard reached previously unexplored artistic heights.

> *"Though God has raised me high, yet this I count the glory of my crown, that I have reigned with your loves."*
>
> Elizabeth I in a speech to the House of Commons, November 30, 1601

LEFT: Elizabeth stage-managed her cult as the Virgin Queen. Unauthorized portraits of her were banned from 1563 onward.

1500–1799

198 ROYALTY

AMINA

Zazzau (now Zaria, Nigeria)
1533–1610

Hausa warrior queen who expanded Zazzau in northwest Nigeria.

Queen Amina's wars of expansion greatly enlarged the territory of the Hausa city-state of Zazzau (now Zaria) in northwest Nigeria. Many oral legends have collected around her. The daughter of King Nikatau, she was raised by her grandfather, who instructed her in matters of state when she was an infant. She rejected many suitors who asked for her hand in marriage, and proved herself the equal of any male warrior in her brother's cavalry when he became king around 1566. After he died in 1576, she took the throne and one of her first acts was to tell her people to "resharpen their weapons." Over thirty-four years, she led a great expansion of Zazzau at the expense of other Hausa states such as Daura, Kano, and Katsina. She reputedly took a new lover in every town where she stopped for the night and each morning he was executed, so none could tell the secrets of the bedroom. She ordered the building of earth walls around cities, and many of these survive today; they are still called "Amina's walls." She also developed trade with northern Africa and introduced the farming of kola nuts.

KNOWN FOR
- Expanding Zazzau
- Building defensive walls
- Developing trade

199 POLITICAL LEADER

TOYOTOMI HIDEYOSHI

Nakamura, Owari (now Aichi, Japan)
c. 1537–1598

As chancellor and chief imperial minister in 1585–1598, Toyotomi Hideyoshi finished the national unification of Japan started earlier in the century by Oda Nobunaga. Born a peasant, he was elevated to the samurai (warrior) ranks in the service of Nobunaga. His introduction of *shi-no-ko-sho* divided people into warriors, farmers, artisans, and tradesmen, with only the warriors permitted to keep their swords. He had ambitions to conquer China and even India, but his attempts at overseas expansion—invasions of Korea in 1592 and 1597—failed, in part as a result of the defensive heroics of Korean admiral Yi Sun-shin.

ABOVE: Toyotomi Hideyoshi's reforms, picked up by Tokugawa Ieyasu, set the scene for the peace and prosperity of the Tokugawa era.

200 ROYALTY

AKBAR

Umarkot (now Sindh province, Pakistan)
1542–1605

The greatest Mughal ruler expanded his empire and was a major patron of the arts.

Jalal al-Din Muhammad Akbar (r. 1556–1605) extended Mughal territory from the Punjab and Delhi area to encompass the whole of northern India and eventually much of the subcontinent. His rule is remembered for fairness, benevolence, and religious tolerance. He promoted a new faith, *Din-e Ilahi* (Divine Religion), that blended elements of Hinduism, Christianity, Zoroastrianism, Buddhism, and Jainism with Islam. His court was a great center of artistic achievement, frequented by bookbinders, scribes, artists, translators, scholars, and calligraphers. During his reign, a distinctive Mughal style emerged in fine art and architecture through the combination of Persian and Timurid (Turko-Mongol) Islamic approaches with Indigenous Indian traditions.

"Truth is the means of pleasing God; I never saw any one lost on the right road."

Akbar's seal

RIGHT: A page from the *Akbarnama* (*Book of Akbar*) depicts an incident early in Akbar's reign in which he arrests a rebellious lord, Shah Abul-Maali.

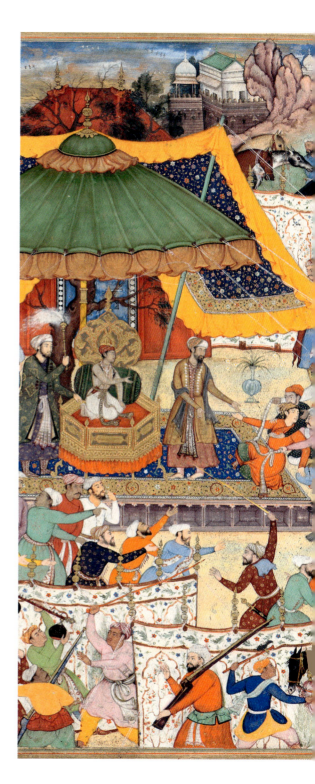

1500–1799 167

ABOVE: Ieyasu was known for his loyalty to Oda Nobunaga. Sometimes cautious, he was also bold and decisive in action.

201   MILITARY LEADER

TOKUGAWA IEYASU

Okazaki, Honshu, Japan
1543–1616

The third unifier of Japan, after Oda Nobunaga and Toyotomi Hideyoshi, Ieyasu won the power struggle that followed his former ally Hideyoshi's death in 1598. He seized power in 1603 and ruled until his death in 1616. Ieyasu founded the Tokugawa shogunate (military government) that endured until 1867.

202   ACTIVIST

GASPAR YANGA

Gabon
1545–1618

Celebrated as "the First Liberator of the Americas," Gaspar Yanga led a slave revolt in Mexico in 1570 and established a colony of maroons (descendants of African slaves) in the highlands near Veracruz, New Spain (now Mexico)—one of the first Black settlements in the New World. It became a refuge for fugitive slaves from other areas. An attack by the Spanish authorities on the settlement in 1609 led to years of struggle, until a settlement based on self-rule was agreed on in 1618. Yanga was originally a member of the royal family in Gabon, but was taken into slavery and sold in Mexico.

YI SUN-SIN

Hansung, Korea
1545–1598

This brilliant Korean admiral defeated the Japanese invasions of the 1590s.

Yi Sun-sin commanded the Korean navy to heroically hold off Japanese invasions in 1592 and 1597. He is revered as a hero in Korea, where the *Nanjung Ilgi*, his war diaries covering 1592 to 1598, are considered to be a national treasure. He initially proved himself a brilliant army general in the 1580s, but was imprisoned and tortured after being falsely accused of desertion. Yi was released and served as an ordinary soldier, then in 1591 was appointed to a regional position with responsibility for the navy and developed the *kobukson* (turtle ship), the first ironclad battleship that had armored plating on the upper deck to shield the crew. In 1592 Yi won a string of naval victories that scuppered the Japanese land invasion by cutting troops off from their supplies. Given full command of the navy in 1593, Yi was again falsely accused and demoted, returning in 1597 to save the day in the Battle of Myeongnyang when the Japanese had almost destroyed the navy. The 1597 Japanese invasion failed, but Yi was killed in the Battle of Noryang in 1598.

RIGHT: This towering bronze statue of Yi Sun-sin reflects his physical presence, but he is celebrated for his intellect as well.

"Yi Sun-sin ... [his] incomparable personality, strategic intelligence, inventiveness, ability as a commander, intelligence, and bravery were all worthy of our admiration."

Lieutenant Commander Kawada Isao, 1905

204 ARTIST

MIGUEL DE CERVANTES

Alcala de Henares, near Madrid, Spain
1547–1616

Spain's greatest author wrote the first novel, *Don Quixote*.

As a soldier, Miguel de Cervantes was captured by Barbary pirates and sold into slavery, then ransomed and briefly imprisoned in Spain. He wrote dramas, a romance, short stories, and poems, as well as his masterpiece *Don Quixote* (two volumes, 1605 and 1615), which is celebrated as the first novel. The tale of an elderly knight and his travels on horseback with his squire Sancho Panza satirizes contemporary chivalric romances.

LEFT: In a famous scene from Miguel Cervantes's *Don Quixote*, the hero mistakes a windmill for a giant and rides toward it with lance extended—the origin of the phrase "tilting at windmills," which means fighting imaginary enemies.

205 ARTIST

AHMAD BABA

Timbuktu, Songhai Empire (now Mali)
1556–1627

This brilliant scholar condemned the enslavement of Muslims.

Legal expert Ahmad Baba wrote more than forty books, was chancellor of the Sankore University in Timbuktu, and issued a well-known legal opinion on slavery. His position was that Muslims could not be enslaved no matter what their color or racial origin. But he did not condemn slavery outright, and allowed for people of other religions to be made and kept as slaves. He studied under his father and the great scholar Mohammed Abu Bekr, whom he revered. After the Sultan of Morocco Ahmad al-Mansur conquered Timbuktu in 1591, Ahmed Baba was accused of disrespect and plotting rebellion, and was exiled with his family to Morocco. His library of more than 1,600 volumes was destroyed. He was initially jailed in Marrakesh, but such was his reputation that Arab scholars persuaded the sultan to release him. Following the sultan's death in 1603, he returned to Timbuktu. Ahmed Baba's books include a biographical history of the major legal experts in the Sunni Muslim Maliki school of law. He also wrote an Arabic grammar that is still used today.

KNOWN FOR
- His wise legal opinions
- Opposing the enslavement of Muslims
- Being exiled to Morocco

1500–1799

PHILOSOPHER

FRANCIS BACON

London, England
1561–1626

This English philosopher was a pioneer of modern scientific methods.

In his book *Novum Organum* (*New Instrument*), written in Latin in 1620, Bacon argued that scientific knowledge should be based on study of nature and inductive reasoning—the process of deriving a principle from a set of observations. He was also a notable statesman under James I, serving as Solicitor General, Attorney General, and Lord Chancellor in 1607–1618. But he was convicted in 1621 of accepting bribes, imprisoned, and permanently excluded from Parliament and public life. The theory that he wrote some—or all—of the plays and poems attributed to William Shakespeare, first floated in the nineteenth century, is mostly discredited, but still has some backers.

> *"If a man will begin with certainties, he shall end in doubts, but if he will be content to begin with doubts, he shall end in certainties."*
>
> Francis Bacon, *The Advancement of Learning*, 1605

LEFT: A patron of libraries, Bacon developed a system of classifying books as either history, philosophy, or poetry.

RIGHT: Galileo was a prolific physicist and engineer. He invented the thermoscope (a device for measuring heat).

SCIENTIST

GALILEO GALILEI

Pisa, Tuscany, Italy
1564–1642

In 1611, Italian mathematician and astronomer Galileo Galilei backed Nicolaus Copernicus's view that the Earth revolves around the Sun. The view was dismissed as heretical and contrary to Holy Scripture by the Inquisition of the Catholic Church in 1615. Galileo restated his position in his 1632 book *Dialogue Concerning the Two Chief World Systems* and was tried by the Inquisition, forced to recant, and put under house arrest. Galileo was also the first to use a telescope to observe the skies, and discovered the moons of Jupiter and the phases of Venus.

"All the world's a stage,
*   And all the men and women merely players;*
*   They have their exits and their entrances."*

William Shakespeare, *As You Like It*, 1599

KNOWN FOR
- Being the most celebrated writer in the world
- Writing at least 37 plays
- Co-owning the Globe Theatre

208 ARTIST

WILLIAM SHAKESPEARE

Stratford-upon-Avon, England
1564–1616

This English poet-playwright achieved greatness "for all time."

English poet and dramatist William Shakespeare is often judged the greatest of all writers. Admiring rival Ben Jonson wrote: "I confess thy writings to be such / As neither man nor muse can praise too much," adding, "He was not of the age but for all time." Shakespeare wrote at least 37 plays, 154 sonnets, and two lengthy narrative poems. He was born in 1564 in Stratford-upon-Avon and in 1582, at the age of 18, he married a local woman, Anne Hathaway. They had three children—Susanna in 1583, and twins Hamnet and Judith in 1585; Hamnet died aged 11 in 1596. By that time Shakespeare was established in the London theater as actor and playwright. He was the principal playwright for the Lord Chamberlain's Company of Players, later granted the royal patent as "the King's Men." They played at court before Queen Elizabeth I and King James I. Initially they performed at the theater in Shoreditch, east London, but after the lease on the site expired they took the theater down, transported it, and rebuilt it as the famous Globe Theatre beside the river Thames. After a stellar career in which he wrote plays whose titles are familiar the world over, such as *Hamlet* (1600–1601), *Othello* (1604–1605), and *Macbeth* (1605–1606), Shakespeare retired in *c.* 1613 to Stratford, where he died on his fifty-second birthday in 1616.

LEFT: One of several possible likenesses of Shakespeare, this (the Cobbe portrait) was probably painted in 1595–1610. The words are from an ode by Horace addressed to a playwright.

RIGHT: Shakespeare was part-owner of the Globe Theatre on the river Thames in London.

209 RELIGIOUS LEADER

POPE URBAN VIII

Barberino, Val d'Elsa, Italy
1568–1644

Pope who oversaw the flowering of the grand Baroque style in Rome.

A great patron of the arts, Urban VIII commissioned architect-sculptor Gian Lorenzo Bernini to create the bronze baldachin (canopy) above the high altar in St. Peter's Basilica, the Triton Fountain in Piazza Barberini, and the pope's family palace, the Palazzo Barberini, all in Rome. Urban also fortified the city, building defenses along the Tiber and strengthening Castel Sant'Angelo. In foreign affairs he generally supported the interests of France and its minister Cardinal Richelieu against those of the Hapsburgs of Spain and Austria.

210 EXPLORER

WILLEM JANSZOON

Amsterdam, Netherlands
c. 1570–1630

Dutch explorer Willem Janszoon (also Jansz) was the first European to land in Australia. In 1606 he brought his ship the *Duyfken* (Little Dove) ashore at Pennefather River on the Cape York Peninsula, Queensland, and charted around 200 miles of the coast. He had been sailing from Indonesia to New Guinea for the Dutch East India Company. Janszoon called the land Nieu Zeelandt after Zeeland, a Dutch province, but the name did not stick and Dutch mapmakers later used it for New Zealand.

BELOW: Going Dutch. A modern replica of Janszoon's ship *Duyfken* on the water in Adelaide, South Australia.

211 ACTIVIST

ST. MARTIN DE PORRES

Lima, Viceroyalty of Peru (now Peru)
1579–1639

Dominican lay brother Martin de Porres worked for the poor in Lima, setting up a children's hospital and an orphanage. He was the son of a Spanish nobleman, Don Juan de Porras, and a freed slave woman of African/Indigenous descent, Ana Velásquez. De Porres performed many miracles. He was canonized by Pope John XXIII in 1962, the first Black saint in the Americas. He is the patron saint of those seeking racial harmony.

212 ROYALTY

NJINGA OF NDONGO AND MATAMBA

Kabasa, Ndongo (now Angola)
c. 1583–1663

Queen Njinga of the kingdoms of Ndongo and Matamba defended her lands and people against the Portuguese empire and the rapidly developing slave trade. She was taught to read and write in Portuguese by missionaries, and this helped her to be an extremely effective diplomat. Giving refuge to runaway slaves and developing militias, she fomented resistance to the Portuguese colony at Luanda. She also built Matamba into a powerful commercial force capable of dealing with the Europeans as equals.

213 ROYALTY

SHAH JAHAN

Lahore (now Pakistan)
1592–1666

The fifth emperor of the Mughal empire, Shah Jahan commissioned the exquisitely beautiful Taj Mahal in Agra in 1631 as a mausoleum for his wife Mumtaz Mahal. He also built the Red Fort in Delhi as an imperial residence when he moved the capital there from Agra, and the elaborately tiled Shah Jahan Mosque in Thatta in Sindh. He waged war on the Deccan sultanates (the medieval kingdoms on the Deccan peninsula in southern India) and the Safavids, as well as fighting the Portuguese. In 1657, in poor health, he made his eldest son Dara Shikoh his successor, sparking a succession conflict that was won by his third son, Aurangzeb. When Shah Jahan recovered, Aurangzeb confined him in the Agra Fort for the rest of his life.

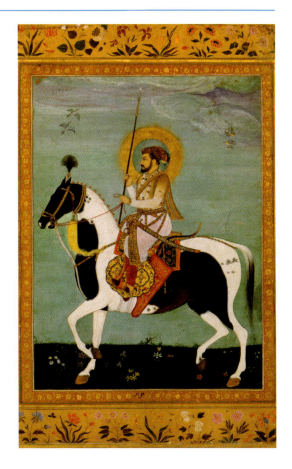

RIGHT: Shah Jahan executed his brother Shahryar Mirza and other rivals to claim power on the death of his father Jahangir in 1627.

MUMTAZ MAHAL

India
1593–1631

The Taj Mahal commemorates this much-loved empress consort.

Mumtaz Mahal was the most favored wife of Mughal emperor Shah Jahan. When she died giving birth to her fourteenth child, a daughter, in 1631, he commissioned the glorious Taj Mahal beside the Yamuna river in Agra as her mausoleum. Born Arjumand Banu Begum in 1593, the daughter of Shah Jahan's grand vizier Abu'l-Hasan Asaf Khan, Mumtaz was betrothed to Shah Jahan at fourteen and married five years later in 1612. He gave her the name Mumtaz Mahal (meaning "exalted one in the palace") as a sign of his great regard. Shah Jahan took two other wives, Kanadahri Begum (in 1610, before marrying Mumtaz) and Izz-un-Nissa Begum (in 1617). These were reputedly marriages of alliance rather than affection and he saved his love for Mumtaz. On becoming emperor in 1628, Shah Jahan declared her Padshah Begum (First Lady of the Great) and Malikia-i-Jahan (Queen of the World). On her death, Shah Jahan could not be consoled. The Taj Mahal mausoleum he built for her took twenty-two years to complete. He was himself later buried beside her in the mausoleum, though this was not his initial intention.

> "[Shah Jahan's] whole delight was focused on this regal lady [Mumtaz] . . . for his other wives he felt less than one-thousandth of the affection he had for her."
>
> Court historian Inayat Khan

LEFT: Mumtaz Mahal was a great linguist who composed poems in Persian and had a good knowledge of Arabic.

ABOVE: Pocahontas and John Rolfe are married by a Christian priest, with the bride's compatriots in attendance.

ABOVE: Descartes has had a huge influence on the history of philosophy; his 1641 *Meditations on First Philosophy* is a set text for students today.

215   EXPLORER

POCAHONTAS

Near present-day Jamestown, Virginia
c. 1596–1617

The daughter of a Native American chief, Pocahontas was captured by colonial settlers at Jamestown, Virginia, in 1613. She converted to Christianity, was baptized as Rebecca, then in 1614 married a tobacco planter, John Rolfe. Together they had a son, Thomas. The Rolfes sailed to London, where Pocahontas, presented in polite society, became a celebrity and attended a masque (courtly entertainment) at Whitehall Palace in 1616. As she prepared to return to Virginia with Rolfe in 1617, she fell ill at Gravesend, Kent, before embarking and died.

216   PHILOSOPHER

RENÉ DESCARTES

La Haye en Touraine, France
1596–1650

French philosopher and mathematician René Descartes emphasized the duality of mind and body and is called the "father of modern philosophy." He is famous for his statement *Cogito ergo sum* ("I think therefore I am") in his book *Discourse on the Method*, written in Latin and French in 1637. In mathematics he combined algebra and geometry to create the field of analytic geometry.

217 EXPLORER

ABEL TASMAN

Lutjeggast, Groningen, Dutch Republic (now the Netherlands)
c. 1603–1659

This explorer was the first European to find New Zealand, Fiji, and Tasmania.

In 1642 Antonie van Diemen, the governor-general of the Dutch East Indies in Indonesia, sent Abel Tasman to search for a southern continent in the Pacific Ocean. When, on November 24, Tasman reached the west coast of Tasmania, he named it Van Diemen's Land. Then, on December 13, he sighted and sailed along the coast of New Zealand's South Island, which he believed to be the continent he was seeking. He found and sailed into the sea between the South and North Islands, thinking it a bay. On his return voyage toward Indonesia, he came across Tonga on January 21, 1643, and Fiji on February 6. On a second trip in 1644 he entered the Gulf of Carpentaria and explored the northern and western coasts of Australia. Before his historic voyages to New Zealand, Fiji, and Tasmania, and while in the service of the Dutch East India Company, Tasman had sailed to Batavia (modern Jakarta), Dutch Formosa (Taiwan), Japan, and Cambodia.

KNOWN FOR
- Being the first European to sight New Zealand, Fiji, and Tasmania
- Exploring the northern and western Australian coasts
- Being the greatest Dutch navigator

218 ARTIST

REMBRANDT VAN RIJN

Leiden, Netherlands
1606–1669

The greatest artist of the Dutch "Golden Age" created penetrating portraits.

Rembrandt was a master of painting, drawing, and etching who worked with equal skill and energy on portraits, landscapes, still lifes, biblical and historical scenes, and studies of animals. He was supremely observant and skilled at representing human emotions and behavior—he is celebrated as one of the finest storytellers in painting. His magnificent self-portraits, which make up one-tenth of his entire work, are very moving. Throughout his career, but especially in his later years, he explored the effects of light and shade.

219 ROYALTY

AURANGZEB (MUHI AL-DIN MUHAMMAD)

Dahod, Gujarat, India
c. 1618–1707

The Mughal Empire reached its greatest extent under Aurangzeb, encompassing almost all of South Asia, and he established Sharia law and Islamic economics (economics administered in line with the teachings of Islam) throughout these vast territories. Aurangzeb came to power by defeating his brother (and his father Shah Jahan's nominated successor) Dara Shikoh in 1658. Some

"*Compare me with Rembrandt! Sacrilege! With Rembrandt, the Colossus of art! We should prostrate ourselves before Rembrandt and never compare anyone with him!*"

Auguste Rodin (1840-1917)

LEFT: One of Rembrandt's many self-portraits. This one was painted in 1660, when he was in his mid-fifties.

RIGHT: After falling ill in old age, Emperor Aurangzeb spent most of the next two years praying.

Islamic historians identify him as the greatest Mughal emperor, but his religious intolerance, including the 1675 execution of the Sikh guru Tegh Bahadur, exclusion of Hindus from public life, and demolition of Hindu temples, was controversial and some say contributed to the eventual decline of the Mughal Empire in the middle of the eighteenth century.

MOLIÈRE (JEAN-BAPTISTE POQUELIN)

Paris, France
1622–1673

This comic writer and theatrical jack-of-all-trades dazzled the French royal court.

Jean-Baptiste Poquelin, known by his stage name Molière, is celebrated as France's counterpart to Shakespeare, and the country's greatest dramatist. He is a major influence on modern French comedy. With the actress Madeleine Béjart he co-founded the acting troupe the Illustre Théâtre, which toured the provinces from 1645 to 1658. Later, he accessed the royal court through the patronage of Louis XIV's brother Philippe, Duke of Orléans. In 1662 Molière married Armande, Béjart's seventeen-year-old daughter. His celebrated plays include The School for Wives, Tartuffe, The Misanthrope, The Miser, and The Bourgeois Gentleman. They wittily represent and dissect the self-deceptions, self-importance, and vices of French bourgeois and aristocratic society. He was a superb director and actor as well as a playwright. Molière had pulmonary tuberculosis and died on February 17, 1673, after suffering a coughing fit and hemorrhaging during a performance of his play The Imaginary Invalid. The consummate professional, he completed the performance but collapsed and died hours later.

BELOW: Molière delivers a speech from his play Tartuffe in the Parisian salon (drawing room) of author and courtesan Ninon de l'Enclos.

221 SCIENTIST

ANTONIE VAN LEEUWENHOEK

Delft, Dutch Republic (now the Netherlands)
1632–1723

Dutch pioneer of microscopes Antonie van Leeuwenhoek is known as the "father of microbiology"—he made his own single-lens microscopes and was the first to observe bacteria and protozoa. By studying eels, fleas, and mussels, he disproved the theory that life spontaneously generates from non-living matter. He also made the first observations of muscle fibers, spermatozoa, and red blood cells. He initially developed his lens-making to enable him to see the quality of thread better for his work as a draper. He did not publish any books, but wrote 190 letters to the Royal Society in London detailing his findings.

222 ROYALTY

LOUIS XIV

Saint-Germain-en-Laye, France
1638–1715

The French "Sun King" is history's longest-reigning monarch.

Le Roi Soleil (the Sun King) Louis XIV reigned for 72 years and 110 days from his accession aged four years and eight months on May 14, 1643, to his death from gangrene on September 1, 1715. A believer in a king's divinely ordained and absolute authority, he kept a lavish palace at Versailles and governed France in what is arguably the greatest period of its history. He is known as the "Sun King" because he chose the Sun—symbol of Apollo, god of the arts and of peace—as his emblem. He was a great patron of the arts and founded the French Academy of Sciences.

RIGHT: The Sun King adopts a regal pose in this courtly portrait, painted in 1701, when he had already been on the throne for more than half a century.

ISAAC NEWTON

Woolsthorpe, Grantham,
Lincolnshire, England
1642–1727

English mathematician and physicist Isaac Newton was famously inspired to formulate his theory of gravity after watching an apple fall from a tree. He spelled out the laws of motion and the universal law of gravitation in his 1687 book *Philosophiae Naturalis Principia Mathematica* (*Mathematical Principles of Natural Philosophy*). He also made major contributions to the fields of optics and mathematics, was twice member of parliament for the University of Cambridge, and was warden of the Royal Mint and president of the Royal Society.

BELOW: In 1665, Newton demonstrated the spectrum of colors in light by allowing a beam of sunlight coming through a window shutter to pass through a glass prism.

GOTTFRIED WILHELM VON LEIBNIZ

Leipzig, Saxony, Holy Roman Empire (now Germany)
1646–1716

German mathematician, philosopher, and scientist Gottfried Wilhelm von Leibniz developed differential and integral calculus independently of Isaac Newton's discovery of them. As a result the two men were drawn into a struggle for preeminence that served to isolate English mathematics. Leibniz was also a pioneer of mechanical calculators and invented the Leibniz wheel, a device used in the first mass-produced calculator.

225 EXPLORER

WILLIAM DAMPIER

East Coker, Somerset, England
1651–1715

Pirate and naturalist who rescued the original "Robinson Crusoe."

William Dampier was the first Englishman to land on the Australian mainland. He charted parts of the coast and made a scientific study of its animals, plants, and natural landscape. After serving in the Royal Navy and fighting in the Anglo-Dutch War (1672–1674), he turned to privateering (piracy) in 1678–1691, and in 1688 landed in Australia, which Abel Tasman had called New Holland. On returning to England he published *A New Voyage Around the World* in 1697. The Admiralty commissioned him to return to Australia, and he landed at Shark Bay, western Australia, on August 6, 1699. He charted the coast from there to Lagrange Bay, near Broome. He took careful notes and collected biological specimens. His second book, *A Voyage to New Holland*, contained drawings of Australian flora and fauna by James Brand—the first by a European. Later in life Dampier returned to piracy. He rescued castaway Alexander Selkirk, who inspired Daniel Defoe's *Robinson Crusoe*. Dampier was the first European to describe a typhoon.

"It is not yet determined whether it is an island or a main continent, but I am certain that it joins neither Asia, Africa nor America."

Dampier on his first impressions of Australia

ABOVE: With the globe beneath his hand, Dampier appears to conjure a vision of the exotic animals and scenes he witnessed on his world journey.

226 ROYALTY

OSEI TUTU

Anyinam, Ghana
c. 1660–1717

Founder of the powerful Asante Empire in Ghana.

The chief of the state of Kumasi in Ghana, Osei Tutu (r. 1701–c. 1717) led a coalition of small Asante kingdoms to victory over their southern neighbors, the Denkyera, in 1699–1701. In the following years, he enlarged Asante territory roughly three times, trading slaves for guns with Dutch and British merchants. Before the war, he had been a hostage at the Denkyera court, but escaped to the state of Akwamu. In c. 1695, he met and returned to Kumasi with the priest Okomfo Anokye, who introduced the celebrated Golden Stool as a symbol of Osei Tutu's authority as Asantehene, ruler of the newly created empire, and of the bond between the Asante peoples. During the war, Anokye reputedly played a key role when the Asante were being overpowered—when he called out incantations in battle the tide of the war turned, and many Denkyera generals joined the Asante army. Osei Tutu was succeeded by Opoku Ware, who expanded the empire to its greatest territorial extent.

KNOWN FOR
- Founding the Asante Empire
- Engaging in the slave and gun trade

227 MILITARY LEADER

CHANGAMIRE

Mutapa Empire (now Zimbabwe)
c. 1660–1695

Changamire Dombo rose from being a herdsman to become Shona leader. In c. 1684 he founded the Rozwi Empire in what is now Zimbabwe. As the head of an army equipped with traditional spears and shields, he conquered fertile lands rich in minerals and drove back an attempt by the Portuguese to take control of the region's gold mines. He established a capital at Danangombe, near Gweru, in central Zimbabwe. By tradition he had magical powers and could turn a red cow white.

PETER THE GREAT

Moscow, Russia
1672–1725

This revered tsar established Russia as a European power.

Peter I modernized the Russian government and military, introduced Western technology, and established a new capital, St. Petersburg, in 1703. He created the modern Russian navy and oversaw advances in education, culture, and science, establishing the country's first university, in St. Petersburg, in 1724. He fought against the Ottoman Empire in 1695–1696 and defeated Sweden in the Great Northern War of 1700–1721, gaining access to the Baltic Sea. The son of Tsar Alexis, Peter co-ruled with his brother Ivan and their sister Sophia as regent from 1682 to 1689, then as co-tsars until Ivan's death in 1696. After this he was sole tsar, and took the title of emperor in 1721. On his death he was succeeded by his consort, Empress Catherine I.

> "*Peter the Great is indeed the inventor of modern Russian policy.*"
>
> Karl Marx, *The Free Press*, 1857

RIGHT: Peter painted in 1697. He introduced the Julian Calendar in Russia, and the first Russian newspaper was founded during his reign.

ARTIST

JOHANN SEBASTIAN BACH

Eisnach, Saxony, Germany
1685–1750

This baroque composer created profound choral works and joyful instrumental music.

Johann Sebastian Bach was celebrated by his contemporaries as the most skillful organist and harpsichord player of his day, but it was only in the nineteenth century that he was recognized as the finest baroque composer—and possibly the greatest composer—in musical history. Orphaned at age ten, he was raised by his brother Johann Christophe, an organist, who taught him to play the organ and clavier. After various roles as organist and choirmaster, in 1717–1723 he was director of music for Prince Leopold of Köthen, and wrote the celebrated *Brandenburg Concertos*, *The Well-Tempered Clavier*, and his *Cello Suites*. After 1723 he was cantor (choirmaster and singer) at St. Thomas Church in Leipzig. There he wrote the *St. Matthew Passion*, *Mass in B Minor*, and around 300 cantatas. He was married twice, first to a cousin, Maria Barbara Bach, and after her death to Anna Magdalena Wilcken; he had twenty children, but only ten survived to adulthood. His other great works include the *Goldberg Variations* for keyboard (1741), the *Schubler Chorales* (1747–1748) and *Toccata and Fugue in D Minor* (c. 1704).

RIGHT: Music in hand and positioned before an organ, Johann Sebastian Bach stands outside St. Thomas Church, Leipzig, scene of many triumphs.

KNOWN FOR
- Being the greatest composer of baroque music
- Composing the *Brandenburg Concertos* and the *Goldberg Variations*

NADIR SHAH

Dargaz, Safavid Iran (now Iran)
1688–1747

The "Napoleon of Persia" was the founder of the Afsharid dynasty in Iran.

Initially the leader of a bandit group, Nadr Qoli Beg brilliantly led the Iranian army to restore Safavid shah Tahmasp II to the throne, ousting the usurping Afghan ruler Mahmud. He later deposed Tahmasp, declaring himself regent for Tahmasp's son Abbas III, and then from 1736 took power under the title "Nadir Shah." He loved nothing except campaigning and conquest—and getting the better of the Ottoman Turks, Russia, the Mughals, and the Uzbeks. He built a vast territory that matched the ancient Iranian empires in size, running from the Caucasus Mountains to the Indus. He has been dubbed "the Napoleon of Persia" by historians. But he could be volatile and cruel, and was assassinated by his own army.

"How can there be any delights there then?"

Nadir Shah, when told there is no war in paradise

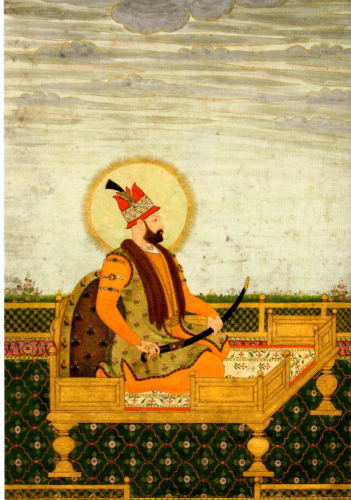

RIGHT: He lived by the sword—and died by it. Nadir Shah hero-worshipped Genghis Khan and Timur and, like the latter, made towers of his victims' skulls.

231 PHILOSOPHER

MONTESQUIEU

La Brède, France
1689–1755

In 1748 French philosopher Charles-Louis de Secondat, baron de la Brède and de Montesquieu (known as Montesquieu) anonymously published *The Spirit of the Laws*, a significant influence on the American Founding Fathers when they were drafting the United States Constitution of 1789. He developed the theory of the separation of powers (the division of government into independent arms, such as the legislative, executive, and judicial) and classified three government types (monarchical, republican, and despotic).

ABOVE: An academic study revealed that the American Founding Fathers cited Montesquieu more than any other book save the Bible.

232 MILITARY LEADER

ABRAM PETROVICH HANNIBAL

Logon (now Cameroon)
c. 1696–1781

Black African slave Abram Hannibal (also known as Gannibal) was adopted by Peter the Great and became a Russian general and military engineer. Sold into slavery in Cameroon, he was brought to Peter's court at the age of eight. With Peter's backing he studied engineering in Paris. He married the daughter of a German officer and had eleven children. His great-grandson was the great Russian poet Alexander Pushkin.

233 RELIGIOUS LEADER

MARIE-MARGUERITE D'YOUVILLE

Varennes, Quebec, Canada
1701–1771

The first Canadian-born saint, Marie-Marguerite d'Youville founded the Sisters of Charity of the Hôpital Général de Montreal, better known as the Grey Nuns, in 1744. The order began with the founding of a home for the poor in 1737. The nuns later took over the General Hospital in Montreal. D'Youville was canonized by Pope John Paul II in 1990.

234 SCIENTIST

BENJAMIN FRANKLIN

Boston, Massachusetts
1706–1790

This inventor, scientist, philosopher, statesman, and diplomat was one of America's Founding Fathers.

One of the most remarkable men in United States history, Benjamin Franklin helped draft the Declaration of Independence and the U.S. Constitution. He was the first U.S. ambassador to France, and played a crucial role in winning French support for the American Revolution. He developed, and was first president of, the Philadelphia Academy that became the University of Pennsylvania, and was president of the American Philosophical Society. As a writer and publisher, he was behind the *Pennsylvania Gazette* and *Poor Richard's Almanack*. He invented the Franklin stove, bifocal spectacles, and the lightning conductor. In his scientific work he established that lightning is electricity, mapped and named the Gulf Stream, and identified the Aurora Borealis (northern lights) as an electrical event. At one time he kept slaves, but from the late 1750s onward was an abolitionist. He was president of Pennsylvania and the first U.S. Postmaster General. He was largely self-taught, and learned Latin, French, Italian, and Spanish.

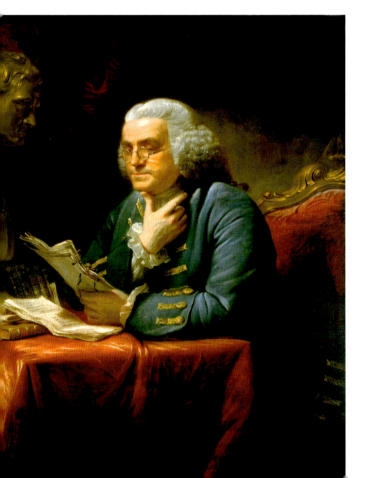

"There never was a good war or a bad peace."

Benjamin Franklin in a letter to Sir Joseph Banks, 1783

LEFT: Benjamin Franklin in 1767. He was an early campaigner for unity of the colonies, which earned him the title of "the First American."

235 SCIENTIST

CARL LINNAEUS

Rashult, Smaland, Sweden
1707–1778

Swedish botanist Carl Linnaeus established the system called binomial taxonomy used for naming organisms—dividing the natural world into the animal, plant, and mineral kingdoms. He published his *Systema Naturae* (*System of Nature*) in 1735, though the tenth edition of 1758 was the most influential. His system was based on work done by Swiss botanists and brothers Gaspard and Johann Bauhin.

ABOVE: Much of Linnaeus's work was in Latin. He was professor of medicine and botany at Uppsala University, Sweden.

236 SCIENTIST

LEONHARD EULER

Basel, Switzerland
1707–1783

One of the greatest mathematicians of all time, Leonhard Euler made contributions to number theory, geometry, mechanics, and calculus, and was also a notable astronomer. He was born in and studied in Basel, Switzerland, then became professor of physics in 1731 and mathematics in 1733 in St. Petersburg. He went to Berlin in 1741 at the invitation of Frederick the Great, and stayed there as a member of the Berlin Academy for twenty-five years.

"Read Euler, read Euler, he is the master of us all."

Scientist Pierre-Simon Laplace (1749–1827)

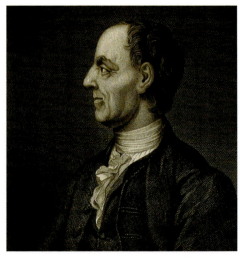

ABOVE: Euler popularized the use of the Greek letter pi (π) to refer to the ratio of a circle's circumference to its diameter.

237 PHILOSOPHER

JEAN-JACQUES ROUSSEAU

Geneva, Switzerland
1712–1778

"Man is born free, but he is everywhere in chains."

Jean-Jacques Rousseau, The Social Contract, 1762

His political philosophy was a major influence on the "Age of Enlightenment" and the French Revolution.

Jean-Jacques Rousseau argued that humans were naturally good, but civilization and society were corrupting influences. His *Discourse on the Origin and Foundations of Inequality Among Men* (1755) proposed that, before the organization of society and introduction of private property, people were free and happy. His masterpiece *The Social Contract* (1762) influenced French revolutionary thinking, developing the idea of "liberty, equality, fraternity," and contended that individuals could find genuine freedom in obedience to the "general will" of the people, and that governments could be overthrown if they were not aligned with this general will. Born in Geneva, he moved to Savoy and then, in 1741, to Paris, where he wrote for Denis Diderot's *Encyclopédie*. He lived in Luxembourg in 1757, but, when his novel on educational themes, *Emile*, provoked outrage, escaped to Switzerland and then England. He wrote one of the first autobiographies, *Confessions*, posthumously published in 1782, and also seven operas.

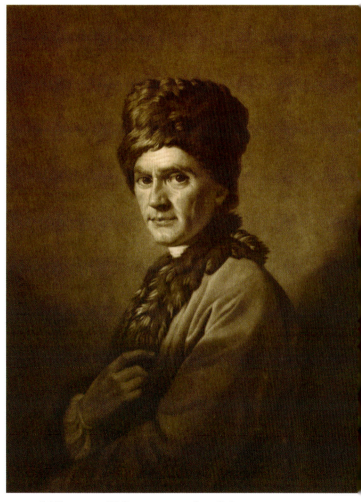

ABOVE: Told "men are evil," Rousseau reputedly replied "but man is good." Late in life his health declined after he banged his head in a 1776 collision with a dog.

238 POLITICAL LEADER

PONTIAC

Maumee River (now in Ohio)
c. 1720–1769

This Native American chief led a revolt against the British.

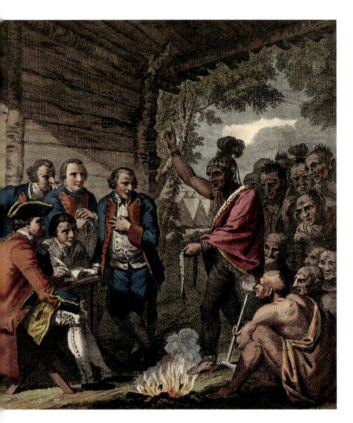

> **KNOWN FOR**
> - Leading Pontiac's War against British forts
> - Being the subject of a play by frontiersman Robert Rogers
> - Victory in the Battle of Bloody Run
> - Being a great strategist

Pontiac, chief of the Ottawa people, inspired a widespread rebellion against British control in the Great Lakes in 1763–1764. Following their victory in the French and Indian War (1754–1763), the British had taken over a series of forts. In May 1763, Pontiac planned a coordinated campaign by Native American groups against the forts, with each group attacking its local fort. Pontiac was to lead an assault on the Detroit fort, but when his plans were discovered, what was to have been a surprise strike became a siege, culminating in Pontiac's victory at the Battle of Bloody Run—an engagement at Parent's Creek near the fort so called because the creek reputedly ran red with the blood of British troops. Frontiersman Robert Rogers (of Rogers' Rangers militia fame) fought in the battle, and later wrote a 1766 play about Pontiac—*Ponteach, or the Savages of America*—that made the leader famous. Nevertheless, after the fort was reinforced, Pontiac was forced to retreat. The wider attack was a success, with eight out of twelve forts captured; "Pontiac's War" ended in a 1766 peace treaty. However, Pontiac had aroused resentment among other Native American groups and he was assassinated in Illinois by a warrior of the Peoria people. This led to a bitter tribal war.

ABOVE LEFT: The Native American leader confronts Swiss-born British soldier Colonel Henry Bouquet in 1764 during Pontiac's War.

239 POLITICAL LEADER

AHMAD SHAH DURRANI

Herat (now Afganistan) or Multan, Punjab (now Pakistan)
c. 1722–1772

Ahmad Shah Durrani created the Durrani Empire and was the founder of modern Afghanistan. His father was the leader of the Abdali confederation and a cavalry commander under Nadir Shah; when Nadir Shah was assassinated, Ahmad Shah Durrani was elected shah. He was crowned in 1747, and established his capital at Kandahar. He built an empire that stretched west to east from Khorasan to northern India, and north to south from the Amu Darya river to the Arabian Sea. He changed the name of the Abdali to Durrani.

ABOVE: Ahmad Shah Durrani is known as the father of Afghanistan and he is often called Ahmad Shah Baba ("Ahmad Shah the Father").

240 PHILOSOPHER

ADAM SMITH

Kirkcaldy, Scotland
1723–1790

Philosopher who wrote the first book of political economy.

Adam Smith is known as the "father of economics" for his 1776 work *An Inquiry into the Nature and Causes of the Wealth of Nations*. The book argues that rational self-interest is the basis for prosperity, and the division of labor (into separate tasks done by different groups) is the driver of productivity. He studied at Glasgow and Oxford, and at Glasgow University was professor of logic (1751) and professor of moral philosophy (1752–1763). He also wrote *The Theory of Moral Sentiments* (1759), and traveled to France as tutor to the Duke of Buccleuch from 1763 to 1766.

> "By pursuing his own interest [a person] frequently promotes that of the society more effectually than when he really intends to promote it."
>
> Adam Smith, *An Inquiry into the Nature and Causes of the Wealth of Nations*, 1776

241 PHILOSOPHER

IMMANUEL KANT

Königsberg, Prussia (now Kaliningrad, Russia)
1724–1804

Immanuel Kant was one of the leading thinkers of the Enlightenment. The son of a saddlemaker, he studied and taught at the University of Königsberg, becoming professor of logic and metaphysics in 1770, a post he held until 1797. His most important work, *Critique of Pure Reason* (1781), examined the role of the mind in building our knowledge of objective reality. He was famous for his regular habits; German writer Heinrich Heine said that the people of Königsberg could set their watches by his daily walk.

242 ACTIVIST

JOHN NEWTON

London, England
1725–1807

Sailor John Newton worked on slave ships, and was himself briefly enslaved in what is now Sierra Leone. After being rescued, he invested in the slave trade, but later converted to Christianity and became a staunch abolitionist. Back in England, he became a Church of England cleric and wrote the celebrated hymns "Amazing Grace" and "Glorious Things of Thee Are Spoken."

ABOVE: Kant believed that objects of everyday experience are "appearances" and that people cannot know "things-in-themselves."

243 EXPLORER

JAMES COOK

Marton-in-Cleveland, England
1728–1779

This explorer was the first European to sail around New Zealand and land in Hawaii.

Royal Navy captain James Cook circumnavigated New Zealand—proving that its North Island was not part of the supposed *Terra Australis Incognita* (unknown southern territory)—on HMS *Endeavour* in 1770. It was part of the first scientific voyage to the Pacific (1768–1771) to view the transit of Venus across the Sun from Tahiti. During the voyage he explored the eastern coast of Australia. He also circumnavigated Antarctica in 1772–1775. He was killed in a quarrel with Indigenous people in Hawaii after becoming the first European to land there during an expedition (1776–1779) seeking the Northwest Passage between the Atlantic and Pacific Oceans. He was also celebrated for preventing scurvy (a disease caused by long-term lack of vitamin C in the diet and common in the navy at the time) by including sauerkraut, orange extract, and cress in the sailors' rations. He was made a Fellow of the Royal Society and awarded a prestigious Copley Medal for his paper on this subject.

ABOVE RIGHT: Cook made his name serving in the Royal Navy in the Battle of Quebec during the Seven Years' War.

"Ambition leads me not only farther than any other man has been before me, but as far as I think it possible for man to go."

James Cook in his journal, 1774

244 ROYALTY

CATHERINE THE GREAT

Stettin, Prussia (now Szczecin, Poland)
1729–1796

Empress who made Russia one of the great powers of Europe.

In power for thirty-four years, the longest-reigning Russian empress oversaw a renaissance of the arts and sciences, reorganized the country's legal code and government administration, and enlarged Russian territory by incorporating Crimea and the bulk of Poland. Catherine was a Prussian princess who married the Russian heir Karl Ulrich aged sixteen, and came to power by forcing her husband, now Emperor Peter III, to abdicate. She was known for taking many lovers. Scurrilous rumors that she died on the toilet or while attempting to have sexual relations with a horse are untrue—she suffered a stroke in her bathroom and died in bed the following day.

LEFT: Catherine admired Peter the Great and continued his work of modernizing and westernizing Russia. During her reign, the Russians colonized Alaska.

245 ARTIST

JOSIAH WEDGWOOD

Burslem, England
1730–1795

The "Father of English potters" was also a noted antislavery campaigner.

The founder of the Wedgwood pottery company pioneered the industrialization of European pottery manufacture. He developed a green glaze that is still used in the twenty-first century, as well as the enormously popular creamware, a cream-colored earthenware approved by Queen Charlotte, consort of George III, and named Queen's Ware; pieces were even ordered by Catherine the Great of Russia. Wedgwood's jasperware, a colored, unglazed stoneware, was also highly prized. He invented the pyrometer for measuring very high kiln temperatures, and used marketing techniques such as money-back guarantees and buy-one-get-one-free offers. He was also a prominent figure in the abolitionist antislavery movement and, in 1787, produced a widely distributed antislavery medallion representing a kneeling Black man bound in chains with hands raised as if in prayer and the phrase "Am I not a man and a brother?" It was a seal for the British Society for Effecting the Abolition of the Slave Trade. He was the grandfather of Charles Darwin, father of evolutionary theory, through his daughter Sarah.

"The demand for Queen's Ware . . . still increases. It is really amazing how rapidly the use of it has spread almost all over the whole globe, and how universally it is liked."

Josiah Wedgwood in a letter to Thomas Bentley, September 8, 1767

GEORGE WASHINGTON

Westmoreland County, Virginia
1732–1799

This Revolutionary War commander became the first president of the United States.

George Washington was hailed by fellow Americans in his own lifetime as "the father of the country." He was commander-in-chief of the Continental Army in the Revolutionary War of 1775–1783, oversaw the drafting of the U.S. Constitution in 1787, and in 1789 was elected as the first U.S. president. He remains the only president to be unanimously elected by members of the electoral college. Earlier in life he was a colonel in the French and Indian War and, in 1755, was made commander of the Virginia forces. He was an imposing figure, standing 6 feet 2 inches tall, and was a strict disciplinarian with his troops. He was elected president as a nonpartisan candidate and, in government, avoided factionalism. He maintained U.S. independence when the UK and France went to war—saying, "I want an American character that the powers of Europe may be convinced that we act for ourselves and not for others." After two terms as president, he declined a third and retired to his Mount Vernon estate. He died there in 1797 after developing laryngitis. Henry Lee III, governor of Virginia, wrote that he was "first in war, first in peace, and first in the hearts of his countrymen."

RIGHT: In the latter part of his life, Washington was content to be celebrated as "father of the country." This portrait shows him in c. 1795.

KNOWN FOR
- Being commander-in-chief in the Revolutionary War
- Overseeing the drafting of the U.S. Constitution
- Being the first U.S. president

247 SCIENTIST

JAMES WATT

Greenock, Scotland
1736–1819

Watt's improved steam engine helped to drive the Industrial Revolution.

In 1769, inventor James Watt patented the addition of a separate condenser to the single-cylinder steam engine produced by Englishman Thomas Newcomen. This reduced heat loss and made the machine much more efficient and cheaper to operate. He began manufacturing the engine with English businessman and engineer Matthew Boulton in 1775, later making several other improvements to the design. Their engine was used in many industries. Watt worked as an instrument maker and engineer on the Forth and Clyde canal in Scotland before developing his steam engine. The unit of power—the watt—is named after him.

> "I can think of nothing else than this machine."
>
> James Watt in a letter to a friend, Dr. Lind, April 29, 1765

ABOVE: One of Scotland's greatest inventors, Watt first took an interest in steam engines while working as an instrument maker at the University of Glasgow.

248 POLITICAL LEADER

ARTHUR PHILLIP

London, England
1738–1814

Arthur Phillip was the first governor of the British penal colony in New South Wales, Australia. Sent from England with the First Fleet, comprising eleven ships in 1787, he was meant to establish the colony at Botany Bay. He found the proposed spot unsuitable and instead settled at Port Jackson (the site of modern Sydney). Further convicts were sent in the Second Fleet (1789) and the Third Fleet (1791). Phillip was unable to prevent conflict with the Indigenous peoples, and poor health forced his return to England in 1792.

249 SCIENTIST

ANTOINE LAVOISIER

Paris, France
1743–1794

Antoine Lavoisier is called "the father of modern chemistry." He identified and named oxygen and hydrogen, disproved the then-accepted theory that an element named phlogiston was released during combustion, wrote the first major list of elements, revised the method of naming chemical compounds, and proved the conservation of mass—the mass of the elements in a chemical reaction remains the same after the reaction. He also worked on developing the metric system. His wife Marie-Anne provided drawings and translations from English and was essential to his work. He was executed by guillotine during the French Revolution on a charge of tax fraud.

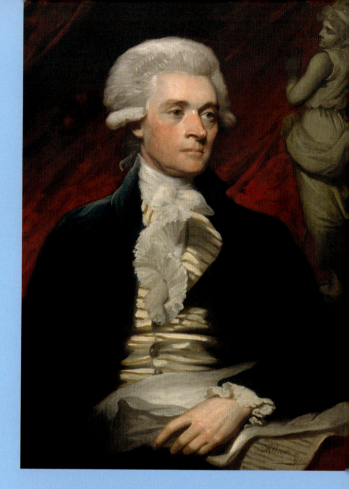

250 POLITICAL LEADER

THOMAS JEFFERSON

Shadwell, Virginia
1743–1826

Thomas Jefferson was a Founding Father of the United States who drafted the Declaration of Independence in 1776, was governor of Virginia in 1779–1781, minister to France in 1785–1789, first U.S. Secretary of State under George Washington in 1789–1794, and third U.S. president, after Washington and John Adams, in 1801–1809. His presidency saw the Louisiana Purchase (1803) and the Lewis and Clark Expedition of 1804–1806 across the newly acquired territory, as well as the 1807 Act Prohibiting Importation of Slaves.

ABOVE RIGHT: The earliest known likeness of Jefferson was painted in spring 1786 when he was visiting John Adams, another future U.S. president.

251 MILITARY LEADER

TOUSSAINT LOUVERTURE

Bréda, near Cap-Français, Saint-Domingue (now Haiti)
1743–1803

The "Father of Haiti" led a slave revolt and launched the Haitian Revolution.

Born into slavery on the French colony of Saint-Domingue, Toussaint Louverture was freed in 1776 and, in 1791, joined and became a leader of a slave revolt. He aligned his guerrilla army with the Spanish against the French, but switched sides in 1794 when the French abolished slavery. The rebellion established Latin America's first independent country. He drove out the British and reached trade agreements with Britain and the United States. Then, in 1801, he evicted the Spanish from the Spanish half of Hispaniola, Santo Domingo, and freed its slaves. He became governor general for life. However, Napoleon reimposed slavery and Louverture was captured and imprisoned in France, where he died. Nevertheless, the revolution he had begun was completed by his lieutenant Jean-Jacques Dessalines—after the French withdrew, he proclaimed independence in 1804. Louverture was a devout Roman Catholic and opponent of the native Voodoo religion, a vegetarian, a man of enormous energy, and an inspirational leader.

252 ARTIST/ACTIVIST

JOSEPH BOLOGNE, CHEVALIER DE SAINT-GEORGES

Baillif, Guadeloupe
1745–1799

The son of a planter and an enslaved Senegalese woman named Nanon, Joseph Bologne was educated from the age of seven in Paris, where he established himself as a violin virtuoso, composer, and concertmaster as well as a renowned fencer. He was friends with Mozart, Gluck, and Salieri. After the French Revolution, he was a colonel in the Légion-St.-Georges, the first all-Black military regiment in Europe.

ABOVE: The first composer of African descent to be widely acclaimed, Bologne was blocked from becoming conductor of the Paris Opera because of his color.

253 ARTIST/ACTIVIST

OLAUDAH EQUIANO

Essaka (now Nigeria)
c. 1745–1797

Olaudah Equiano escaped slavery to become a notable author and abolitionist. Forced into slavery as a child in the Kingdom of Benin (Nigeria), he was transported to the Caribbean and bought and sold three times as a slave before he bought his freedom in 1766. He was a co-founder of the antislavery campaigning group Sons of Africa (British-based Africans) and his autobiography *The Interesting Narrative of the Life of Olaudah Equiano* (1789) was important for the antislavery cause in England.

254 ARTIST

JOHANN WOLFGANG VON GOETHE

Frankfurt am Main, Holy Roman Empire (now Germany)
1749–1832

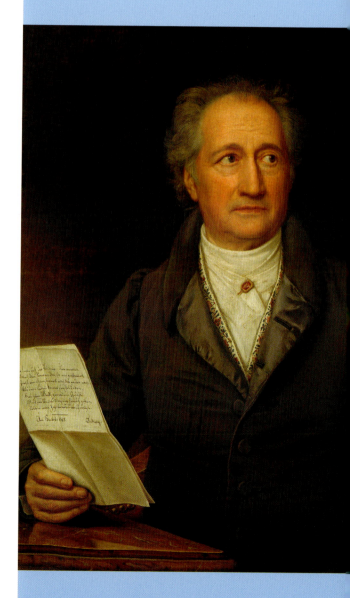

The greatest modern German writer mastered a wide range of forms.

Poet, playwright, and novelist Johannn Wolfgang von Goethe wrote the novel *The Sorrows of Young Werther* (1774) and the poetic drama *Faust* (two parts, 1808 and 1832), and is celebrated as the foremost figure of modern German literature and the early Romantic *Sturm und Drang* (Storm and Stress) movement in the country. He studied law; worked as a newspaper critic; was a scientist who wrote treatises on anatomy, botany, and color; a lyric poet; and an official at the court of Weimar in 1775–1785. In Weimar he was also a theater manager, became friendly with the dramatist Friedrich Schiller, and gave premieres of his plays. Other works include the plays *Iphigenia in Tauris* (1787) and *Torquato Tasso* (1790), and the poems *Roman Elegies* (1795), in which he gave expression to his love for Christiane Vulpius, whom he married in 1806. He died in Weimar.

"One ought, every day at least, to hear a little song, read a good poem, see a fine picture, and, if it were possible, to speak a few reasonable words."

Johannn Wolfgang von Goethe, *Wilhelm Meister's Apprentice Years*, 1796

LEFT: Goethe in 1828. In his scientific writing—and his poetry—he aimed to see the individual element as part of an organic, changing whole. He continued to challenge himself and be open to change throughout a long career.

255 POLITICAL LEADER

ALEXANDER HAMILTON

Charlestown, St. Kitts and Nevis
c. 1757–1804

Born to unmarried parents and orphaned in childhood on the Caribbean island of Nevis, Alexander Hamilton rose to become General George Washington's aide in the Revolutionary War, and later U.S. Secretary of the Treasury in Washington's first cabinet as president. He was a leading anti-slavery campaigner. He was killed in a duel by Vice President Aaron Burr, after he had denounced Burr as unprincipled.

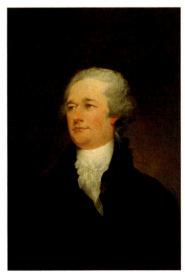

ABOVE: Hamilton supported the Haitian Revolution and helped draft the Haitian constitution.

1500–1799 205

256 ROYALTY

MARIE ANTOINETTE

Vienna, Austria
1755–1793

Marie Antoinette, queen consort of Louis XVI, was the last queen of France before the French Revolution. She was attacked for her extravagant way of life, jailed in 1792 when the monarchy was overthrown, and executed by guillotine in 1793. She is famous for declaring "Let them eat cake" when told the people did not have enough bread—but she probably never said it.

ABOVE: During the revolution, Marie Antoinette was called "Madame Déficit" because people said her extravagance had caused France's financial troubles.

257 ARTIST

WOLFGANG AMADEUS MOZART

Salzburg, Austria
1756–1791

This musical genius excelled in every genre.

Austrian child prodigy Wolfgang Amadeus Mozart, who performed on keyboards and violin by the age of six for appreciative noblemen and women in the main cities of Europe, grew up to become one of the greatest composers in the history of Western music, creator of more than 600 works, including over fifty symphonies, twenty-five piano and many instrumental concertos, fifteen masses, and twenty-two operas. He worked as Konzertmeister (concertmaster) to the Archbishop of Salzburg, and later was court composer to Emperor Joseph II from 1787. He excelled in every musical genre, and is revered for his graceful melodies and complete command of form. His operas, including *The Marriage of Figaro* (1786) and *The Magic Flute* (1791), are widely loved and often performed. He died aged only thirty-five in Vienna. Mozart's father Leopold called his son "the miracle which God let be born in Salzburg."

RIGHT: Mozart at the clavier aged seven, with his father Leopold and his sister Nannerl. She reported that he began composing aged five.

HORATIO NELSON

Burnham Thorpe, England
1758–1805

England's most famous admiral, known for his naval victory at Trafalgar.

Admiral Horatio, Viscount Nelson, was fatally wounded while winning his most famous victory, defeating the combined fleets of Spain and France at the Battle of Trafalgar in 1805. His body was carried home and buried in St. Paul's Cathedral, London, and his statue later erected atop Nelson's Column in the city's Trafalgar Square. Born the son of the village rector in Burnham Thorpe, Norfolk, he joined the navy aged twelve in 1770, and in 1777 was sent to the West Indies. In 1794 he lost the use of his right eye, and in 1797 he had his arm amputated after being injured in action. He won a great victory over the French fleet in the Battle of the Nile (1798), and afterward embarked on a scandalous affair with Emma, Lady Hamilton, despite their both being married. In 1801, during a campaign against Denmark, he won the Battle of Copenhagen and was made a viscount and commander-in-chief of the navy.

BELOW: Nelson was shot by a French sniper in the Battle of Trafalgar and died three hours later—but not before being told that the British had won the battle.

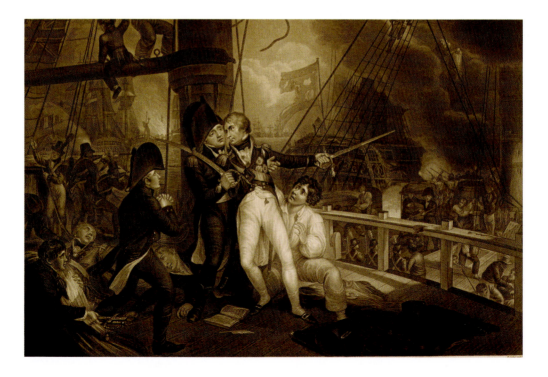

259 ARTIST/ACTIVIST

MARY WOLLSTONECRAFT

London, England
1759–1797

This author of an early feminist classic pushed for women's equality in education and life.

In her 1792 book *A Vindication of the Rights of Woman*, the trailblazing feminist philosopher Mary Wollstonecraft argued that women and men are naturally equal and should be given the same opportunities as men in learning, life, and work. At the time, women were not treated as rational beings and not properly educated, and so they did not appear to be men's equals.

Wollstonecraft was a teacher and governess, and published *Thoughts on the Education of Daughters* in 1787, before learning German and French, becoming a translator for the London publisher Joseph Johnson, and publishing the novel *Mary: A Fiction* in 1788. After a failed relationship with the married artist Henry Fuseli, she went to France in 1792 in the aftermath of the French Revolution and fell in love with American adventurer Gilbert Imlay—they had a daughter, Fanny, but the relationship collapsed and Wollstonecraft, devastated, attempted suicide before returning to London. There she mixed with a radical crowd including poet William Wordsworth, political theorist Thomas Paine, and early anarchist William Godwin. In 1796 she began a relationship with Godwin and, after she became pregnant, they married on March 29, 1797. Wollstonecraft died on September 10 that year, eleven days after the birth of their daughter, who would grow up to be Mary Shelley, author of *Frankenstein, or The Modern Prometheus* (1818).

ABOVE: Mary Wollstonecraft in 1791. She published a history of the French Revolution ("and the effect it has produced in Europe") in 1794.

> "I do not wish them [women] to have power over men; but over themselves."
>
> — Mary Wollstonecraft, *A Vindication of the Rights of Woman*, 1792

KNOWN FOR
- Being an early feminist
- Writing *A Vindication of the Rights of Woman*
- Being the mother of Mary Shelley, author of *Frankenstein*

260 ACTIVIST

WILLIAM WILBERFORCE

Kingston upon Hull, England
1759–1833

This reforming politician led the movement to abolish the slave trade.

Politician, evangelist, philanthropist, and reformer William Wilberforce helped to found the Society for Effecting the Abolition of the Slave Trade. He led the campaign in the British parliament to end the slave trade for two decades from 1787, resulting in the Slave Trade Act of 1807 that banned the slave trade in the British West Indies. He continued to push for the full abolition of slavery in the empire, and the Slavery Abolition Act was passed in 1833, just three days before his death, and became law a month later. He was a lifelong friend of prime minister William Pitt the Younger from their student days at the University of Cambridge. He also founded a society for the "reformation of manners."

"God Almighty has set before me two great objects, the suppression of the slave trade and the reformation of manners."

William Wilberforce, A Letter on the Abolition of the slave trade, Addressed to the Freeholders and Other Inhabitants of Yorkshire, 1807

RIGHT: Wilberforce was Member of Parliament for Yorkshire when, in 1785, he experienced a religious conversion and became an evangelical Christian.

ABOVE: Allen worked very closely with his two wives—first Flora and afterward Sarah—in establishing the church. Sarah became known as "Founding Mother."

261 RELIGIOUS LEADER

RICHARD ALLEN

Philadelphia, Pennsylvania
1760–1831

Former slave who founded the first independent Black Christian denomination in the United States.

Richard Allen founded the African Methodist Episcopal Church (AME) in Philadelphia and was elected its first bishop in 1816. Born the son of slaves in Delaware, he taught himself to read and write, and joined the Methodist Society aged seventeen. In 1782, aged twenty-two, he was

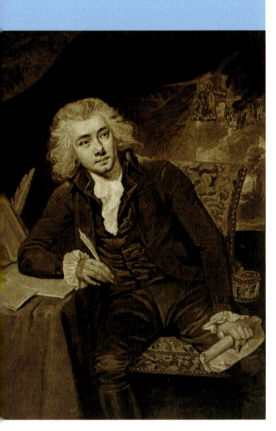

262 ROYALTY

NANDI BHEBHE

Melmoth, now South Africa
c. 1760–1827

Nandi Bhebhe was mother of the famous southern African king Sigidi kaSenzangakhona—better known as Shaka Zulu, ruler of the Zulu kingdom in 1816–1828. Shaka was born out of wedlock. His father was Prince Senzangokhona, son of the Zulu king Jama. Nandi initially lived with the prince at his *kraal* (settlement) then, when they fell out, she left Shaka with his father. He was later returned to Nandi, who kept him safe through famine and even attempted assassinations, taking him to live with the Qwabe people, and then the Mthethwa in southeastern Africa. There, Shaka trained as a warrior in fighting units under King Dingiswayo. Nandi was an important influence through Shaka's reign until her death from dysentery in 1827, just one year before his assassination.

---

allowed to preach. A traveling preacher convinced Stokley Sturgis, the owner of the plantation on which Allen lived, to give his slaves the chance to buy their freedom, and Allen did this in 1786. He went to Philadelphia, where he preached in St. George's Methodist Episcopal Church and, in 1787, founded the first church for Black Americans. In 1799, he was the first African American ordained in the Methodist Episcopal Church. He gathered five African American congregations of the Methodist Episcopal Church—three in Philadelphia, one in Delaware, and one in Baltimore—to found the AME in 1816.

The church became popular with freed slaves. In 1830 it hosted the Negro Convention, with Black delegates from seven states, the first African American engagement on this scale.

"This land which we have watered with our tears and our blood, is now our mother country, and we are well satisfied to stay where wisdom abounds and the gospel is free."

Richard Allen, *David Walker's Appeal*, 1829

263 POLITICAL LEADER

WOOLLARAWARRE BENNELONG

near Port Jackson, Australia
c. 1764–1813

Woollarawarre Bennelong was a leader of the Eora Aboriginal Australian people who was captured on the orders of Governor Arthur Phillip and interacted with the first British settlers in the Port Jackson area. With another Indigenous Australian man, Yemmerrawanne, he visited England with Phillip in 1792, going to the theater and visiting St. Paul's Cathedral in London. Yemmerrawanne died in England from a chest infection, but Bennelong returned to Australia in 1795.

264 POLITICAL LEADER

TECUMSEH

near Old Chillicothe (now Xenia), Ohio
c. 1768–1813

Chief of the Shawnee people, Tecumseh built a confederation of Native American tribes to resist expansion by U.S. colonists, but most of Ohio was lost to the United States in 1795. He fought with the British in the War of 1812 and captured Detroit, but was killed at the Battle of the Thames in 1813. After his death he became a folk hero.

265 MILITARY LEADER

NAPOLEON BONAPARTE

Ajaccio, Corsica, France
1769–1821

This military genius conquered much of Europe and became emperor of France.

Napoleon Bonaparte is revered as one of the finest military commanders in history. He came to prominence in the French Revolution, was a successful commander in the French Revolutionary Wars (1792–1802), then the effective leader of the French Republic (1799–1804), and emperor of France (1804–1814). Defeat by a coalition of European powers in the 1813 Battle of Leipzig forced his abdication and exile to the island of Elba, but he escaped and regained power. A further defeat, in the celebrated Battle of Waterloo in 1815, meant he was exiled a second time to St. Helena in the Atlantic Ocean, and he died there in 1821 aged fifty-one. Napoleon was bold, brave, and decisive when opportunity presented itself, a brilliant leader whose men affectionately nicknamed him "the Little Corporal." He stood 5 feet 6 inches tall—which, though his enemies made much of it, was not unusually short for the time.

"In this age, in past ages, in any age: Napoleon."

The Duke of Wellington (1769–1852), when asked who was the greatest general of the age

RIGHT: This portrait by Jacques Louis David shows Napoleon in spring 1800, leading his troops to Italy through the St. Bernard Pass in the Alps.

LUDWIG VAN BEETHOVEN

Bonn, Germany
1770–1827

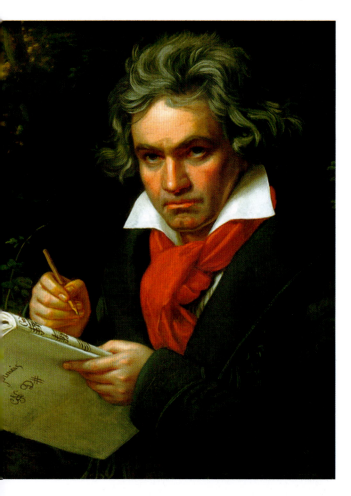

German composer who lifted instrumental music to the level of vocal works.

Supremely gifted pianist and composer Ludwig van Beethoven was instrumental in the development of music from the classical era of Josef Haydn and Wolfgang Amadeus Mozart to the Romanticism of the nineteenth century. His vast output included nine symphonies, the opera *Fidelio* (1805), five piano and one violin concertos, two masses including the *Missa Solemnis* of 1824, and thirty-two piano sonatas including the celebrated *Moonlight Sonata* of 1801. He was the first major composer to make his living without being employed either by the Church or at court. Beethoven famously became deaf, beginning to lose his hearing in 1795 and becoming completely deaf by 1819—he never heard his great *Symphony No. 9*, which includes a choral finale and was the first symphony to include sung elements. He was born into a musical family, and his father tried unsuccessfully to make him a child prodigy like Mozart. He met and impressed Mozart with his ability to improvise in 1727; Mozart said, "This young man will make a great name for himself in the world." He studied under Haydn.

KNOWN FOR
- Writing *Moonlight Sonata* and *Fifth Symphony*
- Creating the first symphony with sung sections
- Composing while deaf

ABOVE LEFT: Beethoven composing the *Missa Solemnis* in 1820. It was first performed in 1824 and is celebrated as one of his greatest works.

267 POLITICAL LEADER

BUNGAREE

Broken Bay, near Port Jackson (now Sydney), Australia
1775–1830

Aboriginal Australian community leader Bungaree was the first native-born Australian to circumnavigate the mainland of the country. A member of the Guringai people, he sailed with British navigator-cartographer Matthew Flinders on a 1798 trip to Norfolk Island in the Pacific Ocean and a later coastal survey; then, in 1802–1803, he joined Flinders on his circumnavigation of the mainland aboard the *Investigator*. Bungaree often served as a go-between, and defused potentially threatening encounters with Indigenous groups. He was later granted fifteen acres of land on George's Head by Governor Lachlan Macquarie and named chief of the Broken Bay tribe.

"Friendship is certainly the finest balm for the pangs of disappointed love."

Jane Austen, *Northanger Abbey*, 1818

RIGHT: In the fist three months of 1817 Austen wrote eleven chapters of a new novel (later called *Sanditon*). She stopped, probably due to illness, and died that July.

268 ARTIST

JANE AUSTEN

Steventon, England
1775–1817

This shrewd and insightful novelist wrote elegant comedies of English manners.

The daughter of a Church of England rector in Steventon, Hampshire, Austen wrote four novels anonymously issued in her lifetime—*Sense and Sensibility* (1811), *Pride and Prejudice* (1813), *Mansfield Park* (1814), and *Emma* (1815), as well as two published posthumously in 1817, *Northanger Abbey* and *Persuasion*. She also lived in Bath and Southampton, before returning to Hampshire to live with her brother Edward. She never married, and her closest relationship was with her sister Cassandra. Her books combine discriminating insight, psychological realism, and brilliant wit, and she is often celebrated as the greatest woman novelist. She died in Winchester, aged forty-one, possibly from Addison's disease.

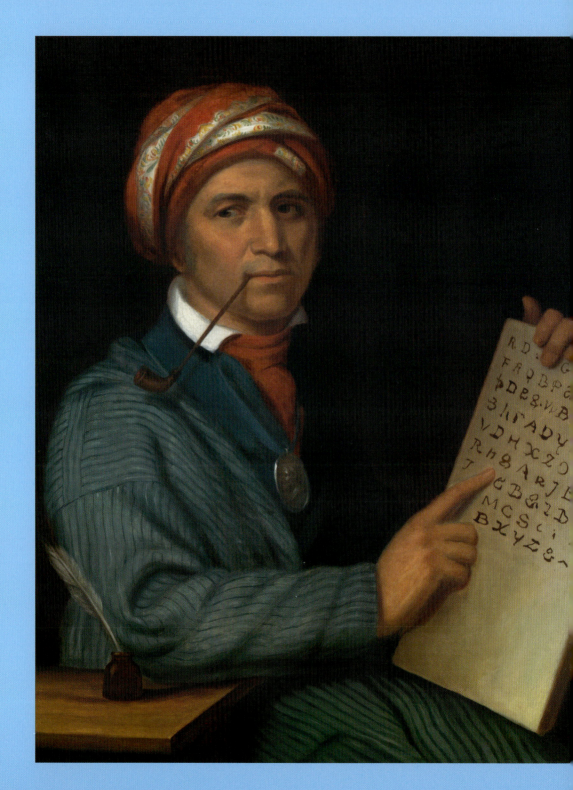

269 POLITICAL LEADER

SEQUOYAH (GEORGE GIST)

Taskigi, Cherokee Nation
(near Knoxville, Tennessee)
c. 1775–1843

Cherokee leader who developed a written language.

Convinced that the lack of a written language was holding his people back, Sequoyah—also known as George Gist—developed a "syllabary" (list of symbols representing the syllables of the spoken language) in 1809–1821. He adapted Greek, Hebrew, and English letters to create eighty-six symbols that gave written form to the syllables spoken by the Cherokee. The Cherokee Nation officially adopted the syllabary, which was easy to learn and use, in 1825, and by the 1850s had a literacy rate of close to 100 percent—far higher than that of white settlers. They published books and a newspaper using the language. Sequoyah was the son of a fur trader and a Cherokee woman, Wuh-teh, a member of the Paint clan. In addition to his linguistic achievements, he was a painter, blacksmith, and silversmith, and as a soldier he fought for the U.S. Army in the Creek War of 1813–1814. Although he never learned to speak or write English, Sequoyah represented the Cherokee in Washington, D.C.

"Sequoyah is the only person in recorded history who created a writing system without first knowing a written language himself."

Dr. Duane King (1947–2017),
director of the Gilcrease Museum, Tulsa, Oklahoma

LEFT: Sequoyah demonstrates his Cherokee syllabary. The coast redwood tree *Sequoia sempervirens* was named in his honor.

270 POLITICAL LEADER

SIR RICHARD BOURKE

Dublin, Ireland
1777–1855

As governor of New South Wales in 1835, Sir Richard Bourke made the infamous proclamation that Australia was *terra nullius* (nobody's land)—the land belonged to no one until the British crown claimed it. Indigenous Australians had no legal claim to land under colonial law. It followed an attempt by a settler named John Batman to buy land at Port Phillip from Aboriginal Australians.

ABOVE: Bourke served in the army and in Cape Colony before being appointed governor of New South Wales in 1831.

271 ARTIST

GEORGE BRIDGETOWER

Biała Podlaska, Poland
1778–1860

Child prodigy violinist George Bridgetower was educated under the supervision of the Prince Regent (the future King George IV of England). He was the son of a German woman and a West Indian (possibly Barbadian) manservant at the court of the Hungarian prince Esterházy. In Vienna in 1803, George became friends with Beethoven. He was the original dedicatee of the composer's *Violin Sonata No. 9 in A Minor* (later known as the Kreutzer Sonata) and gave its first performance, with Beethoven on piano.

272 ROYALTY

RANAVALONA

Merina Kingdom (now Madagascar)
1778–1861

Redoubtable queen (r. 1828–1861) following the death of her husband Radama I, Ranavalona was one of the few African rulers to hold off European powers in a time of colonial expansionism. She drove out the Christian missionaries her husband had welcomed and persecuted their converts, pursued political and economic self-sufficiency, and established a strong standing army that defeated a French attack on Foulpointe (now Mahavelona).

273 POLITICAL LEADER

VICENTE GUERRERO

Tixtla, Mexico
1782–1831

Freedom fighter and Mexican leader who was the first Black president in the Americas.

Vicente Guerrero, whose mother was of African descent and his father a mestizo (of Indigenous/Spanish birth), became a major figure in the Mexican struggle for independence from Spain, leading guerrilla forces from 1810, at first in the service of José Maria Morelos, and then independently after Morelos's execution in 1815. In 1821, with Agustin de Iturbide (later briefly the emperor of Mexico), he issued the Iguala Plan for independence—and the Mexicans achieved independence in August that year. Guerrero came second to conservative candidate Gomez Pedraza in the presidential election of 1828, but was then carried to power by a liberal revolt in 1829. He served as president for less than a year (April to December 1829) before being ousted—but not before he had issued the Guerrero Decree on September 16, 1829, prohibiting slavery in the bulk of the country (apart from ranchlands in Tehuantepec). Taking command of rebel troops, he was betrayed, captured, and executed on February 14, 1831.

RIGHT: A statue of Guerrero in Mexico. He is revered as a national hero.

"General Guerrero [is] one of the most distinguished chiefs of the revolution. Guerrero is uneducated, but possesses excellent natural talents, combined with great decision of character and undaunted courage."

Joel R. Poinsett, U.S. minister for Mexico, 1825–1829

274 POLITICAL LEADER

SIMÓN BOLÍVAR

Caracas, New Granada (now Venezuela)
1783–1830

"The Liberator" led the struggle for independence in Latin America.

Political visionary Simón Bolívar led revolutions that freed Venezuela, Ecuador, Peru, Panama, and Bolivia from Spanish rule. Born to a wealthy family in the Captaincy General of Venezuela, part of the Spanish Empire, he was orphaned in childhood and went to Europe, where he encountered Enlightenment thinking that inspired him. In 1805 in Rome, Bolívar vowed to bring Spanish control of the Americas to an end. The initial attempt, the First Republic of Venezuela, lasted two years from 1810 but ended with the return of Spanish rule in July 1812; after a period of exile, Bolívar invaded and—hailed as "the Liberator"—took Caracas and established the Second Republic on August 6, 1813. When this too failed, he fled into exile once more. Back in Venezuela, he established a base in the southeast and then surprised and defeated the Spanish at the Battle of Boyocá on August 7, 1819. He was named president and military dictator, and won a final victory two years later at the Battle of Carabobo: the Republic of Gran Colombia (incorporating much of Colombia, Panama, Venezuela, Ecuador, and northern Peru) was established on September 7, 1821. Bolívar defeated the Spanish in Peru, and the republic of Bolivia in what was formerly upper Peru was established and named in his honor in 1825. However, facing increasing opposition, Bolívar stood down as president in 1830, then died of tuberculosis en route for European exile.

RIGHT: Bolívar honors the flag after victory in the Battle of Carabobo on June 24, 1821.

KNOWN FOR

- Freeing Venezuela, Colombia, Panama, Ecuador, Peru, and Bolivia from Spanish rule
- Bolivia is named in his honor

SHAKA ZULU

South Africa
1787–1828

Ruler who built a ruthless force to create the Zulu Empire.

Warrior-king Sigidi kaSenzangakhona—better known as Shaka Zulu—was in power for just twelve years (1816–1828), but in his short reign he created a formidable Zulu Empire in southern Africa. At the time that he took power by ousting his half-brother, Sigujana, the Zulu was a small clan of perhaps 1,500. But the young chieftain had had an extensive military education as a warrior in the army of Mthethwa king Dingiswayo, and on becoming Zulu chief, he created a formidable fighting machine with regiments, set tactics, and the use of long-blade *assegai* swords in place of spears. He assimilated some rival clans and swept aside others by force, bringing together more than 100 chiefdoms in his empire, and killing vast numbers in the process. He was assassinated in a plot led by two of his half-brothers, Dingane and Mhlangana. His behavior had become unpredictable after the 1827 death of his mother, Nandi, who was a major force in his life.

LEFT: Shaka replaced the long throwing *assegai* spear shown with a shorter stabbing one (*iklwa*). He introduced the large shield shown here.

276 POLITICAL LEADER

JOHN ROSS

**Turkeytown, Cherokee territory
(near Centre, Alabama)
1790–1866**

After his long campaign to prevent the seizure of Cherokee lands in Georgia failed, Cherokee leader John Ross (also known as Tsan-Usdi) led the relocation of the Cherokee to lands west of the Mississippi on the infamous 5,000-mile "Trail of Tears" in 1838–1839. After the relocation, Ross helped to draft a constitution for the Cherokee in 1839 and served as chief of government.

LEFT: Son of a Cherokee woman and a Scottish store owner, Ross was principal chief of the Cherokee from 1828 to 1866.

ABOVE: After signing a treaty with the British in 1855, Dost Mohammad held back from helping the uprising in the Indian Rebellion of 1857.

277 ROYALTY

DOST MOHAMMAD SHAH

**Kandahar, Durrani Empire
(now Afghanistan)
1793–1863**

Emir in 1826–1839 and 1843–1863, Dost Mohammad was a major figure in the establishment of modern Afghanistan, and founder of the Barakzai dynasty that ruled until 1978. He was deposed in 1839 by a British invasion, which imposed Shah Shuja as ruler. Dost Mohammad surrendered to the British in 1840 and was deported to India, but when the British withdrew in 1843 he returned to power. He took Kandahar in 1855 and Herat in 1863. He was succeeded by his son Sher Ali Khan.

ACTIVIST

SOJOURNER TRUTH

Swartekill, New York
c. 1797–1883

This former slave campaigned for abolition and women's rights.

Sojourner Truth declared "The Spirit calls me, and I must go" when she set out from New York City as a traveling preacher in 1843. She drew large crowds, urging the abolition of slavery and promoting women's rights and suffrage. An off-the-cuff speech she made at the Ohio Women's Rights Convention in 1851 became enduringly famous after it was later published in a different form as "Ain't I a Woman?" Born into slavery as Isabella Baumfree, she was cruelly abused by a succession of masters before she escaped in 1826 with her baby daughter. Then, two years later, she became the first Black woman to succeed in a court case against a white man when she won freedom for her son Peter, who had been sold illegally in Alabama. She worked as a domestic servant in New York City, and changed her name in 1843 when she heard the call to preach the truth. She also recruited Black soldiers for the Union Army in the Civil War and, in Washington, D.C., took part in efforts to desegregate streetcars.

> "I have borne thirteen children, and seen most all sold off to slavery, and when I cried out with my mother's grief, none but Jesus heard me! And ain't I a woman?"
>
> Sojourner Truth, in a speech to the Women's Rights Convention, Akron, Ohio, 1851

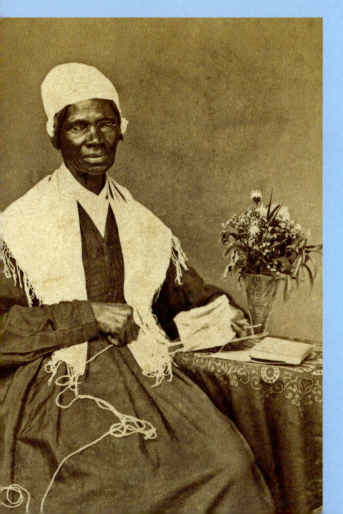

LEFT: Sojourner Truth in 1864. She sold portraits such as this, and her autobiography, to support herself and the cause in which she so passionately believed.

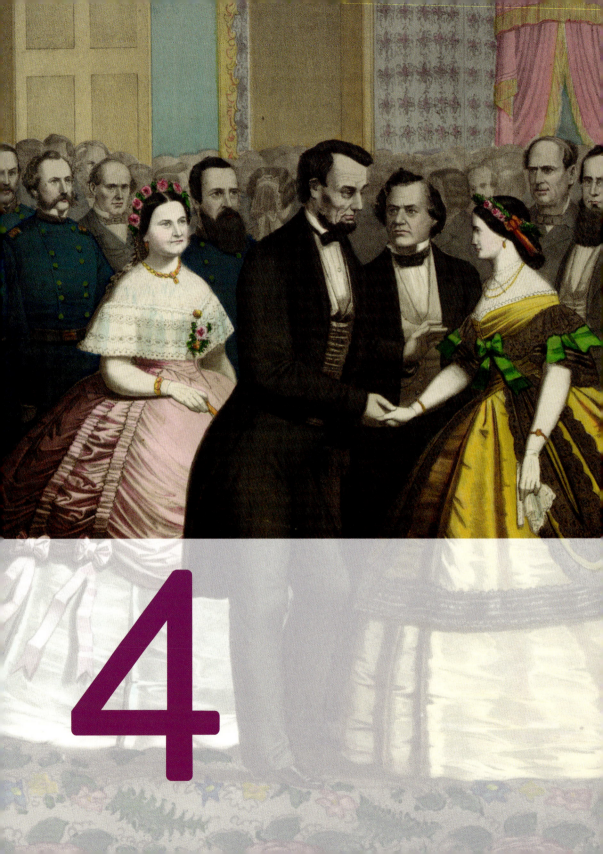

4

Industries and Empires
1800–1899

VICTOR HUGO

Besançon, France
1802–1885

Romantic novelist who had huge success with *Les Misérables* and *The Hunchback of Notre Dame*.

Victor Hugo achieved success as a playwright and poet as well as a novelist, but is celebrated worldwide as the author of historical novels. His *The Hunchback of Notre Dame* (originally published as *Notre-Dame de Paris*, 1831) inspired plays and several hit movies including a Disney animation in 1996, while *Les Misérables* (1862) was made into one of the most successful stage musicals of all time. The son of a general, Hugo studied law in Paris before launching a literary review in 1819, publishing a book of poems in 1822, and his first novel, *Hans of Iceland*, in 1823. His verse drama *Cromwell* (1827) contains a famous preface laying out his literary beliefs, much influenced by the eighteenth- and nineteenth-century Romantic movement. From the 1830s onward Hugo was a celebrated and prolific author and was elected to the Académie Française in 1841. He fled into exile in Brussels under the Second Empire in 1851, and returned only with the reestablishment of the French Republic in 1870. He died in Paris in 1885 and was buried in the Panthéon—the resting place of many great French citizens.

RIGHT: Hugo in 1879. In addition to *Les Misérables*, many musical works have been based on his stories—including Verdi's opera *Rigoletto*, and *Lucrezia Borgia* by Donizetti.

KNOWN FOR

- Author of *Les Misérables* and *The Hunchback of Notre Dame*
- Prolific and revered poet
- Major figure of Romanticism and symbol of French republicanism

280 ARTIST

HANS CHRISTIAN ANDERSEN

Odense, Denmark
1805–1875

This Danish author captured children's hearts with his fairy tales.

Hans Christian Andersen's immortal fairy tales include "The Little Mermaid," "The Ugly Duckling," "The Snow Queen," "The Princess and the Pea," and "Thumbelina." They have been translated into more than 125 languages and are the inspiration for many movies, television shows, plays, and ballets. Andersen published nine books containing a total of 156 tales from 1835 onward, as well as writing plays, novels, poems, and travel books. Among his plays he achieved some success with an antislavery work, *The Mulatto*, in 1840. The son of a washerwoman from Odense, Denmark, Andersen was sponsored to go to school by Jonas Collin of the Royal Theater, Copenhagen, and afterward attended the university in that city. He traveled widely in Europe, Africa, and Anatolia (now part of Turkey).

ABOVE: Some people speculate that Andersen was an illegitimate son of King Christian VIII of Denmark.

281 MILITARY LEADER

GIUSEPPE GARIBALDI

Nice, France
1807–1882

Giuseppe Garibaldi was a general in the *Risorgimento* movement that resulted in the unification of the Kingdom of Italy in 1861. A follower of Italian nationalist Giuseppe Mazzini, Garibaldi took part in a republican mutiny in 1834 while in the Piedmont-Sardinia navy, and was sentenced to death. However, he escaped to South America, where he fought in Brazil and raised a troop, called the Garibaldini or Redshirts, to fight in the Uruguayan Civil War. He returned to Italy with sixty Redshirts in 1848. Garibaldi won key victories, capturing Varese, Como, and later Sicily, before the unification of the country. He was a national hero, promoter of republicanism, and inspiration to later freedom fighters such as Che Guevara.

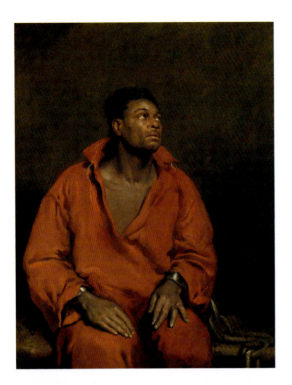

282 ARTIST

IRA ALDRIDGE

New York, New York
1807–1867

Black American actor Ira Aldridge began his career as a teenager at the African Grove Theatre in New York City, but achieved his major success in Europe, particularly performing as Othello in Shakespeare's play of that name in London in 1833, and later as Othello, Macbeth, and King Lear in Switzerland, Austria, and Russia.

LEFT: Aldridge performed in the musical drama *The Slave*, by Thomas Morton, and was the model for John Philip Simpson's 1827 painting *The Captive Slave*.

283 SCIENTIST

CHARLES DARWIN

Shrewsbury, England
1809–1882

In his 1859 book *On the Origin of the Species*, English naturalist Charles Darwin revealed the theory of evolution by natural selection, from which modern evolutionary science derives. He developed the theory after returning from his voyage to South America and around the globe aboard the HMS *Beagle* in 1831–1836.

LEFT: This celebrated portrait of Darwin was taken by British photographic pioneer Julia Margaret Cameron in 1868.

POLITICAL LEADER

ABRAHAM LINCOLN

Larue County, Kentucky
1809–1865

Lincoln was an inspirational president who guided the United States through the Civil War and abolished slavery in the nation.

Abraham Lincoln, the sixteenth U.S. president, led the nation through the American Civil War and issued the Emancipation Proclamation of January 1, 1863, which freed slaves in the Confederate states, which had seceded from the Union. Subsequently, the Thirteenth Amendment to the U.S. Constitution, ratified on December 6, 1865, ended slavery—which Lincoln called "this gigantic evil"—in the country. Lincoln qualified and worked as a lawyer in Springfield, Illinois, then, after being elected to Congress in 1846, won the 1860 presidential election. His inspirational Gettysburg Address on November 19, 1863, at a ceremony for Union soldiers killed in the Battle of Gettysburg the previous July, famously declared, "We here resolve that these dead shall not have died in vain—that this nation, under God, shall have a new birth of freedom—and that government of the people, by the people, for the people, shall not perish from the earth."

"Four score and seven years ago our fathers brought forth on this continent a new nation, conceived in liberty, and dedicated to the proposition that all men are created equal."

Abraham Lincoln, Gettysburg Address, November 19, 1863

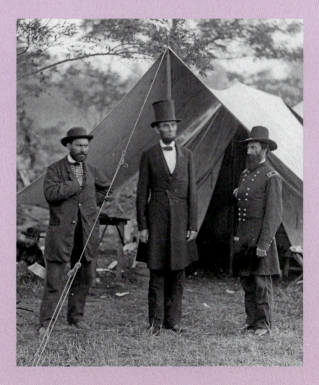

RIGHT: Lincoln (center) at Antietam in 1862. The battle there is remembered as the bloodiest day in U.S. history, with 22,727 missing, wounded, or killed.

285 ARTIST

FRÉDÉRIC CHOPIN

Zelazowa Wola, Duchy of Warsaw
(now Poland)
1810–1849

This Polish-born musician composed a peerless solo piano repertoire.

Frédéric Chopin is celebrated as one of musical history's greatest composers for solo piano, creator of nuanced and sensitive short pieces including 61 mazurkas, 26 preludes, 21 nocturnes, and 20 waltzes, as well as three sonatas and two concertos. He invented the genre of the instrumental ballade. Born to a French father, Chopin was a child prodigy who first performed publicly aged eight, and had his first work published at fifteen. After studying at Warsaw Conservatory, he emigrated to France and settled in Paris aged twenty-one. After this he gave only thirty public performances, though he attended and played at French *salons* (drawing-room gatherings), largely making a living by selling his works and giving piano lessons. He was friends with the Hungarian composer-virtuoso Franz Liszt, and had a long relationship with French novelist Aurore Dupin, who wrote under the name George Sand, while he also received financial support from his former pupil Jane Stirling, to whom he dedicated the *Nocturnes, Op. 55*. Often in poor health, Chopin died in Paris aged just thirty-nine, probably of pericarditis (inflammation of the heart).

KNOWN FOR
- Musical prodigy and celebrity
- Composer of masterpieces for solo piano
- Attended and played at Parisian salons

LEFT: Chopin entertains the guests in the salon of his patron Prince Radziville in 1829. He dedicated his *Piano Trio Op. 8* to him.

ARTIST

CHARLES DICKENS

Portsmouth, England
1812–1870

One of England's greatest novelists who created a cast of unforgettable characters.

The miser Ebenezer Scrooge, thief-handler Fagin, and jilted bride Miss Havisham are just three of the myriad of highly colored characters produced by masterful novelist Charles Dickens. He was a truly great comic writer, who also delivered Gothic thrills while summoning righteous anger at the sufferings of the poor of Victorian London. Dickens shot to national and international fame with his first novel, *The Pickwick Papers* (1836–1837) which, like all his novels, first appeared in serial form. His masterpieces include the story *A Christmas Carol* (1843), and novels *Bleak House* (1852–1853), *A Tale of Two Cities* (1859), and *Great Expectations* (1860–1861). Dickens was a tremendously hard worker, often writing more than one book at a time, and died of a stroke aged just fifty-eight.

ABOVE RIGHT: Dickens in 1868. The dramatized readings he gave of scenes from his novels—such as the confrontations between Sykes and Nancy in *Oliver Twist*—were hugely popular but left him badly drained.

"He was conscious of a thousand odours floating in the air, each one connected with a thousand thoughts, and hopes, and joys, and cares long, long forgotten."

Charles Dickens, *A Christmas Carol*, 1843

287 POLITICAL LEADER

OTTO VON BISMARCK

Schönhausen, Prussia (now Germany)
1815–1898

Statesman Otto von Bismarck transformed Europe, unifying the German states to create a German empire in 1871. Becoming prime minister in 1862, he made Prussia a military force to be reckoned with, having declared, "The great questions of the day will be decided not through speeches and majority decisions ... but by blood and iron." Wars with Denmark, Austria, and France led to German unification. After his retirement in 1890 at the age of eighty-five, he wrote best-selling memoirs that launched a "cult of Bismarck" in Germany.

288 ACTIVIST

ELIZABETH CADY STANTON

Johnstown, New York
1815–1902

This women's rights campaigner and abolitionist led a movement for the right to vote.

In partnership with Massachusetts-born Quaker Susan B. Anthony, Elizabeth Cady Stanton was a driving force for women's suffrage in the United States for decades. Stanton studied law, and in 1848 was behind the Seneca Falls Convention, the first convention called to debate women's rights, and issued a demand that women be granted the vote. With Anthony, she ran the Women's National Loyal League during the Civil War, to drive for the abolition of slavery, and organized the American Equal Rights Association, campaigning for equal rights for African Americans and women. After the war she was co-editor of the women's rights newspaper *The Revolution* and president of the National Woman Suffrage Association. She drafted the 1878 federal suffrage amendment that eventually led to women being granted the right to vote under the Nineteenth Amendment to the U.S. Constitution in 1920.

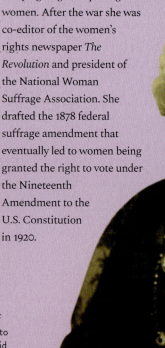

> "We hold these truths to be self-evident: that all men and women are created equal."
>
> Elizabeth Cady Stanton, "Declaration of Sentiments," 1848

RIGHT: Stanton was the author of *The Women's Bible*, which set out to challenge religious dogma that said women should be subservient to men.

289 SCIENTIST

ADA LOVELACE

London, England
1815–1852

Ada King, Countess of Lovelace, has been called the first computer programmer after she created the first algorithm for mathematician Charles Babbage's mechanical computer, the analytical engine. She met Babbage through their mutual friend, Scottish polymath Mary Somerville. Ada was the only legitimate child of English Romantic poet Lord Byron and Lady Byron. Her father died when she was eight years old.

290 ARTIST

HENRY DAVID THOREAU

Concord, Massachusetts
1817–1862

Writer Henry David Thoreau was an advocate of civil disobedience who influenced later figures such as Leo Tolstoy, Mohandas Gandhi, and Martin Luther King Jr. He was also the author of *Walden* (1854), an account of his simple life over two years spent in a cabin he built at Walden Pond near Concord, Massachusetts. He was a follower of the American Transcendentalist philosophical movement, which argued for the essential goodness of people and nature.

ABOVE: Ada Lovelace had the insight that the analytical engine could be used for more than calculation.

ABOVE: Thoreau in 1856. He was a committed abolitionist and his writing on natural history anticipated some aspects of modern environmentalism.

291 ACTIVIST

FREDERICK DOUGLASS

Talbot County, Maryland
1818–1895

Douglass was a former slave who became an abolitionist leader.

Born into slavery on a Maryland plantation, Frederick Douglass's mother was named Harriet Bailey and his father was probably the plantation master; he was separated from his mother and raised by his grandmother, who called him "Little Valentine." For this reason his birthday is often given as February 14. After his escape to New York City in 1838, Douglass proved himself an immensely powerful abolitionist orator. He published his first autobiography, *Narrative of the Life of Frederick Douglass, an American Slave*, in 1845, then made a campaigning tour of England and Ireland in 1845–1847, returning to the United States to buy his freedom and launch an antislavery newspaper, *The North Star*, in Rochester, New York. He served as a consultant to President Abraham Lincoln in the American Civil War, in 1877 he became the first Black U.S. marshal, and toward the end of his life was the American minister to Haiti in 1889–1891 under President Benjamin Harrison. He was the most photographed American man in the nineteenth century.

> "I would unite with anybody to do right and with nobody to do wrong."
>
> Frederick Douglass, in a lecture to the Ladies of Rochester Anti-Slavery Sewing Society, 1855

RIGHT: A talented writer and orator, Douglass was a walking, talking counterargument to the claim that slaves lacked the mental capacity to be full citizens.

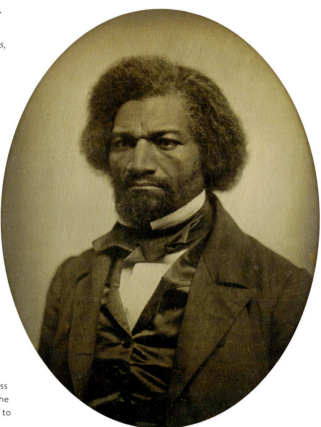

234 INDUSTRIES AND EMPIRES

292 PHILOSOPHER

KARL MARX

Trier, Prussia (now Germany)
1818–1883

Historian-economist Karl Marx wrote the four-volume *Das Kapital* (1867–1883) and with Friedrich Engels, *The Communist Manifesto* (1848). According to his critical theories (known as Marxism), societies develop through class conflict under the capitalist mode of production between the ruling classes (bourgeoisie), who control the means of production and the working classes (proletariat), who must sell their labor for wages to survive.

LEFT: Marx's analysis was that capitalism's internal tensions would lead it to destroy itself, with the socialist mode of production replacing it.

293 ROYALTY

VICTORIA

London, England
1819–1901

Queen Victoria gave her name to the Victorian era and oversaw the establishment and consolidation of the British Empire, the world's largest. Her reign of 63 years and 216 days was the longest in British history until she was overtaken by Queen Elizabeth II (70 years and 214 days). She restored the prestige of the British monarchy after difficult years. Victoria built the Royal Albert Hall and Albert Memorial to commemorate her beloved husband Prince Albert after he died in 1861.

RIGHT: Victoria was crowned queen on June 28, 1838, at Westminster Abbey, and was the first monarch to take up residence in Buckingham Palace.

GEORGE ELIOT (MARY ANN EVANS)

Chilvers Coton, England
1819–1880

Author recognized for developing psychological characterization in the novel.

Mary Ann Evans, who wrote under the male name George Eliot—partly to get around preconceptions about women writers—published a series of psychologically incisive, realistic books, including her masterpiece, *Middlemarch* (1871–1872), which is hailed as one of the finest novels ever written. The daughter of a Warwickshire estate manager, she had a religious schooling but later became friendly with and was influenced by "free thinkers," who questioned aspects of religious belief. She moved to London in 1851 and became assistant editor of *The Westminster Review*, worked as a translator, and began a relationship with a married man, George Henry Lewes, which scandalized polite society. Her first novel, *Adam Bede*, appeared in 1859, and was followed in quick succession by *The Mill on the Floss* (1860), *Silas Marner* (1861), *Romola* (1862–1863), *Felix Holt the Radical* (1866), and then *Middlemarch*. Her final novel, *Daniel Deronda*, was published in 1876. After the death of Lewes, she became friendly with a commission agent named John Walter Cross, whom she married in 1880 even though he was twenty years younger than her. She died the same year, aged sixty-one.

> *"The first condition of human goodness is something to love; the second something to reverence."*
>
> George Eliot, *Scenes of Clerical Life*, 1857

LEFT: Early readers of Eliot's books, speculating about the identity of the author, guessed that "he" was a clergyman.

KNOWN FOR
- Developing psychological characterization familiar from modern fiction
- Being the author of *Middlemarch*
- Writing under a male pseudonym

295   ACTIVIST

HARRIET TUBMAN

Dorchester County, Maryland
c. 1820–1913

"General Tubman" led slaves to freedom.

Escaped slave and leading abolitionist Harriet Tubman helped as many as seventy enslaved people flee to freedom along the "Underground Railroad" of safe houses—reputedly never losing a single escapee en route. She would famously brandish a gun to threaten any who lost their nerve and wanted to turn back, telling them, "You'll be free—or die." Born into slavery in Maryland, from where she fled to freedom in 1849, she was hailed as "General Tubman" by abolitionist John Brown. In the American Civil War she was a scout for Union forces. She later opened the Harriet Tubman Home for Indigent Aged Negroes in Auburn, New York.

"I have heard their groans and sighs, and seen their tears, and I would give every drop of blood in my veins to free them."

Comment attributed to Harriet Tubman, in *Harriet, the Moses of Her People*, Sarah Hopkins Bradford, 1869

LEFT: Tubman was a profoundly moving speaker at abolitionist and women's rights conventions from the 1850s onward.

296   ACTIVIST

FLORENCE NIGHTINGALE

Florence, Italy
1820–1910

British social reformer Florence Nightingale, celebrated by Victorians as the "Lady with the Lamp" and known for tirelessly caring for British soldiers in Constantinople during the Crimean War of 1853–1856, was the founder of modern nursing. After the war, she set up a school of nursing at St. Thomas's Hospital, London, in 1860, and two years later founded a school for midwives. She wrote the widely used manual *Notes on Nursing: What It Is and What It Is Not* and, in 1907, was the first woman to be awarded the Order of Merit, a British honor.

ABOVE: Nightingale in her most famous guise—"the lady with the lamp"—checking the wounded on the ward at night.

1800–1899   **237**

297 ACTIVIST

CLARA BARTON

Oxford, Massachusetts
1821–1912

Clara Barton, founder of the American Red Cross (1881), nursed the wounded and helped search for missing soldiers and baggage in the American Civil War, then worked in Europe with the International Red Cross in the Franco-German War of 1869–1870. Back in the United States, she was president of the American National Red Cross.

298 ARTIST

FYODOR DOSTOEVSKY

Moscow, Russia
1821–1881

This writer cheated death and became a literary giant.

Russian journalist and novelist Fyodor Dostoevsky, author of thirteen novels including *Crime and Punishment* (1886) and *The Brothers Karamazov* (1879–1880), as well as the acclaimed existentialist novella *Notes from Underground* (1864), had a major influence on writing and philosophy in the twentieth century, including on the work of philosophers Friedrich Nietzsche and Jean-Paul Sartre. In 1849, as a young writer-journalist, he was arrested and sentenced to death for being part of the Petrashevsky Circle, a literary group that discussed books that had been banned in Tsarist Russia. But, at the very last moment, the death sentence was commuted to imprisonment in a Siberian camp—a traumatic experience that had a profound effect on him and which he described in *The Idiot* (1868–1869). Dostoevsky spent four years in Siberia, and then endured six years of enforced military service, and later worked as a journalist. He became addicted to gambling, which inspired his 1866 novel *The Gambler*.

> "To be acutely conscious is a disease, a real, honest-to-goodness disease."
>
> Fyodor Dostoevsky, *Notes from Underground*, 1864

LEFT: In prison Dostoevsky had a religious awakening, and his socialism gave way to a belief in the Russian people and the Orthodox Church.

SCIENTIST

LOUIS PASTEUR

Dole, France
1822–1895

"In the fields of observation chance favors only the prepared mind."

Louis Pasteur, lecture, University of Lille, December 7, 1854

Pasteur saved lives with vaccines and invented pasteurization.

Louis Pasteur saved the French beer and wine industries from collapse when, in the 1860s, he developed pasteurization—the process of heating liquids such as wine, beer, and milk to kill microorganisms that would otherwise make them go bad. In 1863, the French emperor Napoleon III asked him to study why wines were becoming contaminated during production and export, and Pasteur had the idea of briefly heating wine to 120–140°F to kill microorganisms. He went on to save the European silk industry, working from 1865 to 1870 to establish that the silkworms' eggs were being attacked by two parasitic microbes and that the problem could be solved by disinfecting the nurseries in which they were kept. In an extraordinary career, Pasteur made a host of other breakthroughs. He argued that microorganisms caused disease in humans and animals, and this drove English surgeon Joseph Lister to develop antiseptic surgery methods, which had a major effect on the development of medicine and public health planning. Pasteur developed the vaccines for rabies and anthrax that would eventually save millions of lives, administering the first rabies vaccine in 1885 to a nine-year-old boy named Joseph Meister, who had been bitten by a rabid dog. Pasteur laid to rest the old theory that life could generate spontaneously with an experiment

ABOVE: Pasteur in the laboratory. He was professor of chemistry in the Sorbonne from 1867, and worked at the Institut Pasteur, Paris, from 1888.

showing that microorganisms could grow in sterilized flasks that were left open, but not in identically sterilized containers that were sealed. Pasteur was not so much a scientific genius as a very hard worker—he put in long hours, even after he suffered a stroke aged forty-five, and then carried on working at a mobile laboratory set up beside his bed. He was inspired to find a cure for infectious diseases, he wrote, by the tragic experience of losing three of his five children to typhoid.

ABOVE: As president, Grant restored the union and brought stability to the postwar economy. He also took on the white supremacist organization Ku Klux Klan.

300   MILITARY AND POLITICAL LEADER

ULYSSES S. GRANT

Point Pleasant, Ohio
1822–1885

General Ulysses S. Grant led the Union army to victory in the American Civil War, receiving the surrender of Confederate general Robert E. Lee on April 9, 1865, then became the eighteenth president of the United States in 1869. He supported Reconstruction and backed the rights of African Americans with the ratification in 1870 of the Fifteenth Amendment to the Constitution, which forbids the denying of the right to vote on grounds of race or previously being a slave.

ABOVE: Red Cloud In 1909. He said, "They made us many promises . . . but they kept but one—they promised to take our land . . . and they took it."

301   MILITARY LEADER

RED CLOUD

North of the Platte River, Nebraska
1822–1909

Dakota Sioux chief Mahpiua Luta, or "Red Cloud," led Native American opposition to the U.S. government's attempts to construct the Bozeman Trail to access the goldfields in western Montana. He captured troops sent to construct the trail and, for two years, led a guerrilla campaign of harassment known as Red Cloud's War, which ended only with the signing of the Second Treaty of Fort Laramie in 1868. He settled on a reservation in Nebraska, but some elements of his Native American coalition continued the war.

LEO TOLSTOY

Yasnaya Polyana, Russia
1828–1910

This profound novelist commanded the respect of writers, religious thinkers, and pacifists.

Russian nobleman and author Count Leo Tolstoy produced two works—*War and Peace* (1865–1869) and *Anna Karenina* (1875–1878)—often counted as among the greatest realist novels of all time. His other works include the highly praised novella *The Death of Ivan Ilych* (1886) and the philosophical treatise *The Kingdom of God Is Within You* (1893) which, with its explication of nonviolent resistance, was a major influence on Indian campaigner Mohandas Gandhi and, through him, on American civil rights leader Martin Luther King Jr. After receiving a private education, Tolstoy attended university but left without a degree, joining the army, fighting in the Crimean War, and publishing his first works, including *Sevastopol Sketches* (1855). He married Sophie Andreyvna Behrs in 1862 and they had thirteen children. Tolstoy settled on his estate and wrote his masterpieces, then, after a spiritual crisis, lived more or less as a peasant after passing his wealth over to his wife. He died at Astapovo railway station of pneumonia after secretly leaving home and embarking on a wandering winter journey.

ABOVE: Tolstoy argued that governments and churches should be abolished. He was excommunicated by the Russian Orthodox Church in 1901.

> "The only thing that we know is that we know nothing—and that is the highest flight of human wisdom."
>
> Leo Tolstoy, *War and Peace*, 1867

303 ACTIVIST

GERONIMO

No-Doyohn Canyon
(now Arizona/Mexico border)
1829–1909

Native American shaman, or medicine man, Goyathley—or Geronimo—led his Bedonkohe Apache people in their struggles against Mexicans and the U.S. authorities in the 1870s and 1880s after they were forcibly moved to a reservation in Arizona. He finally surrendered in 1886. Geronimo dictated his life story *Geronimo: His Own Story* before his death in Oklahoma in 1909.

ABOVE: Geronimo in 1904. He led attempts by the Apache to escape confinement on reservations and return to their traditional nomadic lifestyle.

304 MILITARY LEADER

SITTING BULL

Grand River, Dakota Territory
(now South Dakota)
1831–1890

This Native American chief humbled Custer at Little Bighorn.

Teton Sioux chief Sitting Bull had a vision that seemed to predict a great triumph before his famous victory over Lt. Col. George Custer in the Battle of the Little Bighorn. The chieftain thought he saw soldiers "as thick as grasshoppers" tumbling into the Sioux camp—and in the battle on June 25, 1876, Custer's battalion was annihilated. By this date Sitting Bull had been fighting the U.S. Army for more than a decade—struggles in the years 1863–1868, during which Sitting Bull fought in support of Red Cloud, ended when the Sioux accepted settlement on a reservation, but flared up again in the 1870s in response to attempts by the Northern Pacific Railroad to survey a route directly across Sioux lands. Thousands of U.S. Army troops flooded the area after Little Bighorn, and in 1876 Sitting Bull retreated with his followers to what is now Saskatchewan in western Canada. Because buffalo had been driven close to extinction, Sitting Bull and his followers found it impossible to survive and had to return to the United States and surrender in 1881. Later, Sitting Bull and twenty of his warriors performed in *Buffalo Bill's Wild West Show* touring attraction, but he was arrested and, on December 15, 1890, was fatally wounded after being shot by a policeman at the Standing Rock reservation in South Dakota during a struggle as his followers tried to free him.

"The whites provoked the war; their injustices, their indignities to our families, the cruel, unheard of and wholly unprovoked massacre at Fort Lyon ... shook all the veins which bind and support me. I rose, tomahawk in hand ..."

Sitting Bull to Jesuit priest Pierre-Jean De Smet, June 19, 1868

KNOWN FOR
- Defeating Colonel Custer in the Battle of the Little Bighorn
- Leader of Native American resistance for more than twenty years
- Performing in *Buffalo Bill's Wild West Show*

RIGHT: Sitting Bull in c. 1885 when he joined *Buffalo Bill's Wild West Show*. He was a major attraction and earned about $50 a week. Sitting Bull reputedly often gave his money to beggars.

305 INDUSTRIALIST

ALFRED NOBEL

Stockholm, Sweden
1833–1896

The chemist, industrialist, and inventor of dynamite used his fortune to fund the Nobel Prize.

Chemist, engineer, and businessman Alfred Nobel invented dynamite while seeking a safer way to handle the explosive liquid nitroglycerine. He patented the new invention in 1867, one of more than 350 patents he registered in his lifetime. Nobel was a pacifist, but became known as the "merchant of death" because the explosives he unleashed on the world were used in war. He made a great fortune, establishing factories to make dynamite and businesses to sell his explosives, which he bequeathed to set up the Nobel Prize, awarded since 1901 in physics, chemistry, physiology or medicine, literature, and peace. A sixth prize, in economic sciences and funded by the Bank of Sweden, was added in 1969. The son of an inventor, Nobel learned six languages and knew English well enough to write poetry in the language. Late in life he also wrote a tragic play, *Nemesis*, about sixteenth-century Italian noblewoman Beatrice Cenci.

> *"The capital, invested in safe securities by my executors, shall constitute a fund, the interest on which shall be annually distributed in the form of prizes to those who, during the preceding year, shall have conferred the greatest benefit to mankind."*
>
> From Alfred Nobel's will

RIGHT: Nobel wrote: "dynamite will sooner lead to peace than a thousand world conventions." He explained that if "in one instant, whole armies can be utterly destroyed" people will avoid conflict.

244 INDUSTRIES AND EMPIRES

DMITRI MENDELEEV

Tobolsk, Siberia, Russia
1834–1907

Dmitri Mendeleev created the periodic table of the chemical elements in 1869. It arranged the elements in order of their atomic weight (roughly equal to their number of protons and neutrons), and he used it to predict the existence of several unknown elements that were later discovered. He was professor of chemistry at the University of St. Petersburg from 1867 to 1890, and was later director of the Russian bureau of weights and measures. Element 101 (mendelevium), discovered in 1955, was named after him.

LEFT: Mendeleev used his periodic table to predict the properties of three yet-to-be-discovered elements—gallium, germanium, and scandium.

307 INDUSTRIALIST

ANDREW CARNEGIE

Dunfermline, Scotland
1835–1919

Industrialist who went on to become a great philanthropist.

Andrew Carnegie emigrated from Scotland to the United States with his family in 1848, aged twelve, and, embarking on a career with the Pennsylvania Railroad Company and making a series of canny investments, became wealthy by the time he was thirty. With the Carnegie Steel Company in Pittsburgh, Pennsylvania, which he sold to financier J. P. Morgan in 1901, he became one of the richest Americans in U.S. history. He was a major philanthropist, who gave around $350 million (equivalent to $5.5 billion today) to fund scientific research, libraries, and educational establishments including Carnegie Mellon University in Pittsburgh. Other bodies he founded include the Carnegie Corporation of New York and the Carnegie Endowment for International Peace.

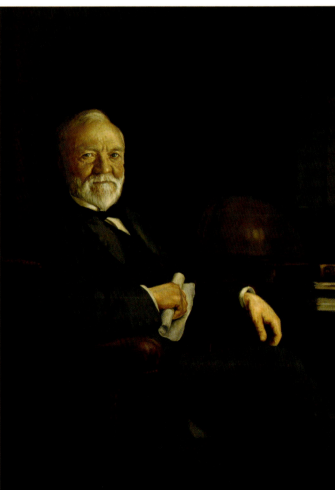

> "The 'good old times' were not good old times. Neither master nor servant was as well situated then as today."
>
> Andrew Carnegie,
> "The Gospel of Wealth," 1889

RIGHT: Carnegie explained his belief that the wealthy have a moral obligation to use their riches for the public good in an 1889 article, "The Gospel of Wealth."

308 ARTIST

MARK TWAIN

Florida, Missouri
1835–1910

American author and humorist Samuel Langhorne Clemens, who wrote under the name Mark Twain, achieved huge success with his boyhood adventure books *The Adventures of Tom Sawyer* (1876) and *Adventures of Huckleberry Finn* (1885). Twain grew up in Missouri alongside the Mississippi River and, in 1859, acquired a riverboat pilot's license. He took his pen name from the riverman's word for water two fathoms (12 feet) deep. He traveled far and wide, and his first book, *The Celebrated Jumping Frog of Calaveras County and Other Sketches* (1867) was based on a story he heard in a mining camp in California. Other books include *The Innocents Abroad* (1869) and *A Connecticut Yankee in King Arthur's Court* (1889). In the 1890s he was bankrupted by ill-advised financial deals.

ABOVE: Twain was a powerful satirist with a great ear for language, who brought colloquial speech into American fiction.

309 ACTIVIST

SAKAMOTO RYŌMA

Shikoku island, Kochi, Japan
1836–1867

This samurai laid the groundwork for the restoration of imperial rule in Japan.

Sakamoto Ryōma rose from humble origins in a low-ranking family to become an important figure in the events that led to Japan's 1868 Meiji Restoration, the sweeping away of the feudal system and return of imperial rule following the Tokugawa shogunate (military government). Leaving the Tosa *han,* or feudal area, in which he was born, Ryōma worked with Katsu Kaishū to establish a naval training establishment, then settled in Satsuma *han,* where he prevailed upon the local leaders to ally with their traditional enemies, Chōshū han, against the Tokugawa shogunate. Ryōma set up a shipping enterprise that was also a navy and, returning to his native area, backed the *daimyo* (lord) Yamanoiuchi Yōdō in his efforts against the shogunate. He promoted modernization and industrialization, democracy and nationalism, as well as the end of feudalism and return of imperial rule. Ryōma did not live to see the Meiji Restoration—he was killed in Kyoto by supporters of the shogunate aged just thirty-one.

KNOWN FOR
- Proponent of democracy based on the U.S. Congress and British Parliament
- Key figure in *Bakumatsu*—the period before the Meiji Restoration
- Committed samurai, gifted swordsman

310 ACTIVIST

ELIZABETH GARRETT ANDERSON

London, England
1836–1917

Elizabeth Garrett Anderson was the first woman to qualify as a physician and surgeon in the UK. Refusing to take no for an answer when blocked from attending medical school on the grounds she was a woman, she studied with doctors and was granted a license to practice by the Worshipful Society of Apothecaries in 1865. Then, in 1866, she was appointed medical attendant at the Marylebone Dispensary, London (later the New Hospital for Women). In 1870 she received a medical degree from the University of Paris. She campaigned for women's education, particularly in medicine.

RIGHT: In addition to her breakthrough in medical access for women, Anderson was the first woman mayor in England— elected in Aldeburgh, Suffolk, in 1908.

311 ACTIVIST

OCTAVIA HILL

Wisbech, England
1838–1912

Housing and charity reformer who pioneered home visits and founded the National Trust to safeguard open spaces and heritage.

Social reformer and housing activist Octavia Hill was a co-founder, in 1895, of the National Trust, the British body established to preserve places of natural beauty and historic interest. In 1853, she became friends with art critic John Ruskin, who gave financial backing to her first housing initiative in London. She went on to expand her work with the poor of the city, later managing the Southwark property of the Ecclesiastical Commissioners. As part of her drive to keep open spaces available for the city's poor, she was instrumental in saving Hampstead Heath and Parliament Hill Fields from being developed for housing. She also founded the Charity Organisation Society (now Family Action), which developed a system of home visits that was the basis of modern social work. Hill had no formal schooling after the age of fourteen, and grew up in relative poverty following the failure of her father's business. Her work inspired housing projects in the United States and on the European continent, as well as elsewhere in the UK.

ABOVE: Hill was one of nine children, and her parents were social reformers. She started work aged fourteen in a cooperative her mother managed.

312 ROYALTY

YAA ASANTEWAA

Besease, Ghana
1840–1921

Yaa Asantewaa I led the 5,000-strong Ashanti army in what is now Ghana in the War of the Golden Stool (a symbol of royal authority) against the British in 1900. The Ashanti uprising ended with the British army annexing the territory as a British Crown Colony. Yaa Asantewaa was captured and exiled with her advisers in the Seychelles.

> "There is perhaps no need of the poor of London which more prominently forces itself on the notice of anyone working among them than that of space."
>
> Octavia Hill, "Space for the People," 1883

313 MILITARY LEADER

CRAZY HORSE

Near present-day Rapid City,
South Dakota
c. 1842–1877

This chief led the fight to defend Native American lands.

Chief of the Oglala Band of Teton Sioux, Crazy Horse—known to his fellow Sioux as Ta-sunko-witko (which means "his horse is crazy")—was a redoubtable leader of Native American resistance to the U.S. Army and settlers' incursions into the northern Great Plains for more than a decade. In 1866, combating efforts to build a road to goldfields discovered in Montana, he took part in the Fetterman Fight—the massacre of Captain William Fetterman and eighty men—and in 1867 was involved in the Wagon Box Fight. He refused to accept the 1868 Treaty of Fort Laramie, which sought to limit the Native American tribes to reservations, and then in the Great Sioux War of 1876, after defeating General George Crook in the Battle of the Rosebud, fought alongside Sitting Bull in the annihilation of Colonel George Custer at the Battle of the Little Bighorn. He was forced to surrender to Crook in 1877 and sent to Fort Robinson, Nebraska, where he was killed in a struggle with soldiers attempting to confine him in a guardhouse.

KNOWN FOR
- Took part in the Fetterman Fight and the Battle of the Little Bighorn
- Led struggle to defend the Lakota people's traditional lifestyle

314 POLITICAL LEADER

BLANCHE KELSO BRUCE

Near Farmville, Virginia
1841–1898

Former slave who was the first African American to serve a full Senate term.

Blanche Kelso Bruce was elected by Mississippi to serve in the U.S. Senate in 1875–1881. He was the son of a slave woman, Polly Bruce, and the man who enslaved her, Pettus Perkinson, and was kept as a slave until he escaped to Lawrence, Kansas, during the American Civil War. After the war he moved to Mississippi, where he rose in state

politics and became wealthy enough to purchase a plantation. Bruce was not the first African American senator—that honor goes to Hiram Rhodes Revels, a minister in the AME Church who was elected by Mississippi in 1870–1871—but he was the first to serve a full six-year term, and the first to chair a congressional committee. Bruce was an advocate for justice for Blacks and Native Americans.

> "I am a negro, and proud of my race."
>
> Frequently said by Blanche Kelso Bruce to explain why he refused to use the word "colored"

ABOVE: Before embarking on his political career, Bruce promoted education and, in 1864, founded the first school for African Americans in Missouri.

---

315 RELIGIOUS LEADER

MARY MacKILLOP

Melbourne, Australia
1842–1909

Mary MacKillop—Saint Mary of the Cross—was the first Australian canonized (made a saint) by the Roman Catholic Church. She founded the country's first order of nuns, the Sisters of St. Joseph of the Sacred Heart, in 1866, in Penola, South Australia, with a priest, Father Julian Tenison Woods, and the following year became the order's first Mother Superior. The sisters opened schools, an orphanage, and a refuge for former women prisoners. MacKillop won papal approval for the order after a meeting with Pope Pius IX in 1873. She was beatified by Pope John Paul II in 1995, and canonized by Pope Benedict XVI in 2010. She was briefly excommunicated after exposing the activity of a priest who was sexually abusing those in his charge, but she was later reinstated in the Church.

LEFT: St. Mary MacKillop was made a saint on the basis of reports that a woman's terminal disease was cured after Josephite sisters prayed to her.

1800–1899 **251**

316 POLITICAL LEADER

ABDUR RAHMAN KHAN

Kabul, Afghanistan
1844–1901

The grandson of Dōst Mohammad Khan, who founded the Bārakzai dynasty of Afghanistan, Abdur Rahman Khan lived in exile in Samarkand, Russian Turkistan, while his cousin Shīr Alī was in power. But, following the outbreak of war between the Afghans and the British, and Shīr Alī's death in 1879, Khan returned to Afghanistan and was recognized as emir by the British. Emir from 1891 to 1901, Khan was a key figure in the establishment of modern Afghanistan, unified the country in 1880, and rebuilt its administration.

ABOVE: One of Afghanistan's greatest military figures, Abdur Rahman Khan is known as "the Iron Amir" for his ruthless rule.

317 PHILOSOPHER

FRIEDRICH NIETZSCHE

Röcken, Prussia (now Germany)
1844–1900

German-Swiss philosopher Friedrich Nietzsche declared that "God is dead" and critiqued Christian morality, developing the idea of the individual's driving force as a "will to power" and of the *Übermensch* ("Over-man" or "Beyond-man"), a focus on fulfillment in this world rather than the next world (as in Christianity). His ideas were admired by Adolf Hitler and adopted by the Nazis, but they mispresented his work. His books include *Beyond Good and Evil* (1886) and *Thus Spoke Zarathustra* (1883–1885).

BELOW: Norwegian artist Edvard Munch (creator of *The Scream*) was an admirer of Nietzsche and, though he never met him, painted this portrait of the philosopher in 1906.

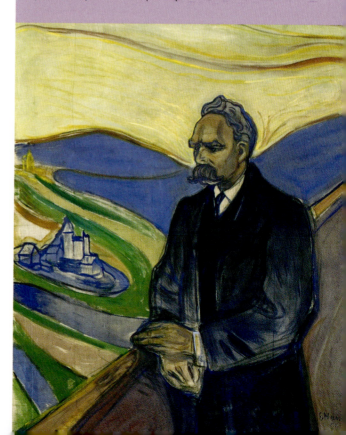

318 INVENTOR

ALEXANDER GRAHAM BELL

Edinburgh, Scotland
1847–1922

LEFT: Alexander Graham Bell presides over the opening of the telephone line from New York to Chicago in 1892.

Pioneering deafness researcher's invention of the telephone went on to transform communication.

"Mr. Watson, come here, I want you." This request, spoken in 1876 by Scottish-born American inventor Alexander Graham Bell to his assistant Thomas Watson, formed the first comprehensible words transmitted by electric wire, the key moment in the invention of the first practical telephone, which Bell patented on February 14 that year. He established the Bell Telephone Company in 1877. Bell had moved to Canada in 1870, and to the United States a year later, and worked as a teacher of the "System of Visible Speech" for deaf students developed by his father, speech therapist Alexander Melville Bell. He continued his work with those who could not hear—and both his mother and wife, Mabel Hubbard, were deaf. He later developed a wireless phone that transmitted sounds using beams of light, and patented what he called his "photophone" in 1880. Bell was also responsible, in 1887, for directing the young author and activist Helen Keller to meet with Anne Sullivan, who became her teacher.

319 INVENTOR

THOMAS EDISON

Milan, Ohio
1847–1931

American inventor Thomas Edison developed the phonograph, the first record player, in 1877, and the incandescent light bulb (1879) as well as—with technician W. K. L. Dickson—the Kinetograph, an early motion-picture camera, and Kinetoscope film projector. He issued 1,093 patents. Edison established the first industrial research establishment at Menlo Park, New Jersey, in 1876.

ABOVE: Edison at his workbench in West Orange, New Jersey, c. 1901. After his death, Edison was buried behind his home there.

320 POLITICAL LEADER

EDMUND BARTON

Sydney, Australia
1849–1920

Edmund Barton was the first prime minister of the commonwealth of Australia in 1901–1903, and afterward was a founding member and senior judge in the High Court of Australia until 1920. He backed the federation of the six British self-governing colonies in Australia—Queensland, New South Wales, Victoria, Tasmania, South Australia, and Western Australia—under the slogan "a nation for a continent, a continent for a nation."

321 POLITICAL LEADER

EMPEROR MEIJI

Kyoto, Japan
1852–1912

Japanese emperor who was the figurehead of the country's modernization.

During the reign of Emperor Meiji (r. 1867–1912) Japan underwent a period of westernization and was transformed from a culturally and economically isolated feudal society to an industrialized modern power. Born Mutsuhito, son of Emperor Komei, he took the name Meiji on being crowned emperor in 1868, following his father's death the previous year. His accession is known as the Meiji Restoration, as it eclipsed the isolationist military government of the Tokugawa shogunate and revived imperial rule. Meiji wore Western-style clothes and ate a Western diet, but also maintained Japanese traditions and was the author of 100,000 traditional poems. During his reign, feudalism was abolished (1871), a new education system was developed (1872), a constitution introduced (1885), and the Japanese Diet (national legislature) established (1890). Japan's engagement in the Sino-Japanese War against China of 1894–1895 and the Russo-Japanese War of 1904–1905 marked its emergence onto the world stage. Two years before Meiji's death in 1910, Japan annexed Korea.

"The Way here set forth is indeed the teaching bequeathed by Our Imperial Ancestors... infallible for all ages and true in all places."

Emperor Meiji's Charter Oath, 1868

LEFT: In 1871 Emperor Meiji issued an edict requiring all courtiers to wear Western dress.

322 ARTIST

VINCENT VAN GOGH

Zundert, Netherlands
1853–1890

This Post-Impressionist painter is one of the most famous in history.

With his love of color and bold brushwork, Vincent van Gogh had a huge influence on the direction of modern art. He was immensely productive, creating 2,100 artworks including 860 oil paintings, but he never achieved commercial success—we can only be certain that he sold one piece in his life—and was plunged into deep depression. After an argument with fellow artist Paul Gauguin on Christmas Eve 1888, he cut off part of his own ear; the next year he was placed in an asylum in Arles, France, for twelve months. He took his own life with a revolver in July 1890. Among his celebrated works are *Sunflowers* (1887) and *The Starry Night* (1889).

> "The work is an absolute necessity for me. I can't put it off, I don't care for anything but the work."
>
> Vincent van Gogh in a letter to his brother Theo, June 3, 1883

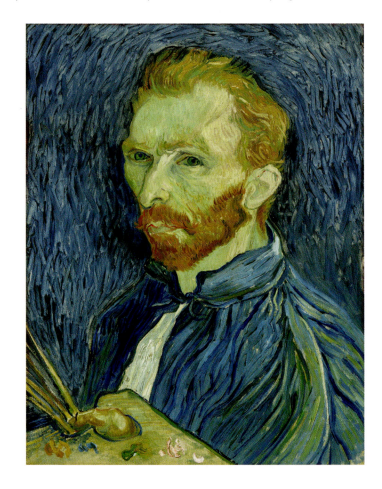

RIGHT: This 1889 self-portrait—like all those in that year—shows the left side of van Gogh's head, so as not to depict his damaged right ear.

323 SCIENTIST

SIGMUND FREUD

Freiberg, Moravia (now Příbor, Czech Republic)
1856–1939

Austrian neurologist who was the founder of psychoanalysis.

Sigmund Freud developed the theory and practice of psychoanalysis for treating mental and behavioral disorders. His work, with its theories of the unconscious mind, repressed infantile sexuality as a source of adult neuroses, and dreams as wish fulfillment, transformed the way people understand psychology and the human condition. It also had a profound influence on the humanities and popular culture. Freud developed the practices of free association and dream analysis, and the theory of the Oedipus complex, named after the Greek myth of Oedipus, according to which the infant boy unconsciously wants to have sex with his mother and grows to hate his father. He also originated the three-part psychic apparatus of the id, ego, and superego—with the id consisting of instinctive desires, the superego imposing critical and moral restraints, and the ego being the individual agent. Freud qualified as a doctor in 1881 in Vienna, where he ran a private practice from 1886 until 1938, before he fled to London to escape Nazi persecution of the Jews. Many of his theories were based on his case studies of wealthy female clients in Vienna.

LEFT: Freud was an excellent writer and subtle critic, and his case studies were praised by author D. M. Thomas as "masterly works of literature."

KNOWN FOR
- Being the founder of psychoanalysis
- Developing the idea of the Oedipus complex
- Theorizing about the id, ego, and superego
- Pioneering the interpretation of dreams

324   INVENTOR

NIKOLA TESLA

Smiljan, Austrian Empire (now Croatia)
1856–1943

The work of Serbian-American inventor Nikola Tesla made modern alternating-current electricity supply possible. A great showman and well-known inventor, he tried to develop wireless electrical power and communication, notably in his Wardenclyffe Tower (or Tesla Tower) on Long Island, New York. Toward the end of his life, running out of money, Tesla lived in a series of hotels in New York City, leaving unpaid bills in his wake. Many of his myriad brilliant inventions were undeveloped and he left notebooks full of ideas.

325   ROYALTY

OVONRAMWEN NOGBAISI

Benin (now Nigeria)
c. 1857–1914

Born Idugbowa, Ovonramwen Nogbaisi took his regnal name, which means "Rising sun that spreads through the atmosphere," on becoming king of Benin in 1888. British colonists were keen to gain access to Benin, to trade in ivory, rubber, and palm oil. Ovonramwen unsuccessfully tried to keep Europeans out of the kingdom and, after a trade dispute and the killing of the UK's acting consul general, the British invaded in January 1897, captured Benin City the following month, and stole the famous Benin Bronzes. Ovonramwen kept up resistance for six months, but then surrendered and died in exile in Calabar.

326   RELIGIOUS LEADER

PIUS XI

Desio, Italy
1857–1939

Pope who had a mixed record in challenging the rise of fascism.

Pius XI (r. 1922–1939) was the first pope of an independent Vatican City, established under the Lateran Treaty signed with Italian fascist leader Benito Mussolini on February 11, 1929. In a time of rising tensions, with the Spanish Civil War and the buildup to World War II, Pius used the motto *Pax Christi in regno Christi* (The Peace of Christ in the Kingdom of Christ) as he attempted to foster international peace. Initially willing to cooperate with rising fascist regimes, he later issued condemnations—his 1937 encyclical *Mit Brennender Sorge* (*With Burning Anxiety*), written in German rather than Latin and smuggled into Germany to be read in Catholic churches—was critical of the Nazis. In 1931 he was the first pope to make a radio broadcast.

> *"None but superficial minds could stumble into concepts of a national God, of a national religion."*
>
> Pius XI, encyclical "With Burning Anxiety," 1937

327 ACTIVIST

EMMELINE PANKHURST

Manchester, England
1858–1928

British women won the right to the vote thanks to this political activist.

Suffragist Emmeline Pankhust worked for forty years to win British women the vote in political elections, and achieved success in 1928 when the Representation of the People Act that gave women full voting equality with men was passed. Born into a radical Manchester family, she founded the Women's Franchise League in 1889 with her husband Richard Pankhurst, a lawyer who had been author of the first women's suffrage bill in the 1860s. Then, after being initially rejected for membership of the Independent Labour Party on account of her sex, in 1903 she founded the Women's Social and Political Union (WSPU), with a commitment to delivering suffrage for women through "deeds not words." Under the leadership of Emmeline and her eldest daughter Christabel, members became notorious for acts of physical protest and civil disobedience, smashing windows, confronting police officers, arson, hunger strikes in prison, and famously in 1913, the attempt by WSPU member Emily Davison to disrupt the Epsom Derby horse race that cost her her life. In 1917, Emmeline and Christabel founded the Women's Party to replace the WSPU. The parliamentary act that delivered Emmeline's lifelong goal was passed on June 14, 1928, a few weeks after her death.

ABOVE RIGHT: Emmeline Pankhurst is arrested after trying to deliver a petition to the king at Buckingham Palace on May 21, 1914.

KNOWN FOR
- Founding the Women's Social and Political Union
- Winning British women full voting equality

328 POLITICAL LEADER

THEODORE ROOSEVELT

New York, New York
1858–1919

This war hero is also the youngest ever U.S. president.

Aged forty-two years and 322 days on becoming president in 1901, Theodore "Teddy" Roosevelt was the youngest U.S. president in history, just under a year younger than John F. Kennedy when he became president in 1963. Roosevelt assumed the presidency on the assassination of President William McKinley by anarchist Leon Czolgosz in Buffalo, New York, and—reelected in 1904—served until 1909. Roosevelt overcame childhood sickness to become a larger-than-life, macho "cowboy" figure and naturalist, who operated a cattle ranch and formed and led the 1st U.S. Volunteer Cavalry, known as the "Rough Riders," in the Spanish-American War. Press coverage of an incident on a 1902 hunting trip, on which he refused to kill a cornered black bear, led to the invention of the "teddy bear," named after him. As president he was known for his "Square Deal" social reform policies, taking on trusts and monopolies, and beginning construction of the Panama Canal (1904–1915). He brokered an end to the Russo-Japanese War (1904–1905) and became the first American to win a Nobel Prize when he was awarded the 1906 Nobel Peace Prize.

> "The welfare of each of us is dependent fundamentally upon the welfare of all of us."
>
> President Theodore Roosevelt, speech at New York State Fair, Syracuse, September 7, 1903

RIGHT: The future president in 1898 after returning from the Spanish-American War with his 1st U.S. Volunteer Cavalry (Roosevelt's Rough Riders).

INDUSTRIES AND EMPIRES

329 ARTIST

ARTHUR CONAN DOYLE

Edinburgh, Scotland
1859–1930

Scottish writer Arthur Conan Doyle created the enduringly popular detective Sherlock Holmes, basing his meticulous powers of observation on those of his professor Dr. Joseph Bell when a medical student in Edinburgh. Holmes first appeared, with Dr. John Watson, in *A Study in Scarlet* (1887), and the pair starred in four novels and fifty-six stories, and would later appear in scores of acclaimed movies and TV series.

ABOVE: His creation, Sherlock Holmes, was devoted to a rational approach, but Doyle was fascinated by psychical research, the paranormal, and spiritualism.

330 ARTIST

RABINDRANATH TAGORE

Calcutta (now Kolkata), India
1861–1941

Bengali poet, painter, dramatist, educator, and songwriter Rabindranath Tagore was the first non-European to win the Nobel Prize for Literature, in 1913. He founded an experimental school at Shantiniketan, West Bengal, which aimed to combine Western and Eastern approaches and became the Visva-Bharat University. Tagore was an important advocate of Indian independence from the British Empire. He took up painting in his sixties and became a major artist.

ABOVE: Tagore was knighted as Sir Rabindranath in 1915, but resigned the honor in 1919 to protest at repressive British actions in the Punjab.

331 INDUSTRIALIST

HENRY FORD

Springwells Township, Michigan
1863–1947

American industrialist Henry Ford founded the Ford Motor Company and pioneered assembly line mass production. He transformed the world by manufacturing the first affordable car, the Ford Model T, in 1908— famously available in any color "so long as it is black." He declared, "I will build a motor car for the great multitude . . . it will be so low in price that no man making a good salary will be unable to afford one." He was a pacifist during World War I, and believed in the power of consumerism to keep peace.

ABOVE: Ford at the controls of the Ford Quadricycle, a forerunner of his first motor car, on the streets of Detroit c. 1893.

332 ARTIST

BANJO PATERSON

Near Orange, Australia
1864–1941

"Waltzing Matilda" was composed by this Australian "Bush poet."

Andrew "Banjo" Paterson was a lawyer and journalist as well as a bestselling poet, whose *The Man from Snowy River and Other Verses* (1890) was a major success. He traveled widely as a journalist, covering the Boer War and events in China, as well as fighting in France and Egypt in World War I. "Waltzing Matilda," generally viewed as Australia's unofficial national anthem, was in his 1917 collection *Saltbush Bill, JP, and Other Verses*. Paterson reputedly wrote the poem in 1895 on a visit to Winton, Queensland, to visit his fiancée Sarah Riley, to music written by Riley's best friend Christina Macpherson.

"For the drover's life has pleasures that the townsfolk never know."

Banjo Paterson, "Clancy of the Overflow," 1889

333 SCIENTIST

GEORGE WASHINGTON CARVER

Diamond Grove, Missouri
c. 1864–1943

Carver was a former slave turned agricultural scientist who promoted soil conservation by varying crops.

A man of many and varied talents, George Washington Carver was dubbed the "Black Leonardo" by *Time* magazine in 1941 in a reference to the famously versatile Renaissance artist, engineer, and architect Leonardo da Vinci. Born into slavery in Missouri, Carver got a high-school education while working on a farm in his late twenties, and then took a degree in agricultural science at what became Iowa State University. He was an artist who exhibited his work at the 1893 Chicago World's Fair, and an academic for five decades at what is now Tuskegee University in Alabama. But Carver is remembered above all as an environmentalist and agricultural scientist who promoted soil conservation through the growing of other crops aside from cotton in the American South—notably peanuts, sweet potatoes, and soybeans. To boost the market for these crops, Carver came up with 300 uses for peanuts, including in cosmetics, ink, soap, and flour, and with many applications for sweet potatoes, soybeans, and pecans. He turned down a 1931 offer from Joseph Stalin to oversee cotton plantations in Russia. On Carver's death, President Franklin D. Roosevelt established the George Washington Carver National Monument in Missouri in his memory.

LEFT: The inscription on Carver's grave reads: "He could have added fortune to fame, but caring for neither, he found happiness and honor in being helpful to the world."

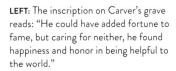

KNOWN FOR

- Promoter of soil conservation in the southern United States
- First African American to have a national park named after him

334 POLITICAL LEADER

SUN YAT-SEN

Xiangshan (now Zhongshan), China
1866–1925

"To understand is difficult; to act is easy."

Sun Yat-sen, quoted in *Great Britain and the East*, Vol. 61, 1944

The "Father of modern China" was the first president of the Chinese republic.

Sun Yat-sen led the overthrow of the Qing dynasty in the 1911 Xinhai Revolution, and then became the first provisional president of the Republic of China and leader of the Nationalist Party of China (Kuomintang). After training as a doctor, he turned to politics and spent years in exile attempting to foment revolution among expatriate Chinese, heading the 1905 United League (Tongmenghui), before returning home in 1911 to be provisional president of a new government. In 1912 he passed control to Yuan Shikai then, when they fell out, was forced into exile once more, in Japan, before returning to be head of a revolutionary government in the south of China. With Soviet assistance, he reorganized the Nationalist Party, made an alliance with the Chinese Communist Party, and oversaw the setting up of a military training section under Chiang Kai-shek. He died of gallbladder cancer before he could see Chiang Kai-shek unify China in 1926.

BELOW: Sun Yat-sen in Shanghai in 1912, when he was briefly "provisional president" after the emperor resigned and Yuan Shikai took power.

335 POLITICAL LEADER

RAMSAY MacDONALD

Lossiemouth, Scotland
1866–1937

Gifted orator who was the first Labour Party prime minister in the UK.

James Ramsay MacDonald was the first Labour Party prime minister of the United Kingdom, leader of the Labour governments in 1924 and 1929–1931, and then a national government in a coalition dominated by the Conservative Party in 1931–1935. He was elected to Parliament in 1906 as a member of the Labour Representation Committee, the forerunner of the Labour Party, and became its parliamentary leader in 1911.

LEFT: MacDonald chose his daughter Ishbel (left) to be his "official hostess" as prime minster at Downing Street. His wife Margaret died in 1911.

1800–1899

336 ARTIST

FRANK LLOYD WRIGHT

Richland Center, Wisconsin
1867–1959

He transformed architecture with the development of the Prairie style.

As well as developing the Prairie style of domestic architecture, Frank Lloyd Wright also designed major public buildings including Unity Temple in Oak Park, Illinois (1905), and the Guggenheim Museum in New York City, and is probably the most celebrated American architect of the twentieth century. He studied briefly at the University of Wisconsin, Madison, before working in Chicago for architectural firms. In 1893 he opened his own practice, developing the Prairie style of low-lying two-story private houses—such as the W. W. Willits House in Highland Park (1902) and the Robie House in Chicago (1910). His career had downs as well as ups: for some time Wright struggled to gain commissions because of his living arrangements—cohabiting with Mamah Cheney, the wife of a former client, despite his still being married, caused controversy—and after the stock market crash of 1929 there was next to no architectural activity in the United States. But Wright became an internationally celebrated architect following his design of Fallingwater, built over a waterfall near Pittsburgh in the Allegheny Mountains (1935–1937). The Guggenheim Museum was commissioned in 1943, but construction did not start until 1956 and was completed in 1959 following his death.

LEFT: Wright designed 800 buildings, of which 380 were built. In 2019, UNESCO designated eight of them as World Heritage Sites.

337 SCIENTIST

MARIE CURIE

Warsaw, Poland
1867–1934

This pioneering scientist was the first woman to win a Nobel Prize and the first person to win a Nobel Prize twice.

Marie Curie won the Nobel Prize for Physics in 1903 with her husband Pierre and colleague Henri Becquerel for their discovery of radioactivity. Eight years later she alone won the 1911 Nobel Prize for Chemistry for isolating pure radium. Born Maria Sklowdowska, she worked first as a teacher and governess then, in 1891, emigrated to Paris and studied at the Sorbonne. In Paris she met and, in 1895, married Pierre Curie and together they discovered the elements polonium (which she named after her native country, Poland) and radium. She was the first female professor at the University of Paris. Curie died in 1934 of aplastic anemia resulting from her exposure to radiation.

"One never notices what has been done; one can only see what remains to be done."

Marie Curie in a letter to her brother, 1894

LEFT: Marie and Pierre Curie at work in 1898 in the converted shed they used as their laboratory. That year she discovered that thorium was radioactive.

1800–1899 **267**

338 ACTIVIST

W. E. B. DU BOIS

Great Barrington, Massachusetts
1868–1963

African American sociologist, author, and civil rights activist W. E. B. Du Bois was one of the founders in 1909 of the National Association for the Advancement of Colored People (NAACP) and author of the influential book *The Souls of Black Folk* (1903). Du Bois objected to Booker T. Washington's argument that Black Americans should accept discrimination and work hard to better themselves, and believed that African Americans should press for full equality. He was a pioneer of Pan-Africanism—the idea that all Blacks of African descent should work together for freedom. In 1961 Du Bois moved to Ghana and spent the rest of his life there.

ABOVE: Du Bois graduated from the historically Black college of Fisk University in Nashville, Tennessee, then received a PhD from Harvard.

339 ACTIVIST

MOHANDAS GANDHI

Porbandar, India
1869–1948

Protest leader faced down the British and won the epithet Mahatma (Great Soul).

Mohandas Gandhi's nonviolent revolution helped propel India to independence from the British Empire in 1947. His powerful strategy of nonviolent resistance—*satyagraha* (holding to truth)—was a major influence on African American civil rights leader Martin Luther King Jr. He declared, "I have nothing new to teach the world. Truth and nonviolence are as old as the hills."

RIGHT: Gandhi said he learned that he needed to conserve and channel the anger he felt at social injustice—"as heat conserved is transmuted into energy, even so our anger controlled can be transmuted into a power that can move the world."

340 POLITICAL LEADER

VLADIMIR LENIN

Simbirsk, Russia
1870–1924

Revolutionary and theorist who was the first leader of Soviet Russia.

From 1917, Russian revolutionary socialist Vladimir Ilyich Ulyanov Lenin was the first head of government of Soviet Russia and, from 1922, leader of the newly formed Soviet Union. A political theorist whose work was integrated with the work of Karl Marx to form Marxism-Leninism—which was adopted by the Soviet Union—Lenin was probably the greatest revolutionary leader in history, and inspired Fidel Castro in Cuba, Mao Zedong in China, and Ho Chi Minh in Vietnam. Lenin committed to revolutionary socialism after the 1887 execution of his brother Aleksandr Ulyanov, who had participated in an attempted assassination of Tsar Alexander III. Expelled from Kazan Imperial University for anti-government protests, Lenin moved to St. Petersburg, then was sent to Siberia in 1897 for sedition. Afterward, in exile in Western Europe, he became leader of the Bolshevik faction of the Russian Social Democratic Workers Party against the Mensheviks led by Julius Martov. Lenin returned to Russia following the 1917 February Revolution, was a key figure in the October Revolution, and became head of government. His health was in decline from 1922, and on his death on January 21, 1924, more than a million mourners came to view his corpse lying in state in Moscow.

RIGHT: Lenin rouses soldiers preparing to fight on the Polish front in Sverdlov Square, Moscow, on May 5, 1920.

KNOWN FOR

- Being a revolutionary leader and first head of the Soviet government
- Developing Leninism, a version of Marxist revolutionary theory
- Being the subject of a personality cult in the Soviet Union after his death

341 ACTIVIST

JOHN CHILEMBWE

Blantyre district, Nyasaland (now Malawi)
1871–1915

"Let us strike a blow and die for Africa."
John Chilembwe's reputed words in a sermon on January 24, 1915

This pastor and hero of Malawi nationalism led a revolt against the British.

Baptist pastor John Chilembwe was born in Nyasaland (now Malawi) but educated in the United States. From 1892, he was a house servant to missionary Joseph Booth and, in 1897, traveled to the United States with him and was educated at what is now Virginia University of Lynchburg. Chilembwe returned to Nyasaland in 1900, and in 1915 led a rebellion against British rule. Angered by the treatment of Blacks on plantations and the British conscription of Nyasa men to fight the Germans in East Africa in World War I, he led an attack on an estate. The revolt was short-lived, and he was shot by African policemen. In Malawi, Chilembwe's memory is celebrated annually on John Chilembwe Day—January 15.

BELOW: Pastor Milembwe with his wife, Ida, and one of their two sons. Ida died during the 1918 flu epidemic.

342 SCIENTIST

ERNEST RUTHERFORD

Spring Grove, New Zealand
1871–1937

Physicist Ernest Rutherford made a series of experimental breakthroughs that were central to twentieth-century scientists' conception of the atom. Traveling from his native New Zealand to study at Cambridge University in England, he discovered alpha and beta radioactivity in 1895–1897. Then, in 1911, after establishing that the alpha particle was a helium atom, he proposed the Rutherford atomic model, according to which the atom has a central dense positively charged nucleus orbited by negatively charged electrons. In 1920 Rutherford proposed the existence of the neutron. He was awarded the 1908 Nobel Prize in Chemistry.

343 ACTIVIST

ROSA LUXEMBURG

Zamosc, Russian Empire (now Poland)
1871–1919

Polish-born German revolutionary who was a founder of the anti-war Spartacus League in World War I.

With fellow radical Karl Liebknecht and others, Rosa Luxemburg founded the anti-war Spartacus League (1916) with the goal of bringing World War I to an end in a revolution that would usher in proletarian government. The movement did not succeed in ending the war, but in 1918 Luxemburg set up the newspaper *The Red Flag*, the Spartacist movement's main publication, and co-founded the German Communist Party. Following the Spartacist Uprising in Berlin in January 1919, she and Liebknicht were murdered by the conservative paramilitary Freikorps (Free Corps). The pair were later celebrated as communist martyrs by the East German communist government. Born in Poland, Luxemburg emigrated to Zurich, where she studied political economy and law, and engaged with the international socialist movement, cofounding the Polish Social Democratic Party, which would become the Polish Communist Party. She argued against nationalism, which she dismissed as a

KNOWN FOR
- Arguing against nationalism in favor of international socialism
- Founding the anti-war Spartacus League
- Being killed by the Friecorps, and revered as a communist martyr

"Socialism in life demands a complete spiritual transformation in the masses degraded by centuries of bourgeois rule."

Rosa Luxemburg, *The Russian Revolution*, 1918

bourgeois concern, and in favor of international socialism. In 1898 she married Gustav Lübeck, took German citizenship, and settled in Berlin. In her 1899 book *Reform or Revolution?* Luxemburg argued against the theory that socialist ends could be best achieved through gradual change and parliamentary politics, stressing the need for revolution. Following the 1905 Russian Revolution she went to Warsaw, where she was jailed, and in 1906 wrote *The Mass Strike, Political Party, and the Trade Unions*, urging mass strike action. Released from prison, she returned to Berlin and the Social Democratic Party school. Under the name Junius, Luxemburg wrote *Crisis in German Social Democracy*, arguing for a new international socialist movement to prevent the mass killing of the war.

LEFT: Luxemburg in Berlin, 1914. That year she co-founded the International Group, which became the Spartacus League in 1916.

344 ARTIST

MARCEL PROUST

Auteuil, France
1871–1922

This French writer's masterpiece probed the workings of memory.

Marcel Proust's seven-volume *In Search of Lost Time* (1913–1927) is one of the greatest and most influential novels of the twentieth century, a profound and beautifully written examination of love, art, and memory. A sickly child and lifelong sufferer from asthma, Proust studied law and literature in Paris, and attended many refined salons (drawing room gatherings). Following the deaths of his father in 1903 and mother in 1905, Proust was financially secure and devoted himself to writing the great book for which he is remembered. He also translated the work of the English art critic John Ruskin into French.

> "*I had recognized the taste of the crumb of madeleine soaked in her decoction of lime-flowers . . . the old gray house upon the street, where her room was, rose up like the scenery of a theater.*"
>
> Marcel Proust, *In Search of Lost Time*, 1901

345 EXPLORER

ROALD AMUNDSEN

Borge, Norway
1872–1928

Norwegian adventurer Roald Amundsen was the first to take a ship through the Northwest Passage, the sea route between the Atlantic and Pacific via the Arctic Ocean (1903–1906), the first explorer to reach the South Pole (1911), and one of the first to fly over the North Pole (in 1926 in a dirigible). In 1918 he tried but failed to reach the North Pole by ship, on board the *Maud*. In 1928 he disappeared while attempting to locate and help the crashed *Italia* airship. His remains have never been found.

RIGHT: Amundsen began planning his South Pole expedition in 1909. He left Norway in June 1910, reached Antarctica the following January and the pole on December 14, 1911.

ALICE GUY-BLACHÉ

Paris, France
1873–1968

Guy-Blaché was a film pioneer and the first woman to direct a movie.

Alice Guy-Blaché was the first woman to direct a motion picture, and likely the world's only female movie director for the ten years after her 1896 debut, *The Cabbage Fairy*. She rose from secretary to head of production at the French company Gaumont, where she experimented with the use of synchronized sound, close-ups, and special effects such as double exposure and color tinting, making 600-odd shorts there before, in 1906, shooting a biblical epic, *The Life of Christ*, with 300 extras. Two years later she moved across the Atlantic with her husband Herbert Blaché and, in 1910, they founded the Solax Company in New York—the largest U.S. film company before the emergence of Hollywood. In 1912, Guy-Blaché directed the comedy short *A Fool and His Money*, believed to be the first film with an all African American cast. Across her career Guy-Blaché produced, wrote, or directed 1,000 films. Later in life she was angry that she had been written out of history and that her films were credited to male colleagues. She was awarded the French Legion of Honour in 1953. Only a handful of her films have survived.

BELOW: Before her marriage, Guy-Blaché helped to pioneer the development of narrative cinema.

347 INVENTOR

GUGLIELMO MARCONI

Bologna, Italy
1874–1937

Italian inventor Guglielmo Marconi invented the first wireless telegraph (radio), and was awarded the 1909 Nobel Prize in Physics with German physicist Ferdinand Braun. He sent radio signals across the English Channel in 1899 and, in 1901, across the Atlantic Ocean between Poldhu, Cornwall, England, and St. John's, Newfoundland, Canada. In Italy he was made a marquis and was elected to the senate in 1929. In 1932 Marconi installed a radio system at the Vatican for Pope Pius XI. On his death, radio operators around the world maintained radio silence for two minutes.

348 SCIENTIST

CARL JUNG

Kesswil, Switzerland
1875–1961

This psychiatrist developed the idea of the collective unconscious.

Carl Jung's theories of the collective unconscious (mental concepts shared by people at an unconscious level), archetypes (ideas or patterns such as the Mother, the Hero, the Trickster), introvert and extrovert personalities, and synchronicity (seemingly significant events that have no causal connection) have been immensely influential. Jung was a psychiatrist and close ally of Sigmund Freud, but took issue with Freud's insistence on the sexual source of neuroses, and founded his own field of analytical psychology. Jung argued that a human's main task was individuation—putting together the self out of unconscious and conscious parts.

> "We should not pretend to understand the world only by the intellect; we apprehend it just as much by feeling."
>
> Carl Jung, *Psychological Types, or The Psychology of Individuation*, 1921

RIGHT: Jung photographed c. 1935. He proposed that women have an unconscious masculine side (animus) and men an unconscious feminine side (anima).

349 POLITICAL LEADER

WINSTON CHURCHILL

Blenheim, United Kingdom
1874–1965

Iconic wartime leader who defied fascism and won plaudits as an author.

As prime minister from 1940 to 1945, Winston Churchill led the United Kingdom through the severe trials of World War II to emerge victorious. His speeches summoned the defiance that enabled the country to hold off and, eventually, defeat Nazi Germany and its allies, with the essential backing of the United States. Among his immortal rallying cries was the speech he delivered in Parliament on June 4, 1940, defying the threat of a Nazi invasion: "We shall fight on the beaches, we shall fight on the landing grounds . . . We shall never surrender." And on August 20, 1940, he paid stirring tribute to the fighter and bomber pilots he said were turning the tide of the war: "Never in the field of human conflict has so much been owed by so many to so few." He placed great emphasis on perseverance—in his words, to "keep buggering on." Churchill had a long career. After a stint in the army and as a journalist, he served in Parliament from 1900 to 1964—apart from two years from 1922. He held many positions, including Home Secretary (1910–1911) and First Lord of Admiralty (1911–1915 and 1939–1940). In 1945 he warned of the "Iron Curtain" of Soviet influence in Eastern Europe. He also wrote a multivolume history of World War II and was awarded the Nobel Prize for Literature in 1953.

LEFT: In 1929, with a distinguished political career already behind him but his finest hour still ahead, Churchill visited the United States, exploring Civil War sites and, here, visiting the White House.

KNOWN FOR

- Being the defiant leader of the UK in World War II
- Possibly coining the phrase "Iron Curtain"
- Winning the Nobel Prize for Literature

1800–1899 **277**

350 SCIENTIST

HIDEYO NOGUCHI

Inawashiro, Japan
1876–1928

This Japanese bacteriologist was the first to identify the agent that causes syphilis.

Hideyo Noguchi graduated from Nippon Medical College in Tokyo, then worked at the University of Pennsylvania and, from 1905, at the Rockefeller Institute for Medical Research in New York City. In 1913 he showed that *Treponema pallidum* was the causative agent of syphilis. He also demonstrated that *Bartonella bacilliformis* was the cause of Oroya fever and verruga peruana (forms of Carrion's disease). For years he searched for a vaccine for yellow fever, and died in 1928 after contracting the disease in Accra (Ghana).

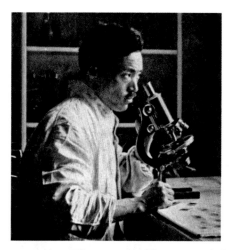

ABOVE: Noguchi is a controversial figure, accused of unethical experimentation for inoculating orphan children as part of syphilis research.

351 POLITICAL LEADER

JOSEPH STALIN

Gori, Georgia, Russian Empire
1878–1953

Dictator who unleashed terror as he made the Soviet Union a superpower.

Joseph Stalin ruled the Soviet Union as a dictator from 1928 to 1953. He transformed a peasant economy into a global superpower, collectivizing agriculture, imposing industrialization in a series of "Five Year Plans" and, after World War II, establishing governments throughout Eastern Europe aligned with the Soviet Union. Under his brutal totalitarianism, millions died in the famine of 1930–1933. In his Great Purge against political opponents, more than 1 million were imprisoned in labor camps, and more than 700,000 executed. Stalin initially signed a nonaggression pact with Nazi Germany, but joined the Allies in 1941 when the Nazis invaded the Soviet Union, driving back the invasion and, in 1945, capturing Berlin to end the war in Europe. In the postwar years the Soviet Union developed an atomic bomb and went toe to toe with the United States in the Cold War.

> *"The leaders come and go, but the people remain. Only the people are immortal, everything else is ephemeral."*
>
> Joseph Stalin, in an address to the Reception of Directors and Stakhanovites of the Metal Industry and the Coal Mining Industry, October 29, 1937

RIGHT: Soviet artist Isaak Brodsky, a key figure in the socialist realism movement, painted this government-commissioned "state portrait" of Stalin in 1933.

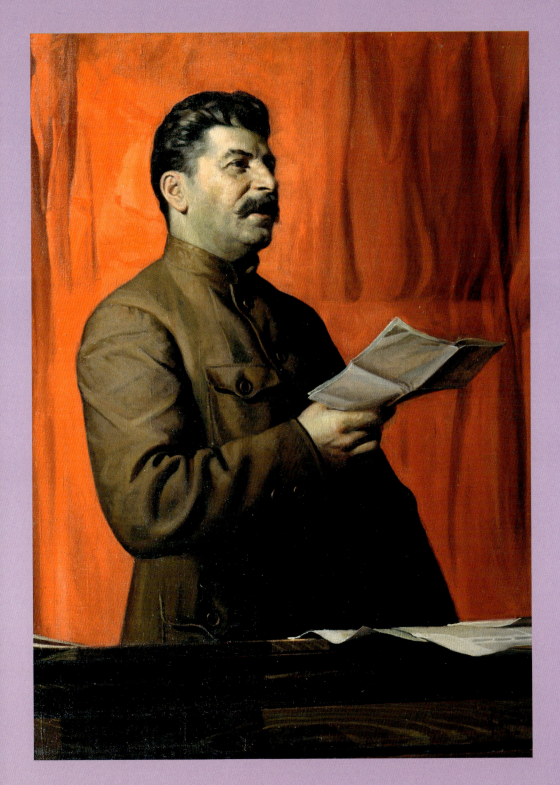

352 SCIENTIST

ALBERT EINSTEIN

Ulm, Kingdom of Wurtemberg (now Germany)
1879–1955

Scientific pioneer who explained gravity, and that mass and energy are equivalent.

Theoretical physicist Albert Einstein has become a byword for genius, and is probably the most celebrated and influential scientist of the twentieth century. He transformed human understanding of the universe with his special and general theories of relativity. Born into a Jewish family, in 1895 he moved to Switzerland, where he studied mathematics and physics in Zurich, then took a job at the Swiss Patent Office in Berne. In a single year—1905—he published four groundbreaking papers. One explained the photoelectric effect (the release of electrically charged particles when a material is exposed to electromagnetic radiation); this opened the way for quantum physics, and later won him the 1921 Nobel Prize in Physics. One laid out experimental proof for the existence of atoms by studying Brownian motion (the movement of particles in water). One was on special relativity, which explained how mass, time, and space are affected by speed, and proposed that space and time are unified as space-time. The fourth explained that mass and energy are two forms of the same thing and can be converted using the formula $E=mc^2$ (energy = mass multiplied by the speed of light squared). He developed the 1905 special theory into the 1916 general theory of relativity, which also included the effects of gravity, explaining that massive objects distort space-time, giving rise to the effects of gravity. Fleeing the Nazis, Einstein settled in the United States, working at Princeton, and became an American citizen in 1940.

> "I believe in intuition and inspiration . . . Imagination is more important than knowledge. For knowledge is limited, whereas imagination embraces the entire world. It is, strictly speaking, a real factor in scientific research."
>
> Albert Einstein in an interview for *The Saturday Evening Post*, 1929

LEFT: Einstein photographed after he began lecturing at Princeton. He said, "Science can flourish only in an atmosphere of free speech."

KNOWN FOR
- Being a theoretical physicist
- Developing the theories of special and general relativity
- Writing the world's most famous scientific equation, $E=mc^2$, which defines equivalence of mass and energy
- Winning the 1921 Nobel Prize in Physics

353 ROYALTY

ABDULAZIZ BIN ABDUL RAHMAN AL SAUD

Riyadh, Emirate of Nejd (now Saudi Arabia)
1880–1953

Tribal and religious leader who founded the kingdom of Saudi Arabia.

Arab tribal leader Abdulaziz bin Abdul Rahman al Saud (Ibn Saud) founded Saudi Arabia and ruled as its first king from 1932 until his death. He fathered forty-five sons and founded a dynasty that continues to rule the kingdom. He retook Riyadh, from which his family had been driven out by their rivals the Rashids, in 1902, and over the next thirty years took control of central and northern Arabia—capturing the holy city of Mecca in 1925. After oil was discovered in 1938, Ibn Saud oversaw the large-scale oil production in the kingdom after World War II that made him, and the country, rich beyond imagining—by the 1950s the king was receiving $2.5 million a week. His promotion of Wahhabi Sunni Islamic fundamentalism and backing for Islamic revivalists around the world was a major factor in this growth of pan-Islamism (the promotion of the unity of Muslims under one rule or international body).

354 ACTIVIST

MARIE STOPES

Edinburgh, Scotland
1880–1958

An advocate for birth control, Marie Stopes established the United Kingdom's first contraception clinic in Holloway, north London, in 1921. She studied at University College, London, and received a doctorate in paleobotany at the Botanical Institute Munich in 1904. She wrote the books *Married Love* and *Wise Parenthood* (1918).

ABOVE: Stopes was a geologist as well as a paleobotanist, and is seen here in her laboratory, probably in Manchester in 1905, studying coal slides.

355 ACTIVIST

HELEN KELLER

West Tuscumbia, Alabama
1880–1968

This deaf-blind activist and author was an inspiration to her fellow Americans.

Helen Keller was the first deaf-blind person to be awarded a Bachelor of Arts degree in the United States. She received her degree from Radcliffe College, Harvard University, in 1904. Having lost her sight and hearing due to illness at the age of nineteen months, she was educated by her teacher and later companion Anne Sullivan (introduced to her by telephone inventor Alexander Graham Bell), who taught her to read and write using Braille. Keller wrote fourteen books, including *The Story of My Life* (1903), which was adapted as a play, *The Miracle Worker* (1959), and later a film with the same title (1962), and toured the United States and the world as an advocate for those affected by loss of vision. She worked for the American Foundation for the Blind from 1924 to 1968. She was also a campaigner for women's suffrage, peace, and labor rights, and joined the Socialist Party of America in 1909.

ABOVE RIGHT: Keller's portrait accompanied a magazine article in which she described how she used touch to understand the world. "Paradise," she wrote, "is attained by touch; for in touch all is love and intelligence."

356 ARTIST

LU XUN

Shaoxing, China
1881–1936

Poet, short-story writer, and literary critic Lu Xun was a major figure in modern Chinese literature, and is often considered the greatest twentieth-century Chinese author. He was admired by Mao Zedong, and was head of the League of Left-Wing Writers in Shanghai. His 1923 book *Call to Arms* made his name.

PABLO PICASSO

Málaga, Spain
1881–1973

*"Art is never chaste . . .
Art is dangerous."*

Comment attributed to Pablo Picasso, in
Picasso by Antonina Vallentin, 1963

This genius occupied a central place in twentieth-century art.

The son of a professor of drawing, Pablo Picasso began exhibiting his work at the age of thirteen and moved to Paris aged twenty-three. His early works are known by their predominant coloration—the Rose Period (1904–1906) followed the Blue Period (1901–1904). An early masterpiece, *Les Demoiselles d'Avignon* (1907), an angular and confrontational portrait of five nude prostitutes on the Carrer d'Avinyó in Barcelona, appears to anticipate his development, with fellow artist Georges Braque, of Cubism from 1909 to 1912, which rejected perspective and often used geometric forms to emphasize the two-dimensional image. He worked as a sculptor, ceramicist, and printmaker and, from 1917 to 1924, designed stage sets for five ballets for the Ballets Russes led by Russian impresario Serge Diaghilev. The horrors of the Spanish Civil War inspired the anti-war masterpiece *Guernica* (1937). Picasso joined the French Communist Party in 1944. In the postwar years he produced reinterpretations of works by great masters of art such as Velázquez, Goya, and Manet.

BELOW: During the Spanish Civil War, Picasso was named director of the Museo del Prado in absentia and arranged for the Madrid museum's key artworks to be taken to Geneva.

358 POLITICAL LEADER

ATATÜRK (MUSTAFA KEMAL)

Salonkia (now Thessalonniki), Greece
1881–1938

Mustafa Kemal—celebrated as Atatürk (Father of the Turks)—founded the Republic of Turkey in 1923 and served as its first president until his death. Following the defeat of the Ottoman Empire in World War I, Kemal prevented the partition of the country among the Western Allies in the Turkish War of Independence, then abolished Ottoman rule. He transformed the country's education system, introduced a Latin alphabet, and gave equal rights to women, creating a modern secular republic.

ABOVE: Mustafa Kemal with Turkish army officers in 1923, shortly after his marriage to Latife Uşaki.

359 ARTIST

JAMES JOYCE

Dublin, Ireland
1882–1941

Irish writer James Joyce's *Ulysses* (1922), structured around Homer's *Odyssey* and describing the events of June 16, 1904, in Dublin, is revered as one of the great novels of the modernist movement and pioneered stream-of-consciousness writing. He followed it up with the dense, allusive, complex *Finnegans Wake* (1939). Joyce left Ireland in 1904 and lived in Switzerland, Italy, and France.

RIGHT: Joyce photographed c. 1920. His other masterpieces are *Dubliners* (1914) and *A Portrait of the Artist as a Young Man* (1916).

360 POLITICAL LEADER

FRANKLIN D. ROOSEVELT

Hyde Park, New York
1882–1945

FDR led the United States through the Great Depression and World War II.

Franklin D. Roosevelt was U.S. president from 1932 to 1945, the only U.S. president elected to the role four times. "FDR" was a cousin of the twenty-sixth U.S. president, Theodore Roosevelt, and married a distant cousin, Eleanor, in 1905. He entered the Senate aged twenty-eight in 1911. Despite being laid low by poliomyelitis in 1921, and thereafter being unable to walk without a cane or brace, FDR persisted with his political career and was elected governor of New York in 1928, and president in 1932. He took on the economic crisis of the Great Depression, providing inspirational leadership and delivering the New Deal of 1933–1939, which substantially increased the role of federal government in providing work and social security payments for the needy and unemployed. FDR pioneered direct communication through the "fireside chats" he delivered on U.S. radio from 1933 to 1944. As war loomed in Europe, there was a strong isolationist sentiment in the United States, but he held the country together and, in 1940, won the support of Congress to give Britain "all aid short of war." Then, in August 1941, he signed the Atlantic Charter that dedicated the United States and Britain to "the final destruction of Nazi tyranny." The country was at war by the end of 1941, but FDR died without seeing victory after a cerebral hemorrhage on April 12, 1945.

RIGHT: The future president while a senator and before he was struck by polio. He worked for a law firm on Wall Street before entering politics.

KNOWN FOR

- Being the only U.S. president elected four times
- Leading the United States in World War II
- Developing the "New Deal" during the Great Depression
- Having "fireside chats" on U.S. radio

361 ARTIST

COCO CHANEL

Saumur, France
1883–1971

Fashion designer who created a casual, chic style.

Gabrielle Bonheur "Coco" Chanel put the emphasis on comfort and simplicity, and is known for her tweed suits and making the "little black dress" fashionable. She opened her first boutique in Deauville, Normandy, in 1913, and established a fashion house in Paris in 1919. She went on to add handbags—she's particularly known for the quilted 2.55 bag that was inspired by a soldier's bag—and costume jewelry, especially strings of faux pearls, and earrings and brooches made from poured glass, to her output. She was also a perfumier; her scents include the still-popular Chanel No. 5 (1922). The company she founded continues to be at the forefront of fashion.

> "*Fashion is a queen and sometimes a slave.*"
> Coco Chanel, "Maximes et Sentences," French *Vogue*, September 1938

ABOVE RIGHT: Chanel in Los Angeles. A 1930s Hollywood engagement did not work out, but she famously designed costumes for the 1939 French movie *The Rules of the Game*.

362 ARTIST

FRANZ KAFKA

Prague, Bohemia, Austria-Hungary (now Czech Republic)
1883–1924

Czech writer Franz Kafka captured the insecurities and alienation of the twentieth century in his story *The Metamorphosis* (1915) and the unfinished novels *The Trial* (1925), *The Castle* (1926), and *Amerika* (1927) that were published after his death in 1924 from tuberculosis. He worked without joy in a Prague insurance office from 1908 to 1922, when illness forced his retirement. Kafka is hailed as one of the great twentieth-century writers, and his unsettling vision remains enormously powerful and influential. This would not have been the case had his executor Max Brod not ignored Kafka's request to destroy his work.

363 ACTIVIST

MARCUS GARVEY

Saint Ann's Bay, Jamaica
1887–1940

Marcus Garvey established branches of his Universal Negro Improvement Association (UNIA) in Harlem and other centers of African American population in the United States from 1916 to the early 1920s, and published a newspaper, *Negro World*, celebrating African culture and Black achievements. But after being imprisoned for mail fraud, Garvey was deported and was unable to revive the organization. He died in London.

ABOVE: Garvey held that Black people needed to achieve economic success to win respect. He set up business ventures and the Negro Factories Corporation.

364 POLITICAL LEADER

ADOLF HITLER

Braunau, Austria
1889–1945

The notorious dictator of Nazi Germany from 1933 to 1945 committed suicide in his bunker when defeat in World War II appeared inevitable. He fought in World War I, became Nazi Party leader in 1921, and Chancellor of Germany in 1933, claiming the superiority of the "Aryan race," and promoting anti-Semitic policy that culminated in the Holocaust.

365 ARTIST

CHARLIE CHAPLIN

London, England
1889–1977

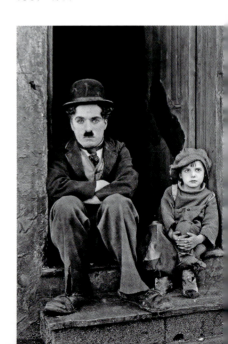

LEFT: Like populist leaders worldwide, Hitler knew how to play a crowd—admirers flocked to see der Führer (the Leader) in the flesh.

This actor-comedian created an immortal Tramp persona and became a global icon in silent films.

Charlie Chaplin escaped a poverty-stricken London childhood through performing in vaudeville and then, after going to the United States with the Fred Karno company, being scouted by Mack Sennett for the movie industry. He created his tramp costume, with baggy trousers, derby hat, and walking stick, as early as 1914, in *Kid Auto Races at Venice*. Chaplin began directing his own movies, and *The Tramp* (1915) propelled him to stardom. From 1919, when he cofounded United Artists Corporation distribution company, Chaplin had complete control over the movies and created a string of masterpieces including *The Kid* (1921, his first film of more than sixty minutes and costarring Jackie Coogan), *City Lights* (1931), and *Modern Times* (1936). His first movie with sound, *The Great Dictator* (1940), made delicious fun of Hitler. He was harassed and investigated by the FBI for supposed communist sympathies and left the United States for Switzerland in 1952. Chaplin received an Honorary Academy Award in 1972.

LEFT: Chaplin, pictured with Jackie Coogan in a publicity photo for the 1921 movie *The Kid*.

"I am a citizen of the world."

Charlie Chaplin in a speech at "Artists' Front to Win the War" at Carnegie Hall, New York, 1942

366 POLITICAL LEADER

CHARLES DE GAULLE

Lille, France
1890–1970

After the fall of France to Nazi Germany in World War II, French military hero and statesman Charles de Gaulle launched the Free French movement in exile. On the liberation of Paris in 1944, he headed a provisional government. He retired, but returned as prime minister in 1958, ended the Algerian War, and was elected president of the Fifth French Republic. De Gaulle retired again in 1969.

367 MILITARY AND POLITICAL LEADER

DWIGHT D. EISENHOWER

Denison, Texas
1890–1967

As Supreme Commander of Allied Forces in World War II, Eisenhower planned the 1944 Normandy Campaign that liberated Paris, and then became army chief of staff in 1945, and supreme commander of NATO in 1951. He went on to serve as the thirty-fourth U.S. president from 1953 to 1961. Eisenhower created NASA in 1958 in response to the Soviet Union's launch of *Sputnik I*.

368 POLITICAL LEADER

HAILE SELASSIE

Harer, Ethiopia
1892–1975

Emperor who was hailed as a divine incarnation.

Haile Selassie was emperor of Ethiopia from 1930 to 1974. Some Rastafari, members of a religious/political movement established in Jamaica in the 1930s, celebrate him as an incarnation of God (Jah), the Messiah or Second Coming on Earth of Jesus; others see him as a prophet. Selassie saw himself as Christian and a member of the Ethiopian Orthodox Church. His original name was Tafari Makonnen; as regent of Empress Zauditu he was named heir apparent and adopted modernizing, internationally focused policies, bringing Ethiopia into the League of Nations in 1923. He took the name Haile Selassie (Strength of the Trinity) on becoming emperor. He was forced into exile by Italy's invasion from 1935 to 1937 but, after appealing to the League of Nations, was returned to power with the help of British troops in 1941. Under Selassie's rule, Ethiopia was a founding member of the United Nations in 1945, and he oversaw the establishment of the Organization of African Unity in 1963 in Addis Ababa. Selassie was assassinated in a coup by the Marxist Derg military government in 1974.

RIGHT: Selassie was celebrated as a member of the Solomonic dynasty, a descendant of Menelik I, who was reputedly the son of King Solomon and the queen of Sheba in the tenth century BC.

369 ARTIST

FATMA BEGUM

India
1892–1983

The first Indian woman movie director was also a major star of the country's silent movies.

Fatma Begum founded her own production company, Fatma Films, and scripted and directed her directorial debut, *Nightingale of Fantasyland*, the first film directed by a woman in India, in 1926. It was a fantasy with special effects set in fairyland (Paristan). She was already an established movie star, particularly after her role in *The Brave Abhimanyu* (1922). Begum directed several films up to *Goddess of Luck* in 1929.

370 POLITICAL LEADER

AMANULLAH KHAN

Paghman, Afghanistan
1892–1960

This Afghan ruler led his country to complete independence.

Taking the throne on the assassination of his father Habibullah Khan on February 20, 1919, Amanullah Khan declared independence from the UK, which provoked conflict with the British. But the war came to little more than a few tussles, in part because the British army in India was still recovering from World War I, and a peace treaty recognizing Afghan independence was signed on August 8, 1919, at Rawalpindi (now in Pakistan). Under Amanullah Khan the Afghans signed a treaty of friendship with the Bolshevik government of the Soviet Union, making Afghanistan one of the first countries to recognize the Soviets, and initiating a special relationship between them that endured until the Soviet invasion of Afghanistan in 1979. Amanullah Khan's attempts at Westernization—especially a drive to emancipate women in 1928—angered Muslim religious leaders and provoked a revolt in which bandit chief Bacheh Saqqaw seized Kabul. Amanullah, unable to reimpose his authority, abdicated and went into exile in 1929. He died in Switzerland in 1960.

RIGHT: Amanullah Khan in 1928 at the height of his campaign to introduce Western customs to Afghanistan.

ARTIST

J. R. R. TOLKIEN

Bloemfontein, South Africa
1892–1973

English author who wrote the fantasy classic *The Lord of the Rings*.

South African-born English writer John Ronald Reuel Tolkien was a professor of Anglo-Saxon and English at Oxford University when he shot to fame with the fantasy epic *The Hobbit* (1937), which introduced Middle-earth, the hobbit Bilbo Baggins, and the wizard Gandalf to the world.

Tolkien followed it up with *The Lord of the Rings* trilogy (*The Fellowship of the Ring*, *The Two Towers*, and *The Return of the King*) from 1954 to 1955. The books were very popular in the 1960s counterculture and became a major movie franchise in the early twenty-first century.

ABOVE: Tolkien was an English professor at Oxford University for thirty-four years from 1925. *The Lord of the Rings* had sold 50 million copies in thirty languages by 2000.

372 POLITICAL LEADER

MAO ZEDONG

Shaoshan, Hunan province, China
1893–1976

The leader of China's revolution became the head of the People's Republic.

Mao Zedong was a founding member of the Chinese Communist Party (CCP) in 1921, and established the Chinese Soviet Republic in Jiangxi province. He held off attacks from the Kuomintang (KMT), or Nationalist army, of Chiang Kai-shek but was eventually forced to retreat in the Long March to Shaanxi. After allying with the KMT to fight Japan from 1937 to 1945, Mao defeated the KMT in 1949. He proclaimed the People's Republic of China.

His attempt to industrialize in the Great Leap Forward was not a success, and the Cultural Revolution, a ten-year effort to drive out "counter revolutionary" elements, led to class struggle and millions of deaths.

RIGHT: The peasant's son who became a twentieth-century political icon. Mao famously said, "Politics is war without bloodshed, while war is politics with bloodshed."

373 ENTERTAINER

HATTIE McDANIEL

Wichita, Kansas
1895–1952

Actor who was the first African American to win an Academy Award.

Actor and singer Hattie McDaniel's performance as Mammy in the 1939 movie *Gone with the Wind* won her the Academy Award for Best Supporting Actress, making her the first African American to win an Oscar. She suffered racial discrimination on many counts, being unable to attend the *Gone with the Wind* premiere in Atlanta on December 15, 1939, because it was held in a whites-only theater, and being made to sit at a segregated table during the Academy Awards ceremony at which she was given her Oscar. Even when she died, McDaniel was unable to be buried in the Hollywood cemetery of her choice since at the time it was whites-only. Early in her career she performed with traveling minstrel groups, released several blues records, and was one of the first African American women to sing on the radio. She made her movie debut, playing a maid, in *The Golden West* (1932), and had her first major role in *Judge Priest* (1934). She performed in more than 300 films, including *Alice Adams* (1935) and *In This Our Life* (1942).

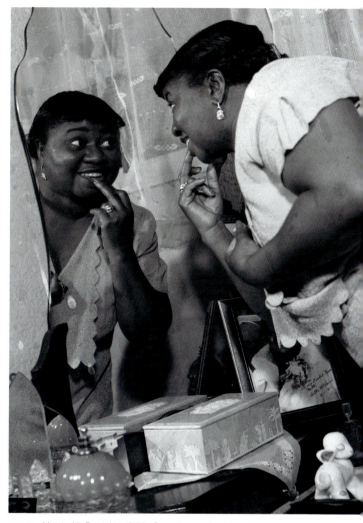

ABOVE: Hattie McDaniel in 1940. Over the previous decade she was cast as a maid or cook in almost forty films.

KNOWN FOR
- Being the first African American to win an Oscar
- Being one of the first Black American women to sing on the radio
- Having a long movie career

374 INDUSTRIALIST

KONOSUKE MATSUSHITA

Wakayama, Japan
1894–1989

In 1918 Konosuke Matsushita founded a company to make and sell the electric lamp plugs and sockets he designed. The operation grew to become the Matsushita Electric Industrial Co., which survived the U.S. occupation after World War II to become the principal maker of television sets, refrigerators, transistor radios, tape recorders, and washing machines for the people of Japan. One of its key brands was Panasonic and, in 2008, it changed its name to the Panasonic Corporation. Orphaned young, Matsushita started work aged nine, first running errands and then as an inspector at the Osaka Electric Light Co. He started his own operation aged twenty-three.

BELOW: Matsushita in 1929, when he split the company into three divisions, making bicycle lamps and batteries, electrical sockets, and radios.

375 EXPLORER

AMELIA EARHART

Atchinson, Kansas
1897–1937

This fearless flier was the first woman to fly solo across the Atlantic—and then disappeared.

On May 21, 1932, Kansas-born aviator Amelia Earhart landed her Lockheed Vega B aircraft in a field in Derry, Northern Ireland, to complete the first nonstop solo flight by a woman across the Atlantic Ocean. She had taken off from Newfoundland fourteen hours and fifty-six minutes earlier. Earhart was already a celebrity, hailed in the press as "Queen of the Air" in 1928 after being the first woman to fly as a passenger across the Atlantic, in a Fokker FVIIb plane piloted by Wilmer Stultz. But this adventurer's biggest drama was still to come—she disappeared on July 2, 1937, during an attempt to become the first woman to fly around the world. She was flying with navigator Fred Noonan in a Lockheed Model 10E Electra over the Pacific Ocean near Howland Island. They were last seen in Lae, New Guinea, the last stop before Howland Island. After months of speculation and searching, she was declared dead on January 5, 1939.

> "Preparation, I have often said, is rightly two-thirds of any venture."
>
> Amelia Earhart quoted in *Last Flight* by George P. Putnam, 1937

RIGHT: In 1929, Earhart helped to establish the female pilot organization the Ninety-Nines, and became its first president in 1931.

376 SCIENTIST

HOWARD FLOREY

Adelaide, Australia
1898–1968

This pathologist played a key role in the development of penicillin.

Howard Florey worked with British biochemist Ernst Boris Chain to develop penicillin, the first antibiotic, as a usable drug. Alexander Fleming had discovered penicillin in 1928, but it was Florey and Chain who purified and tested it and carried out the first clinical trials in 1941. The three men shared the Nobel Prize in Physiology or Medicine in 1945 for their work on penicillin. Florey graduated in Adelaide, then studied in Oxford and the United States, and became director of the Sir William Dunn School of Pathology in Oxford before returning to Australia and helping to cofound the Australian National University in Canberra.

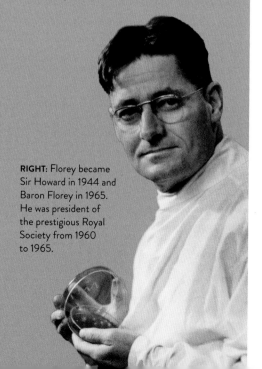

RIGHT: Florey became Sir Howard in 1944 and Baron Florey in 1965. He was president of the prestigious Royal Society from 1960 to 1965.

377 ENTERTAINER

DUKE ELLINGTON

Washington, D.C.
1899–1974

Bandleader who was the greatest jazz composer of the twentieth century.

Pianist Edward Kennedy "Duke" Ellington led his superb big band, which he formed in 1924 aged just twenty-five, for five triumphant decades, often performing at the famous Cotton Club in Harlem, and winning a reputation as probably the top jazz composer of the era. He wrote or collaborated on more than 1,000 pieces. Timeless numbers he wrote include "Mood Indigo" (1930), "Sophisticated Lady" (1933), "In a Sentimental Mood" (1935), "Don't Get Around Much Anymore" (1940), and "Cotton Tail" (1940). From the late 1930s on, the band's signature tune was "Take the 'A' Train" (1939), written by Ellington's frequent collaborator and co-arranger Billy Strayhorn, who was pianist in the band. He also wrote film scores, including for Otto Preminger's *Anatomy of a Murder* (1959)—the first Hollywood picture scored by an African American composer—and pieces for concert performance, including three "Sacred Concerts" in 1965, 1968, and 1973 that he called "the most important thing I have ever done." Ellington made recordings with other jazz greats, including Charles Mingus (1962) and John Coltrane (1963), while famous jazz names such as saxophonist Ben Webster were members of his band. Australian composer Percy Grainger declared that "the greatest composers who ever lived are Bach, Delius, and Duke Ellington."

RIGHT: Jazz nobility, Ellington with band members in 1946. Always well-dressed, he was nicknamed "Duke" by friend Edgar McEntree early in life.

378 ARTIST

ERNEST HEMINGWAY

Cicero, Illinois
1899–1961

Author who set the standard for a generation.

Ernest Hemingway developed a direct, succinct writing style that influenced a host of writers, who were also seduced by his colorful life story, which included being injured while an ambulance driver in World War I and reporting on the Spanish Civil War. His books include *A Farewell to Arms* (1929), *For Whom the Bell Tolls* (1940), and *The Old Man and the Sea* (1952, a Pulitzer Prize winner). Hemingway was awarded the Nobel Prize for Literature in 1954. He lived in Cuba from 1940 to 1960, but in 1961, depressed and unwell, took his own life.

> "Eschew the monumental. Shun the Epic. All the guys who can paint great big pictures can paint great small ones."
>
> Ernest Hemingway in a letter, January 5–6, 1932

379 ROYALTY

SOBHUZA II

Mbabane, Swaziland (now Eswatini)
1899–1982

Southern African monarch Sobhuza II ruled as king of the Swazi from 1921, and ruler of the Kingdom of Swaziland from 1967 to 1982. After Swaziland won its independence from Britain in 1968, Sobhuza suspended the constitution, dissolved parliament, and installed himself as supreme ruler. He established an electoral college of members chosen by local councils in 1979. Sobhuza had seventy wives and 210 children. He was succeeded, after a period of regency, by King Mswati III in 1986.

LEFT: The author at work in 1939.

RIGHT: The first U.S. edition of Hemingway's debut novel, *The Sun Also Rises*, published October 1926.

5

Modern and Postmodern
1900–present

WALT DISNEY

Chicago, Illinois
1901–1966

Family entertainment was transformed by this animator and film producer.

Walt Disney was behind a string of iconic products of twentieth-century American culture including Mickey Mouse, the first feature-length animated movie (*Snow White and the Seven Dwarfs*, 1937), live-action family movies, and the Disneyland amusement park. After working as a commercial illustrator in his native Chicago, Disney moved to California in the 1920s and set up Disney Brothers Studio with his brother Roy. Together with Kansas City–born animator Ub Iwerks, they created the cartoon character Mickey Mouse, who starred in the first animated sound picture, the four-minute-long *Steamboat Willie*, in 1928—Disney provided the voice. Other iconic characters such as Pluto, Goofy, and Donald Duck followed, and then a string of animated triumphs—*Snow White and the Seven Dwarfs*, *Pinocchio* (1940), *Fantasia* (1940), *Dumbo* (1941), and *Bambi* (1942). After World War II Disney moved into live-action films, including *Mary Poppins* (1964), which won five Academy Awards, and television. In 1955 he opened the Disneyland amusement park in Anaheim, California. Disney was the first individual to be nominated for Academy Awards in six different categories, and holds the record for the most nominations (fifty-nine) and wins (twenty-two).

BELOW: Disney presents Mickey Mouse to a cat, in 1931. He later declared, "I only hope that we never lose sight of one thing—that it was all started by a mouse."

381 ACTIVIST

YU GWAN-SUN

Cheonan, South Chungcheong province, Korea
1902–1920

Yu Gwan-sun took part in the March First Independence Movement protests in Seoul that began on March 1, 1919, the late Korean emperor's commemoration day. When schools were closed on March 10 in response, Yu went to the village of Jiryeong-ri (modern Yongdu-ri) and organized a further challenge to the authorities. She was arrested, found guilty of sedition, and jailed for five years. She died in prison on September 28, 1920, after being tortured and beaten. In the twelve months before the movement was stamped out by Japan, 2 million Koreans took part in protests and 7,000 were killed. The movement led to the establishment of the Korean Provincial Government in exile in Shanghai.

BELOW: This statue of Yu Gwan-sun stands near her memorial shrine at a major site celebrating Korean independence in Cheonan.

382 RELIGIOUS LEADER

RUHOLLAH KHOMEINI

Khomeyn, Persia (now Iran)
1902–1989

Islamic Shia cleric Ayatollah Khomeini led the Islamic Revolution that ended the Persian monarchy and deposed Shah Mohammad Reza Pahlavi in 1979, and was the first supreme leader of the Islamic Republic of Iran until his death. In exile before the revolution, he developed the theory of *velayt-e faqih* (guardianship by religious authority) that was the basis of the theocratic rule of the Iranian republic by Islamic jurists. Khomeini led the country in the Iran-Iraq War from 1980 to 1988. He was succeeded by Ali Khameni.

383 POLITICAL LEADER

DENG XIAOPING

Guang'an Sichuan province, China
1904–1997

Leader of the People's Republic of China (PRC) from 1978 to 1989, Deng Xiaoping oversaw market-economy reforms that transformed the country, setting it on the path to being the world's second largest economy after the United States. After playing important roles in the Long March, the war with Japan, and the Chinese Civil War, Xiaoping was Secretary General of the Chinese Communist Party (CCP) and vice-premier of the PRC in the 1950s. He fell from favor during Chairman Mao's Cultural Revolution (1966–1976), but returned to prominence after Mao's death in 1976, developing "socialism with Chinese characteristics."

ABOVE: Deng Xiaoping (right) with Mao Zedong. This image was used on a Chinese postage stamp in the 1990s.

384 ARTIST

FRIDA KAHLO

Coyoacan, Mexico
1907–1954

During her long recovery from childhood polio and a road accident, Frida Kahlo abandoned plans to study medicine and determined to become an artist. After joining the Mexican Communist Party, she met and married fellow artist Diego Rivera in 1929. She is known for her intense self-portraits, many drawing on elements from Indigenous Mexican traditions. Her first solo show was in New York in 1938; this was followed by a show in Paris in 1939. He health was never good, and she died aged just forty-seven. Her art was rediscovered in the 1970s, and she has become a revered feminist and Chicano icon.

ABOVE: In 1937 Kahlo told *Vogue* magazine, "I am happy to be alive as long as I can paint."

ACTIVIST

RACHEL CARSON

Springdale, Pennsylvania
1907–1964

Biologist who left a major legacy in the environmental movement.

Rachel Carson's book *Silent Spring* (1962) made the world aware of the dangers of the pollution of the environment through the use of synthetic pesticides, and was one of the most important books of the nascent environmental movement. She initially planned to be a writer, but changed to biology, studying at Pennsylvania College for Women (subsequently Chatham University) and carrying out graduate work at Johns Hopkins University before becoming an academic at the University of Maryland. In 1936, Carson joined the U.S. Bureau of Fisheries as an aquatic biologist. Her first book, *Under the Sea-Wind* (1941), was followed by *The Sea Around Us* (1951), which was a bestseller and National Book Award winner. *The Edge of the Sea* was published in 1955 before the groundbreaking *Silent Spring*. Her research for the book led her to conclude that synthetic pesticides were not only devastating for bird populations, but also polluted the food chain and could be linked to cancer in humans. She accused the chemical industry of spreading misinformation, and public officials of accepting it uncritically. She stood her ground under attack and threats of lawsuits, and the book led to a nationwide ban on the use of dichlorodiphenyltrichloroethane (DDT) and other pesticides, and sparked a grassroots movement that led to the establishment of the U.S. Environmental Agency in 1970.

LEFT: Carson in 1962, the year of *Silent Spring*'s serialization in the *New Yorker* and publication. In May of that year she attended a White House Conservation Conference.

386 PHILOSOPHER

SIMONE DE BEAUVOIR

Paris, France
1908–1986

This existentialist philosopher and feminist was the author of *The Second Sex*.

French feminist writer Simone de Beauvoir did not think of herself as a philosopher, but her books had a major influence on philosophy. She is known above all for her two-volume *The Second Sex* (1949), a critique of the treatment of women throughout history and in contemporary society that opined that women are defined as "the other" compared to men, and argued for the sweeping away of the myth of the "eternal feminine," envisaging a future in which women and men would be equals. Beauvoir was also a novelist, whose *The Mandarins* (1954) won the Prix Goncourt, and the author of four important volumes of autobiography, from *Memoirs of a Dutiful Daughter* (1958) to *All Said and Done* (1972). As a student at the Sorbonne, Beauvoir met existentialist philosopher Jean-Paul Sartre and entered into a lifelong relationship with him. In 1945 they founded and edited the monthly review *Modern Times* (named after Charlie Chaplin's 1936 film). She wrote of Sartre's last years in *Adieux: A Farewell to Sartre* (1981).

KNOWN FOR
- Being a feminist existentialist philosopher
- Writing *The Second Sex*
- Her relationship with Jean-Paul Sartre

ABOVE: De Beauvoir wrote movingly on aging—issuing a book on her mother's death (1964) and writing a critique of social attitudes to older people (1970).

387 POLITICAL LEADER

THURGOOD MARSHALL

Baltimore, Maryland
1908–1993

Educated at Lincoln University, Pennsylvania, Marshall was rejected from the University of Maryland Law School because he was not white, and instead attended Howard University Law School, where he graduated ranked first in his class, then worked for the National Association for the Advancement of Colored People (NAACP). He is known above all for his successful argument before the Supreme Court in *Brown v. Board of Education*, which established that racial segregation in public schools was unconstitutional. Marshall was solicitor general under President Lyndon B. Johnson (1965), and was nominated to the Supreme Court in 1967. He served on the court until 1991.

BELOW: One of Marshall's first legal victories was a 1935 case against the University of Maryland, which had denied a Black student law-school entry on the grounds of race alone.

388 POLITICAL LEADER

MOHAMMAD DAOUD KHAN

Kabul, Afghanistan
1909–1978

In 1973, Mohammad Daoud Khan led a coup against the Afghan monarch Mohammad Zahir Shah, establishing a republic and declaring himself president. Even though he swept away the monarchy, Khan was a cousin and brother-in-law of the king he deposed. He had a career in the military and was prime minister from 1953 to 1963, with pro-Soviet leanings. Khan ruled until 1978, when he was himself ousted and killed in a communist coup led by Nur Mohammad Taraki.

389 POLITICAL LEADER

KWAME NKRUMAH

Nkroful, Gold Coast (now Ghana)
1909–1972

Kwame Nkrumah was the first president of Ghana after it achieved independence from Britain and became a republic in 1960. After studying in the United States, he returned to Ghana and worked toward independence; he was prime minister from 1952 and president from 1957 until he was deposed in 1966 by the National Liberation Council. Nkrumah lived the remaining eight years of his life in exile in Guinea.

LEFT: Nkrumah promoted pan-Africanism, and under his rule Ghana played an important international role during the period of Africa's decolonization.

390 RELIGIOUS LEADER

MOTHER TERESA

Skopje, Ottoman Empire (now Republic of North Macedonia)
1910–1997

Agnes Gonxha Bojaxhiu founded the Missionaries of Charity, a Roman Catholic order of nuns dedicated to caring for the poor and sick, especially in India, in Kolkata in 1950. She was canonized by Pope Francis as St. Teresa of Calcutta in 2016.

LEFT: Mother Teresa was awarded the 1979 Nobel Peace Prize for her work. She wears the blue-bordered white cotton sari that identified her missionaries.

391 POLITICAL LEADER

RONALD REAGAN

Tampico, Illinois
1911–2004

As U.S. president, this former Hollywood star was the "Great Communicator."

Ronald Reagan, veteran of more than fifty Hollywood movies, is the only movie actor to have become U.S. president. As fortieth president from 1981 to 1989, he was known for his folksy demeanor and as an effective orator—he was celebrated as "the Great Communicator." His movies included *Knute Rockne, All American* (1940) and *Kings Row* (1942), and he was president of the Screen Actors Guild from 1947 to 1952 and 1959 to 1960. He served as governor of California from 1967 to 1975, before defeating Democrat Jimmy Carter in the 1980 presidential election. As president he was known for cuts in tax and government spending, together with economic deregulation in "Reaganomics," and in his second term for a less confrontational engagement with Soviet premier Mikhail Gorbachev and the Intermediate-Range Nuclear Forces Treaty arms control agreement of 1987. There was controversy over the Iran-Contra affair from 1985 to 1987, when secret deals to sell arms to Iran to fund the Contras, a right-wing group active against the Marxist Sandinista government in Nicaragua, were uncovered.

ABOVE: On the presidential campaign trail in 1984. Reagan knew how to please the camera. As president he put his weight behind "the war on drugs."

392 POLITICAL LEADER

KIM IL-SUNG

Mangyondae, Pyongyang, North Korea
1912–1994

Kim il-Sung ruled as premier of North Korea from its establishment in 1948 until 1972, and then president until his death in 1994. He was a Korean freedom fighter against Japanese rule in Korea, and was trained by the Soviets and fought in the Soviet army in World War II. With Soviet backing, Kim founded a communist state in North Korea after the war. He invaded South Korea in 1950, but was driven back by U.S. and United Nations forces in the Korean War of 1950–1953.

LEFT: Kim is viewed almost as a god in North Korea and was declared the country's "eternal president" on his death.

393 SCIENTIST

CHIEN-SHIUNG WU

Liuho, Jiangsu province, China
1912–1997

Chinese-American particle physicist Chien-Shiung Wu made a major discovery in nuclear physics when, in "the Wu experiment" (1956), she showed that in weak subatomic interactions the accepted principle of the conservation of parity (symmetry) did not apply. Her work was not properly recognized because she was a woman—her colleagues Tsung-Dao Lee and Chen Ning Yang won the 1957 Nobel Prize for Physics. She was later celebrated with the 1978 Wolf Prize in Physics, and is hailed as "the First Lady of Physics."

ABOVE: Wu was Dupin professor of physics at Columbia University from 1957 to 1981. In 1975 she became president of the American Physical Society.

394 SCIENTIST

ALAN TURING

London, England
1912–1954

Genius known as the "father of artificial intelligence," who broke the Nazi code and then became an LGBTQ icon.

Mathematician Alan Turing made key contributions to the development of computers and artificial intelligence. In a 1936–1937 paper, he proposed a computing apparatus, the Turing machine, which became the model for digital computers. Arguing that computers would be capable of "thought" hard to distinguish from human mental processes, he devised what he called the "imitation game" or "Turing test" to distinguish them, in which a human questioner asks questions of two sources, one human and one a computer—if the questioner does not notice a difference between the responses, then the computer has passed the test. During World War II, Turing led a team that broke the code of the German Enigma machine used for sending military information, saving many lives. Turing was homosexual and was prosecuted for committing homosexual acts in 1952; rather than be sent to prison, he accepted hormone treatment—commonly known as "chemical castration." He was found dead on June 7, 1954, having apparently taken his own life. He has become an icon for the LGBTQ community, and the British establishment has expressed remorse for his treatment. In 2013, Queen Elizabeth II issued a posthumous pardon for his conviction. When, in 2016, the British government announced it would issue further historic pardons for homosexual men convicted in this way, it became known as "the Alan Turing law."

LEFT: Turing received an official apology in 2009, fifty-five years too late. Prime Minister Gordon Brown wrote, "We're sorry, you deserved so much better."

KNOWN FOR
- Developing the Turing test
- Breaking the code of the German Enigma machine
- Being an LGBTQ icon

395 ACTIVIST

ROSA PARKS

Tuskegee, Alabama
1913–2005

The "First Lady of civil rights" inspired the 1955 Montgomery Bus Boycott.

On December 1, 1955, Rosa Parks repeatedly refused to move when a white bus driver in Montgomery, Alabama, ordered her to vacate her seat for a white passenger on the racially segregated bus. Some reports suggested she was tired, but she later said, "The only tired I was was of giving in." She was arrested and charged with violating the segregation law of the city code and, in court, was fined $10 plus $4 in fees, but with the help of E. D. Nixon, president of the Montgomery chapter of the National Association for the Advancement of Colored People (NAACP), appealed the conviction and challenged the legality of segregation in Alabama. Her case inspired a 381-day boycott of Montgomery buses by the local Black population, which led to protests against segregation of public places across the nation and was a key event in the launch of the U.S. civil rights movement. On November 13, 1956, after the Supreme Court upheld a decision that segregated bus seating in Montgomery was unconstitutional, a court order to end segregation on Montgomery buses was issued on December 20, and the boycott ended the next day. In 1999 Parks was awarded the highest civilian honor: the Congressional Gold Medal of Honor.

ABOVE: Parks in her rightful place at the front of a Montgomery bus after the Supreme Court ruled that segregation on the city's buses was unconstitutional.

396 ATHLETE

JESSE OWENS

Oakville, Alabama
1913–1980

African American athlete who won four golds at the Berlin Olympics.

James Cleveland "Jesse" Owens took four gold medals in the 1936 Olympic Games in Berlin—the 100 meters, long jump, 200 meters, and 4 x 100 meter relay—and thereby disproved the Nazi leader Adolf Hitler's claim of Aryan racial superiority. A year earlier, in another extraordinary achievement, Owens set three world records (and tied another) during a single hour at the 1935 Big Ten meet at Ann Arbor, Michigan; he equaled the record in the 100-yard dash and set new records in the 220-yard low hurdles, 220-yard dash, and long jump. Owens moved from his birthplace of Oakville, Alabama, to Cleveland, Ohio, as a child, and set his first record in high school. He then attended Ohio State University. Later in life he worked for the Illinois State Athletic Commission. He was awarded the Presidential Medal of Freedom in 1976.

"Although I wasn't invited to shake hands with Hitler, I wasn't invited to the White House to shake hands with the president either."

Jesse Owens

RIGHT: In the 1936 Berlin Olympics, Owens's 100 meters gold medal (10.3 seconds) was an Olympic record and his 200 meters gold medal (20.7 seconds) a world record.

397 ACTIVIST

OLIVER TAMBO

Nkantolo, Bizano, South Africa
1917–1993

South African anti-apartheid campaigner Oliver Tambo was president of the African National Congress from 1967 to 1991. After being banned by the South African government in 1959 as ANC secretary-general, he lived in exile in London from 1960 to 1990 and worked remotely to organize ANC guerrilla units. He suffered a stroke in 1989, returned to South Africa in 1990, and passed the ANC presidency to Nelson Mandela in 1991.

398 POLITICAL LEADER

INDIRA GANDHI

Allahabad, India
1917–1984

Indira Gandhi was the first female prime minister of India, serving from 1966 to 1977, and from 1980 until she was assassinated in 1984. War with Pakistan in 1971 led to the creation of Bangladesh. Gandhi was the daughter of India's first prime minster, Jawaharlal Nehru. Her son Rajiv Gandhi succeeded her as prime minister from 1984 to 1989.

BELOW: Indira Gandhi pictured in September 1980, four years before her assasination on October 31, 1984, by two of her own Sikh bodyguards.

399 ARTIST

I. M. PEI

Guangzhou, China
1917–2019

Chinese-born American architect Ieoh Ming Pei designed the now-iconic glass-and-steel pyramid at the Louvre Museum courtyard in Paris (1989). His other works include the John F. Kennedy Memorial Library at Harvard University (1964), the East Building at the National Gallery of Art, Washington, D.C. (1978), and the Miho Museum in Shiga, Japan (1997).

400 ARTIST

GWENDOLYN BROOKS

Topeka, Kansas
1917–2000

In 1950, Gwendolyn Brooks was the first African American poet to win the Pulitzer Prize. She won for her 1949 collection *Annie Allen*, describing a young Black girl coming of age on Chicago's South Side. She also published a novel, *Maud Martha* (1953), and the verse collections *The Bean Eaters* (1960) and *The Near-Johannesburg Boy and Other Poems* (1987). She was Poet Laureate of Illinois from 1968 to 2000.

401 POLITICAL LEADER

JOHN F. KENNEDY

Brookline, Massachusetts
1917–1963

This youthful president's hopeful rule was brutally interrupted.

Aged forty-three on entering the White House, John F. Kennedy was the youngest president to be elected to office—Teddy Rooosevelt (1901–1909) was the youngest president at forty-two, but he succeeded to the presidency on the assassination of William McKinley. President at a time of great change—the first Roman Catholic president and the first to be elected following televised presidential debates—JFK seemed to represent a hopeful future, though the Cold War with the Soviet Union was at its height and the Cuban Missile Crisis of 1963 saw perhaps the moment of greatest risk of nuclear war in the entire conflict. Kennedy's assassination in Dallas, Texas, on November 22, 1963, plunged America into mourning and stunned the world.

> "I believe that this nation should commit itself to achieving the goal, before this decade is out, of landing a man on the Moon and returning him safely to the Earth."
>
> John F. Kennedy in a speech to Congress, May 25, 1961

BELOW: Kennedy and rocket scientist Wernher von Braun visit the launch site at Cape Canaveral, Florida, on November 16, 1963—less than a week before JFK was assassinated.

402 POLITICAL LEADER

NELSON MANDELA

Mvezo, South Africa
1918–2013

Leader who delivered a peaceful end to South African apartheid.

Lawyer and Black nationalist campaigner Nelson Mandela negotiated the end of South Africa's racially divisive apartheid system, and became the country's first Black president from 1994 to 1999. After joining the Black nationalist African National Congress in 1944, Mandela set up South Africa's first Black law firm with fellow ANC member Oliver Tambo in 1952. When the ANC was banned by the government, effectively closing off all means of peaceful protest, he became leader of the ANC's armed division, which engaged in acts of sabotage. Mandela traveled to England to drum up support for the anti-apartheid struggle, but on return to South Africa, he was tried for sabotage and imprisoned for life. Mandela was in jail from 1964 to 1990 and was probably the most famous political prisoner in the world. For their work delivering a peaceful transition to majority rule in South Africa, Mandela and President F. W. de Klerk were awarded the Nobel Peace Prize in 1993.

> "The time for the healing of the wounds has come … The time to build is upon us."
>
> _{Nelson Mandela, on his inauguration as president, May 10, 1994}

LEFT: Mandela campaigning in Transvaal for the 1994 presidential election. In South Africa he was celebrated as "Father of the Nation" and called by his clan name, Madiba.

403 POLITICAL LEADER

GAMAL ABDEL NASSER

Alexandria, Egypt
1918–1970

Suez triumph made this leader a hero of the Arab world.

Leader of the 1952 Egyptian revolution, Gamal Abdel Nasser was prime minister of Egypt from 1954 to 1956, and president from 1956 to 1970. His nationalization of the Western-controlled Suez Canal Company in 1956, and success in the Suez Crisis that followed, made him revered throughout the Arab world, with a movement for Pan-Arab unity and the creation of the Egyptian/Syrian United Arab Republic from 1958 to 1961. Nasser resigned after defeat by Israel in the Six-Day War of 1967, returned following public protests, and then, after brokering peace between Jordan and the Palestinian Liberation Organization at the 1970 Arab League Summit, died of a heart attack. Around 6 million people attended his Cairo funeral.

BELOW: Crowds acclaim Nasser and Syrian president Shukri al-Kuwatly en route to signing the papers that created the United Arab Republic in 1958.

404 POLITICAL LEADER

EVA PERÓN (EVITA)

Los Toldos, Argentina
1919–1952

First Lady who won global fame as a backer of the "shirtless ones."

Former actress Eva Perón, First Lady of Argentina from 1946 to 1952 while her husband Juan Perón was president, was a powerful political force in her own right. She backed labor rights and championed the needs of the *descamisadoes* (shirtless ones), established the Eva Perón Foundation charitable organization, promoted the vote for women, and in 1949 founded the Peronista Feminist Party. In 1952, a month before her death from cervical cancer, the Argentine congress declared her "spiritual leader of the nation." She became a global icon, partly through the musical *Evita* (1976).

> "Evita symbolize[s] certain naive, but effective, beliefs: the hope for a better world; a life sacrificed on the altar of the disinherited, the humiliated, the poor of the earth."
>
> Tomas Eloy Martinez, 1996

ABOVE: On October 17, 1950, standing alongside President Juan Perón, Evita celebrates the Peronist movement's fifth anniversary.

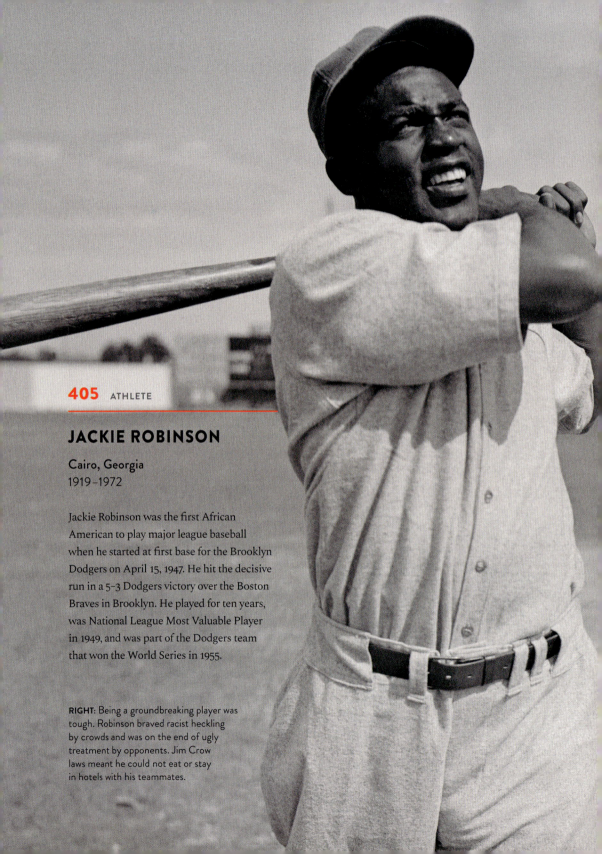

405 ATHLETE

JACKIE ROBINSON

Cairo, Georgia
1919–1972

Jackie Robinson was the first African American to play major league baseball when he started at first base for the Brooklyn Dodgers on April 15, 1947. He hit the decisive run in a 5–3 Dodgers victory over the Boston Braves in Brooklyn. He played for ten years, was National League Most Valuable Player in 1949, and was part of the Dodgers team that won the World Series in 1955.

RIGHT: Being a groundbreaking player was tough. Robinson braved racist heckling by crowds and was on the end of ugly treatment by opponents. Jim Crow laws meant he could not eat or stay in hotels with his teammates.

406 SCIENTIST

ROSALIND FRANKLIN

London, England
1920–1958

British chemist and X-ray crystallographer Rosalind Franklin's X-ray diffraction images of DNA were crucial to the discovery of the DNA double helix for which Francis Crick, James Watson, and Maurice Wilkins won the Nobel Prize in Physiology or Medicine in 1962. In April 2023, scientists determined that Franklin was an "equal player" in the DNA discovery.

407 POLITICAL LEADER

JULIUS NYERE

Butiama, Tanganyika (now Tanzania)
1922–1999

Julius Nyere was the first prime minister of independent Tanganyika in East Africa from 1961 to 1962, and then president of the country, which became the new United Republic of Tanzania in 1964. He remained in power until 1985. Nyere studied history and economics at Edinburgh University in Scotland and, on returning to Tanganyika to teach, became an anti-colonial activist and leader of the Tanganyika African National Union. He worked closely with British governor Sir Richard Turnbull on the path to independence. As leader, his *ujamaa* program—named for a Swahili word meaning "family belonging"—aimed to build a socialist economy based on agriculture; he promoted literacy and delivered universal free education. Nyere was an advocate of Pan-Africanism, a founder in 1963 of the Organization of African Unity, and a forthright opponent of apartheid in South Africa.

> "Freedom to many means immediate betterment, as if by magic... Unless I can meet at least some of these aspirations, my support will wane."
>
> Julius Nyere on becoming prime minister, 1960

LEFT: Nyere is carried aloft by jubilant supporters in 1961 following Tanganyika gaining its independence on December 9 that year.

408 SCIENTIST

CHRISTIAAN BARNARD

Beaufort West, South Africa
1922–2001

South African surgeon Christiaan Barnard performed the first heart transplant in humans. On December 3, 1967, he transplanted the heart of accident victim Denise Darvall into an incurably sick fifty-four-year-old grocer, Louis Washkansky. The operation was a success, but Washansky died eighteen days later after developing double pneumonia because drugs to prevent his body from rejecting the new heart suppressed his immune system. Barnard's subsequent human heart transplants were more successful. He also developed a way to correct the congenital infant defect of intestinal atresia, a gap in the small intestine.

BELOW: Barnard with his second transplant patient, South African dentist Philip Blaiberg (right), who lived a further nineteen months and fifteen days.

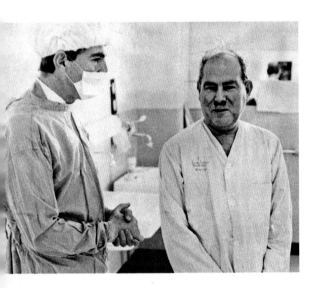

409 ARTIST

STAN LEE

Manhattan, New York
1922–2018

Comic book genius was the creator of Spider-Man.

Stan Lee (born Stanley Lieber) transformed Timely Comics, the comic book division of publisher Martin Goodman, into a household name as Marvel Comics. With other creatives, especially Steve Ditko and Jack Kirby, he was behind world-famous characters such as Spider-Man, Iron Man, Black Widow, Doctor Strange, the Incredible Hulk, the Avengers, and the X-Men. From the 1980s, Lee diversified from comic books into other outlets. He often appeared in cameo roles in the vastly successful movie adaptations of Marvel creations, including the X-Men and Spider-Man franchises. He won in a $10 million lawsuit against Marvel in 2005 on the grounds that he received no profits from the first Spider-Man film.

> "America is made of different races and different religions, but we're all co-travelers on the spaceship Earth and must respect and help each other along the way."
>
> Stan Lee in an interview with *The Washington Post's Comic Riffs*, 2016

RIGHT: Lee and the most famous of his creations, Spider-Man. With Ditko and Kirby, he pioneered an approach in which artists had much more of a say in the plots of stories.

410 ARTIST

CHEIKH ANTA DIOP

Diourbel, Senegal
1923–1986

Senegalese physicist, historian, and anthropologist Cheikh Anta Diop did not call himself an Afrocentrist, but his work was a key influence on the growth of the approach, developed in the 1980s, notably by American academic and philosopher Molefi Kete Asante. Afrocentrism sets out to maintain focus on the experiences and culture of peoples of Africa and the African diaspora—in opposition to Eurocentrism, which views history and culture from a European perspective. Diop studied in Senegal and then in Paris. He proposed that there was a unified Indigenous Black African culture, arguing that the people of the ancient Egyptian civilization were Black Africans, and that Black African culture was a precursor to ancient Greece and Rome and, through them, of all modern Western culture. In a contribution to a UNESCO history of Africa in 1971, he used close reading of art objects and scientific analysis of mummies to argue that ancient Egyptians were genetically linked to sub-Saharan Africans. His books include *Nations nègres et culture* (1954) and *Antériorité des civilisations nègres: mythe ou vérité historique?* (1967, partly published in English in 1974 as *The African Origin of Civilization: Myth or Reality?*).

411 POLITICAL LEADER

KIM DAE-JUNG

Haui Island, South Korea
1924–2009

Kim Dae-Jung, president of South Korea from 1998 to 2003, won the Nobel Peace Prize in 2000 for his efforts to build and maintain peaceful relations with Japan and North Korea, and his support for human rights and democracy in South Korea and East Asia. For decades he was a fearless leader of pro-democracy activism; he survived as many as five assassination attempts, and was jailed and sentenced to death, later commuted to a jail term. As president, Kim was credited with saving South Korea from bankruptcy, and his "sunshine policy" of engagement with North Korea led to a summit meeting with Kim Jong Il on June 15, 2000.

ABOVE: Kim Dae-Jung's election as president with 40.3 percent of the vote was the first power transfer from the governing party to the opposition in modern Korea.

JIMMY CARTER

Plains, Georgia
1924–

President who plotted a path to peace in the Middle East.

James Earl Carter, thirty-ninth U.S. president from 1977 to 1981, delivered the 1978 agreement between Israeli premier Menachem Begin and Egyptian president Anwar Sadat known as the Camp David Accords, which led to a 1979 peace treaty between Egypt and Israel. Carter studied at the U.S. Naval Academy and served in the U.S. Navy, then worked in his family peanut business before being inspired by the civil rights movement to enter politics as Georgia state senator (1963–1967), and then governor (1971–1975). As the Democratic Party candidate, he defeated incumbent president Gerald Ford to win the presidency in 1976. Following the 1979 Soviet invasion of Afghanistan, Carter led the boycott of the 1980 Moscow Olympics and issued the "Carter Doctrine," which stated that, if necessary, the United States would use military force to defend its interests in the Persian Gulf. Carter won the 2002 Nobel Peace Prize for his work looking for peaceful solutions to international conflicts, advancing democracy and human rights, and promoting economic and social development.

BELOW: Carter (center) with Sadat (left) and Begin (reading) present the 1979 Camp David Accords to the media at the White House, Washington, D.C.

413 ARTIST

JAMES BALDWIN

Harlem, New York
1924–1987

This writer was an eloquent commentator on race in America.

James Baldwin was a charismatic and gifted African American essayist, novelist, poet, and playwright. He delivered a powerful critique of race relations in America, and wrote eloquently on the difficulties of life for homosexual and bisexual men in the era. He was active as a preacher in a revivalist church during his teenage years, and poured this experience into his first novel, *Go Tell It on the Mountain* (1953). Baldwin lived in Paris, France, from 1948 until 1957 and published the essays *Notes of a Native Son* (1955) and a second novel, *Giovanni's Room* (1956). After his return to the United States, he was an important voice in the civil rights struggle, writing a book of essays, *Nobody Knows My Name* (1961) and a novel, *Another Country* (1962), followed by another nonfiction book, *The Fire Next Time* (1963), which focused on civil rights. Later works included the play *The Amen Corner* (1965), the short story collection *Going to Meet the Man* (1965), and the novel *If Beale Street Could Talk* (1974).

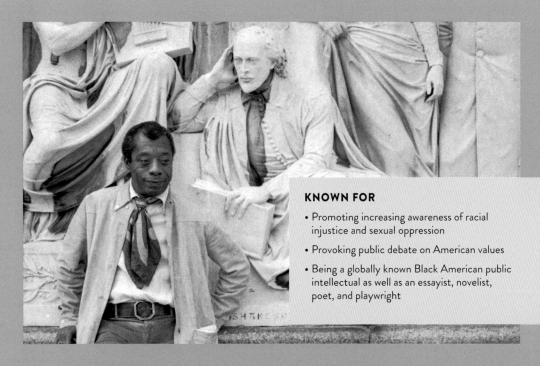

BELOW: Literary giants. Baldwin stands on the Albert Memorial, London, in 1969 beside a statue of Shakespeare.

KNOWN FOR
- Promoting increasing awareness of racial injustice and sexual oppression
- Provoking public debate on American values
- Being a globally known Black American public intellectual as well as an essayist, novelist, poet, and playwright

POLITICAL LEADER

MATATHIR BIN MOHAMAD

Alor Setar, Malaysia
1925–

Leader who was the longest-serving Malaysian prime minister.

Matathir bin Mohamad was prime minister of Malaysia from 1981 to 2003 and 2018 to 2020, serving a total of twenty-four years in office. He was in power during Malaysia's transformation into an industrialized economy, drawing in foreign investment, privatizing many state-owned organizations, and reforming the tax system. The country prospered, literacy and life expectancy rates rose, and the middle class expanded. However, the economy fell into depression in the late 1990s, and he retired in 2003 after growing opposition to him after the dismissal and imprisonment of his deputy Anwar Ibrahim. He returned as prime minister aged ninety-two in 2018, serving a further two years.

POLITICAL LEADER

MARGARET THATCHER

Grantham, England
1925–2013

Margaret Thatcher was the first woman to be prime minister of the United Kingdom, and the first British prime minister to win three consecutive terms. In power from 1979 until her resignation in 1990, she was the country's longest continuously serving prime minister since 1827. She privatized national utilities and industries, followed monetarist economic policy, and engaged in a bruising battle with the miners and other trade unions. She was a member of parliament from 1959, and secretary of state for education and science from 1970 to 1974, in the government of prime minister Edward Heath.

BELOW: International stateswoman. Thatcher waves to curious onlookers in March 1987 during an official visit to the Soviet Union.

416 ACTIVIST

MALCOLM X

Omaha, Nebraska
1925–1965

This civil rights leader advocated Islam and Black empowerment.

Malcolm X was an eloquent and forceful civil rights and Black empowerment campaigner who was under FBI surveillance in the 1950s until his assassination in New York City on February 21, 1965. Born Malcolm Little, he became involved in petty crime and drug dealing as a youth, when he was nicknamed "Detroit Red," and sentenced to ten years in prison for theft and burglary. On joining the Black nationalist religious/political organization Nation of Islam, he adopted X as his second name to be rid of the name Little, given to an ancestor by a white slave-master. As a spokesman for the Nation of Islam, he criticized the mainstream nonviolent civil rights campaign led by Martin Luther King Jr., encouraging Blacks to protect themselves "by any means necessary." But he became estranged from the Nation of Islam and, in 1964, undertook the *hajj* pilgrimage to Mecca, converting to Sunni Islam and changing his name to el-Hajj Malik el-Shabazz. He then founded Muslim Mosque Inc. in 1964, and the Organization of Afro-American Unity in 1965.

ABOVE: Malcolm X received death threats from the Nation of Islam and three of its members were convicted of his killing—but in 2021 two of them were exonerated.

> "They call me 'a teacher, a fomenter of violence.' I would say point blank, 'That is a lie. I'm not for wanton violence, I'm for justice.'"
>
> Malcolm X, *The Autobiography of Malcolm X*, 1965

417 POLITICAL LEADER

FIDEL CASTRO

Biran, Cuba
1926–2016

The Marxist-Leninist leader of the Cuban Revolution (1956–1959) served as prime minister of the country from 1959 to 1976 and president from 1976 to 2008. Under his governance, Cuba was a one-party communist state, aligned with the Soviet Union—his acceptance of Soviet missiles led to the Cuban Missile Crisis of 1962, a key event in the Cold War. Castro was succeeded by his brother Raul.

418 ROYALTY

ELIZABETH II

London, England
1926–2022

With a reign of 70 years and 214 days from February 6, 1952, to September 8, 2022, Queen Elizabeth II was Britain's longest-reigning monarch and the second longest in the world after King Louis XIV of France. She dutifully guided the British monarchy through times of profound social change, and the powerful reaction to her death showed that she had maintained her own and her family's popularity.

LEFT: Queen Elizabeth famously loved corgis, and had more than 30 during the course of her reign.

419 ENTERTAINER

MARILYN MONROE

Los Angeles, California
1926–1962

"Blonde bombshell" who lit up Hollywood with a string of hits.

Norma Jeane Mortenson made her name in Hollywood as Marilyn Monroe, starring in a series of major movies and becoming an enduring icon of popular culture. A contract as a pin-up model launched her into the movies, and she began to make her name in pictures such as the comedy *Monkey Business* (1952). By 1953 she was a star in films such as *Niagara* and *Gentlemen Prefer Blondes*. Contractual clashes led her to start her own film production company in 1954. She won praise for *Bus Stop* (1956), and a Golden Globe for *Some Like It Hot* (1959). Her last picture was *The Misfits* (1961). Her marriages to baseball star Joe DiMaggio and playwright Arthur Miller both ended in divorce. She was found dead, after overdosing on barbiturates, on August 4, 1962.

> *"I think that when you are famous every weakness is exaggerated... Goethe said, 'Talent is developed in privacy,' you know?"*
>
> Marilyn Monroe in an interview for *Life* magazine, August 3, 1962

LEFT: *Bus Stop* (1956) was the first film made by Marilyn Monroe Productions. Its director, Joshua Logan, later likened Monroe to Charlie Chaplin for her capacity to mix tragedy and comedy.

420 ROYALTY

BHUMIBOL ADULYADEJ

Cambridge, Massachusetts
1927–2016

King of Thailand embodied stability during seventy years of change.

King Bhumibol the Great of Thailand reigned for 70 years and 126 days, the third longest reign in history after King Louis XIV of France and Queen Elizabeth II of England. He was a member of the Chakkari dynasty, founded by Rama I in 1782, and was also known as Rama IX. He lived through ten successful coups, seventeen different Thai constitutions, and worked with thirty prime ministers. He was succeeded by his son Maha Vajiralongkorn.

ABOVE: King Bhumibol and Queen Sirikit in London in 1968 during a state visit to the United Kingdom.

1900–present

421 ENTERTAINER

SIDNEY POITIER

Miami, Florida
1927–2022

This Bahamian great changed the rules for Black Hollywood stars.

Sidney Poitier was the first Black Hollywood star and, in 1963, the first African American to win a Best Actor Oscar, for the picture *Lilies of the Field*. He refused roles that derived from racial stereotypes. Poitier was born in the United States while his Bahamian parents were visiting the country, but grew up on Cat Island, Bahamas, before enlisting in the U.S. Army in World War II. He studied acting in New York, appeared on Broadway in *Lysistrata* in 1946, then made his movie debut as a doctor in *No Way Out* (1950). He also played a religious minister in *Cry, the Beloved Country* (1951) and a high school student in *The Blackboard Jungle* (1955). Three 1967 roles made Poitier the year's top box-office attraction: a teacher in *To Sir with Love*, a detective in *In the Heat of the Night*, and a white woman's fiancé taken home to meet her liberal white parents in *Guess Who's Coming to Dinner*. Poitier turned to directing and had a major hit with *Stir Crazy* (1980), before returning to acting in the 1980s and 1990s. He was ambassador of the Bahamas to Japan from 1997 to 2007.

RIGHT: *Buck and the Preacher* (1972) was Poitier's directorial debut. He also starred in the Western that, unusually for the genre, had Black actors as central characters.

KNOWN FOR

- Being the first African American to win the Academy Award for Best Actor
- Being the first Black Hollywood star
- Starring in *In the Heat of the Night*
- Directing *Stir Crazy*
- Being the Bahamian ambassador to Japan

422 POLITICAL LEADER

PATSY MINK

Maui, Hawaii
1927–2002

Attorney was the first Asian American woman in Congress.

Born in Hawaii of Japanese descent, Patsy Mink was the first woman of color and first Asian American elected to Congress. She served in the House of Representatives from 1965 to 1977 and from 1990 to 2002. From 1977 to 1979 Mink was Assistant Secretary of State for Oceans and International Environment and Scientific Affairs. She then returned to Hawaii, and from 1982 to 1985 was chair of the Honolulu City Council.

> "America is not a country which needs to demand conformity of its people, for its strength lies in all our diversities converging in one common belief."
>
> Patsy Mink, in an address to Congress, 1967

ABOVE: Mink campaigning with supporters and family in the 1960s.
In 1971 she ran for president—the first Asian American woman to do so.

423 ACTIVIST

CHE GUEVARA

Rosario, Argentina
1928–1967

Marxist revolutionary and guerrilla fighter Ernesto Guevara de la Serna—Che Guevara—played a key role in the Cuban Revolution (1953–1959) led by Fidel Castro and, afterward, was an important aide in Castro's government. After studying medicine, Guevara traveled in Latin America, settled in Guatemala, then in Mexico where he met Castro. He left Cuba in 1965 to train guerrilla fighters in the Congo and Bolivia, but was shot dead by the Bolivian army. He became a paragon of countercultural style.

ABOVE: Che Guevara and a child depicted in a statue in Santa Clara, Cuba. He had five children, including human rights and debt relief advocate Aleida Guevara.

424 ACTIVIST

MARTIN LUTHER KING JR.

Atlanta, Georgia
1929–1968

Major gains were achieved by this civil rights leader's nonviolent campaign.

Baptist minister and civil rights campaigner Martin Luther King Jr. famously declared, "I have a dream that my four little children will one day live in a nation where they will not be judged by the color of their skin but by the content of their character." He was speaking to 200,000 people on August 28, 1963, at the March on Washington for Jobs and Freedom. He was a superb orator and master strategist, and—inspired by Mahatma Gandhi in India—he used nonviolent civic resistance to combat segregationist Jim Crow laws and push for civil rights for African Americans. He led the Montgomery Bus Boycott initiated by Rosa Parks, and was the first president of the Southern Christian Leadership Conference. In 1964, the year the Civil Rights Act was passed outlawing racial discrimination in public facilities, voting, and employment, he was awarded the Nobel Peace Prize. King was assassinated on April 4, 1968.

425 ARTIST

CHINUA ACHEBE

Ogidi, Nigeria
1930–2013

Nigerian writer Chinua Achebe was a key figure in modern African literature, and his debut novel *Things Fall Apart* (1958) is probably the most widely translated and studied African novel. Working with his publisher, he founded the Heinemann African Writers Series, which boosted the careers of many African writers, including Flora Nwapa.

426 SCIENTIST

YUAN LONGPING

Beijing, China
1930–2021

Chinese crop scientist Yuan Longping created the first hybrid rice, a high-yield crop that saved lives by making it possible to feed more people from a given area of land. He was inspired by witnessing famine and starvation firsthand during the Great Leap Forward (1958–1960). The rice he developed delivered a yield 30 percent higher than existing conventional varieties.

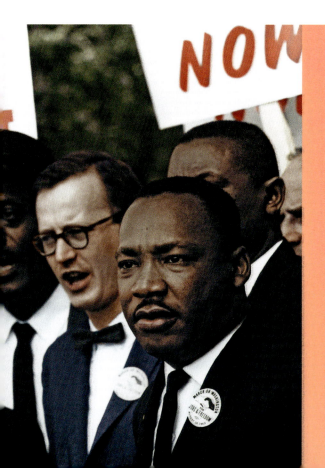

"I've seen the Promised Land. I may not get there with you. But I want you to know tonight that we, as a people, will get to the Promised Land."

Martin Luther King Jr., speaking in Memphis, Tennessee, April 3, 1968

LEFT: King at the March on Washington for Jobs and Freedom before making his celebrated "I have a dream" speech.

427 POLITICAL LEADER

HELMUT KOHL

Ludwigshafen am Rhein, Germany
1930–2017

Chancellor who oversaw the end of the Cold War and reunification of Germany.

German politician Helmut Kohl was chancellor of West Germany from 1982 to 1990, then—having overseen the reunification of the country on October 3, 1990—was chancellor of a united Germany from 1990 to 1998, the first since 1945. His was a tumultuous era, in which the Cold War came to an end and the European Union (EU) was formed. Kohl was a proponent of European integration and German-French cooperation and, with French president François Mitterand, was a driving force behind the 1992 Maastrict Treaty that founded the twelve-member European Union and the euro currency. He also pushed for the EU's eastward spread. In Germany he moved the capital from Bonn back to Berlin.

Kohl studied political science at the University of Heidelberg, graduating in 1958. The following year he was elected to the Rhineland-Palatinate state legislature and, in 1969, became its principal minister—known as the "minister president." He became chairman of the Christian Democratic Union party in 1973, and its candidate in federal elections in 1976 and 1980, then became chancellor after a vote of no confidence in Chancellor Helmut Schmidt in 1982.

BELOW: Kohl (right) in 1978, when he was chairman of the Christian Democratic Party, with Dries van Agt, prime minister of the Netherlands.

428 ACTIVIST

HARVEY MILK

Long Island, New York
1930–1978

When American gay-rights activist Harvey Milk was elected to the San Francisco Board of Supervisors in 1977, he broke new ground as the first openly homosexual elected official in California. However, he and San Francisco mayor George Moscone were shot dead on November 27, 1978, by Dan White, a former supervisor who opposed a bill Milk had sponsored banning discrimination in public accommodation, housing, and employment on grounds of sexual orientation. Milk was a flamboyant character and campaigner. After his death he became an icon and martyr for the gay community. He was posthumously awarded the Presidential Medal of Freedom in 2009.

BELOW: Milk (center) with George Moscone (left) at a restaurant opening in 1978, a few months before both men were murdered.

429 ENTREPRENEUR

WARREN BUFFETT

Omaha, Nebraska
1930–

American businessman Warren Buffett is celebrated as the most successful investor of his era. In 1965, after studying at the University of Nebraska and Columbia Business School, he took control of textile manufacturer Berkshire Hathaway, diversifying it as a holding company and transforming it into one of the leading conglomerates in the world. In March 2023, Buffett's worth was $104 billion. He is one of the world's leading philanthropists and, in 2020, pledged to give away 99 percent of his wealth, principally through the Bill and Melinda Gates Foundation.

430 EXPLORER

NEIL ARMSTRONG

Wapakoneta, Ohio
1930–2012

The first man on the Moon took a "giant leap for mankind."

Apollo 11 astronaut Neil Armstrong made possibly the greatest breakthrough in history when, at 10:56 p.m. Eastern Daylight Time on July 20, 1969, he became the first human to walk on the Moon. As he stepped out of the Lunar Module *Eagle* on the Moon, with an estimated 530 million people watching on television at home, he famously said, "That's one small step for man, one giant leap for mankind." He and Buzz Aldrin spent more than two hours on the lunar surface while the third *Apollo 11* astronaut, Michael Collins, was in lunar orbit on the command module *Columbia*. The moment represented victory for the United States in the "Space Race" with the Soviet Union. Armstrong, Aldrin, and Collins took off from Florida on July 16, and returned to Earth on July 24, splashing down near Wake Island in the western Pacific Ocean.

"Houston, Tranquility Base here. The Eagle has landed."

Neil Armstrong's first words after landing the Lunar Module *Eagle* on the Moon's surface on July 20, 1969

LEFT: Armstrong immediately after completing the historic walk on the Moon, July 20, 1969. The photo was taken by his fellow astronaut Buzz Aldrin.

431 ENTERTAINER

RAY CHARLES

Albany, Georgia
1930–2004

American pianist, singer, bandleader, and composer Ray Charles pioneered soul music by blending elements of jazz, gospel, and rhythm and blues. The man they called "the Genius" lost his sight in childhood, perhaps due to glaucoma, and was blind by the age of seven. His hits included "Georgia on My Mind" (1960) and "Hit the Road Jack" (1961), and he won seventeen Grammy Awards during his career.

432 ACTIVIST

DOLORES HUERTA

Dawson, New Mexico
1930–

Labor leader and civil rights activist Dolores Huerta cofounded the National Farmworkers Association, later part of the United Farm Workers of America (UFW). She was a leader of the 1965 Delano grape strike in California that delivered improved working conditions. She created the UFW motto "Si, si puude" (roughly translated as "Yes, we can!").

RELIGIOUS LEADER

DESMOND TUTU

Klerksdorp, South Africa
1931–2021

Bishop who led a peaceful struggle against apartheid.

Desmond Tutu was the first Black African Bishop of Johannesburg from 1985 to 1986, and then the first Black Archbishop of Cape Town from 1986 to 1996. He was an internationally celebrated leader of the struggle against South African apartheid, emphasizing the role of nonviolent protest and the deployment of economic pressure against the South African regime by countries around the world. He was awarded the 1984 Nobel Peace Prize for this work. Tutu was a schoolteacher before he was ordained as an Anglican priest in 1961. In 1962 he emigrated to London and, from 1972 to 1975, worked as associate director for the World Council of Churches before returning to South Africa and becoming dean of St. Mary's Cathedral, Johannesburg, in 1975 (the first Black South African to hold the post), and general secretary of the South African Council of Churches from 1978 to 1985. After Nelson Mandela was released from jail in 1990, Tutu and Mandela played leading roles in negotiations with the government to end apartheid. In 1995 Mandela put Tutu in charge of the Truth and Reconciliation Commission.

LEFT: Tutu's work with the Truth and Reconciliation Commission won him a great reputation. In 2004 he became Visiting Professor in Post-Conflict Studies at the University of London.

KNOWN FOR
- Being an internationally known anti-apartheid campaigner
- Being the first Black bishop in South Africa

434 POLITICAL LEADER

MIKHAIL GORBACHEV

Privolnoye, Stavropol, Soviet Union (now Russia)
1931–2022

The last leader of the Soviet Union oversaw the end of the Cold War.

In an attempt to preserve the Soviet Union, its leader Mikhail Gorbachev encouraged reform, promoting *glasnost* (openness) and *perestroika* (political and economic restructuring) to enable the decentralization of economic decisions, greater freedom of expression, and democratization. He ended the Soviet-Afghan War and collaborated with U.S. president Ronald Reagan in arms limitation treaties and summits as the Cold War wound down. He did not impose Moscow's authority when eastern European countries broke free from 1989 to 1992. He was the first and only president of the Soviet Union (1990–1991) and, after resigning, founded the Gorbachev Foundation and campaigned for social democracy in Russa.

"We are witnessing most profound social change."

Mikhail Gorbachev, speech to the UN General Assembly, December 7, 1988

ABOVE: Gorbachev and U.S. president Ronald Reagan at the summit in Reykjavík, Iceland, in 1986, which led to the 1987 Intermediate-Range Nuclear Forces Treaty.

435 ENTREPRENEUR

RUPERT MURDOCH

Melbourne, Australia
1931–

Through News Corp. (founded 1979), media entrepreneur Rupert Murdoch built up a large stable of newspapers and media companies around the world—including the *New York Post* and the *Wall Street Journal* in the United States, the *Australian*, *Herald Sun*, and the *Daily Telegraph* in Australia, and the *Times* and the *Sun* in the UK—plus television outlets Fox News and Sky News Australia. He was owner of media companies Sky (to 2018) and 21st Century Fox (to 2019). He built the empire from two Adelaide newspapers, the *Sunday Mail* and the *News*, which he inherited in 1952.

436 ACTIVIST

RUTH BADER GINSBURG

Brooklyn, New York
1933–2020

Ruth Bader Ginsburg was the first Jewish woman and the second woman, after Sandra Day O'Connor in 1981, to be nominated and confirmed to the U.S. Supreme Court. Initially seen as a moderate figure when nominated by President Bill Clinton, she increasingly became known for dissenting statements defending liberal legal views. She embraced the label "Notorious RBG." After graduating first in her class from Columbia Law School, Ginsburg spent many years as an advocate of gender equality and women's rights, and became a general counsel for the American Civil Liberties Union.

BELOW: Despite differing opinions, Ginsburg got on well with many conservative judges on the Supreme Court.

437 ARTIST

WOLE SOYINKA

Abeokuta, Nigeria
1934–

Activist and dramatist Wole Soyinka was the first writer from sub-Saharan Africa to be awarded the Nobel Prize in Literature (1986). He studied at Ibadan in Nigeria, and then in Leeds, England, where he wrote his early plays *The Swamp Dwellers* (1958) and *The Lion and the Jewel* (1959). He worked at the Royal Court Theater, London, then returned to Nigeria to teach drama and literature alongside writing. Soyinka was an outspoken critic of abuses of power, and was imprisoned for two years during the Nigerian Civil War (1967–1970). He fled Nigeria for the United States in 1994 and had a death sentence proclaimed against him while in exile.

438 RELIGIOUS LEADER

DALAI LAMA

Taktser, Amdo, Tibet
1935–

Tenzin Gyatso, the fourteenth Dalai Lama, became a globally renowned figure as spiritual leader of Tibetan Buddhists, living in exile at Dharamshala, India, following the annexation of Tibet by China. He is known for promoting compassion and nonviolence, and communicating Buddhist values. Tibetan Buddhists believe he is the latest in a line of teachers who are incarnations of Avalokiteshvara, *bodhisattva* of compassion. He was awarded the Nobel Peace Prize in 1989.

ABOVE: The Nobel committee praised Soyinka as a writer "who in a wide cultural perspective and with poetic overtones fashions the drama of existence."

ABOVE: The Dalai Lama is often pictured laughing. He has written that while living in exile is difficult, he tries to maintain a happy state of mind.

439 ENTERTAINER

ELVIS PRESLEY

Tupelo, Mississippi
1935–1977

The rock 'n' roll pioneer they called "The King" burst onto the scene in the mid-1950s with a sexually suggestive performance style that earned him the nickname "Elvis the Pelvis" and a string of number-one hits, including "Heartbreak Hotel," "Hound Dog," and "Love Me Tender" (all 1956). He would go on to sell more than 500 million records worldwide—and become among the best-selling solo music artists of all time. After being drafted into the U.S. Army in 1958, in the 1960s he made Hollywood movies and released soundtrack albums before returning to performance with a television comeback in 1968, several tours, and a 636-show Las Vegas residency from July 1969 to his death in 1977. By now he was a reduced figure, as a diet of fast food and addiction to prescription drugs took their toll. But his sudden death of a heart attack aged forty-two shocked the world—some fans refused to accept it, reporting sightings of Presley for years afterward.

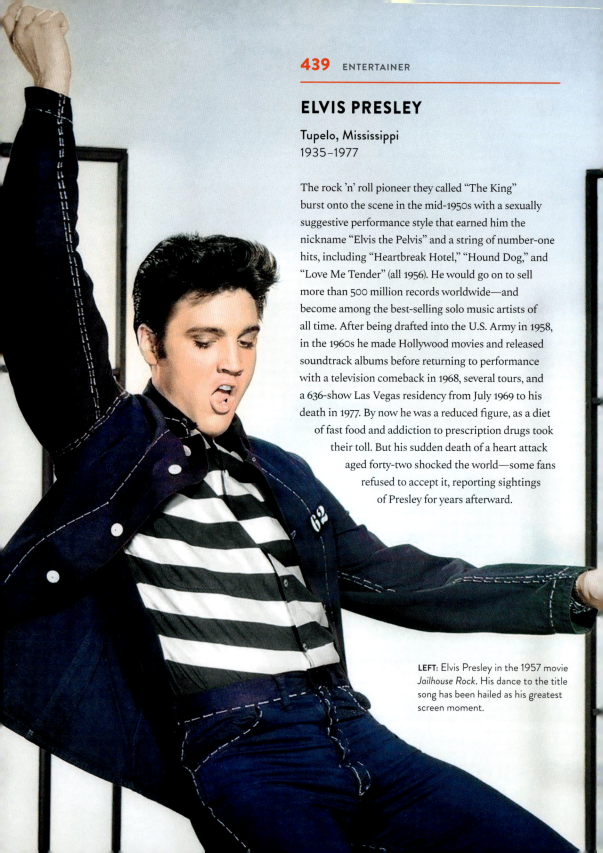

LEFT: Elvis Presley in the 1957 movie *Jailhouse Rock*. His dance to the title song has been hailed as his greatest screen moment.

440 ACTIVIST

EDDIE MABO

Murray Island, Queensland, Australia
1936–1992

Eddie Koiki Mabo was an Indigenous land-rights campaigner who won a landmark ruling in the High Court of Australia in 1992 that led to the establishment of native title in Australia—the rights of Indigenous Australians to land. Mabo brought the High Court case in 1982 after discovering that his family did not legally own the land on Mer (Murray) Island in the Torres Strait, where they had lived for generations. He died on January 21, 1992, less than six months before the judgment was delivered on June 3—now celebrated as "Mabo Day."

441 RELIGIOUS LEADER

POPE FRANCIS

Buenos Aires, Argentina
1936–

Argentinian cardinal Jorge Maria Bergoglio became the first Jesuit pope, the first Latin American pope, and the first pope from the Southern Hemisphere when he was elected leader of the Roman Catholic Church aged seventy-six in 2013. He chose the name Francis in honor of St. Francis of Assisi, "the man who gives us the spirit of peace, the poor man."

BELOW: Pope Francis among admirers. His papacy has focused on mercy, and he has committed the Church to working to end the death penalty worldwide.

442 MILITARY LEADER

OLESEGUN OBASANGO

Abeokuta, Nigeria
1937–

Olesegun Obasango was Nigeria's military ruler from 1976 to 1979, and civilian president from 1999 to 2007. He came to power when Brigadier General Murtala Ramat Mohammed was assassinated in 1976, and handed power to a civilian government in 1979—the first military ruler in Africa to do this. Obasango was jailed in 1995 by General Sani Abacha, but was released in 1998 in time to run for and win the country's presidency in 1999.

443 POLITICAL LEADER

COLIN POWELL

Harlem, New York
1937–2021

Colin Powell was the first African American to be chairman of the Joint Chiefs of Staff (1989–1993) and Secretary of State (2001–2005). In 1989 he oversaw the invasion of Panama and, from 1990 to 1991, Operation Desert Shield and Operation Desert Storm in the Persian Gulf War. His 2003 speech to the United Nations Security Council on the rationale for the Iraq War was later shown to contain inaccuracies. The son of Jamaican immigrants, he served in Vietnam and was the U.S. national security advisor under President Ronald Reagan.

444 POLITICAL LEADER

KOFI ANNAN

Kumasi, Gold Coast (now Ghana)
1938–2018

Secretary-General of the United Nations from 1997 to 2006, Ghanaian diplomat Kofi Annan—together with the UN—won the Nobel Peace Prize in 2001. As Secretary-General he worked to relieve HIV/AIDS, especially in Africa, and established the UN Global Compact, a nonbinding pact to persuade businesses to adopt socially responsible, sustainable policies. After his time at the UN, he founded the Kofi Annan Foundation to promote international development.

ABOVE: Annan, seen here visiting Syrian refugee camps in Turkey in 2012, was UN-Arab League Special Representative to Syria.

POLITICAL LEADER

ELLEN JOHNSON SIRLEAF

Monrovia, Liberia
1938–

This Liberian president was the first woman elected to lead an African country.

Ellen Johnson Sirleaf was president of Liberia from 2006 to 2018. She worked in the finance ministry under President William Tolbert and military dictator Samuel K. Doe, but then was arrested and jailed for criticizing the government. She was released and went into exile for twelve years, then returned and defeated soccer player George Weah to become president in 2005. She managed to get Liberia's debt canceled, brought in foreign investment, and established a Truth and Reconciliation Commission to heal wounds after years of civil war. She was reelected in 2011. The same year she received the 2011 Nobel Peace Prize for work promoting women's rights, with fellow Liberian activist Leymah Gbowee and Yemeni campaigner Tawakkul Karman.

"Once the glass ceiling has been broken, it can never be put back together, however one would try to do that."

Ellen Johnson Sirleaf, "How women will lead us to freedom, justice and peace," TED Talk, June 2020

BELOW: Johnson Sirleaf was a trailblazer for women in African politics. In 2021 she urged girls and women everywhere, "find your voice."

446 ACTIVIST

WANGARI MAATHAI

Ihithe village, Nyeri district, Kenya
1940–2011

Activist who fought deforestation with an environmental NGO.

Wangari Maathai established the Green Belt Movement, a grassroots organization focused on forest conservation and women's rights, in 1977. In 2004 she became the first Black African woman to be awarded the Nobel Peace Prize. She studied in the United States under the Kennedy Airlift, a program started in 1959 to give Kenyans educational opportunities in the United States, then took a PhD at the University College of Nairobi, the first woman in East or Central Africa to receive a doctorate. Maathai was elected to the Kenyan parliament in 2002, and in 2003 was made Assistant Minister of Environment, Natural Resources and Wildlife. Her organization brought about the planting of 30 million trees in Kenya. On her death, UN Secretary-General Ban Ki-moon said she was "a pioneer in articulating the links between human rights, poverty, environmental protection, and security." Maathai herself made a connection between environmental damage and deprivation: "The more you degrade the environment the more you dig deeper into poverty." But she also linked a positive response and social change, saying, "The tree became a symbol for the democratic struggle in Kenya."

> "When we plant trees, we plant the seeds of peace and hope."
>
> Wangari Maathai

ABOVE: Maathai's connection of the environment, women's rights, and internationalism led the Nobel Committee to say, "She thinks globally but acts locally."

KNOWN FOR
- Founding the Green Belt Movement
- Being the first African woman to win the Nobel Peace Prize

447 ACTIVIST

MUHAMMAD YUNUS

Chittagong, East Bengal (now Bangladesh)
1940–

In 1976, academic and social entrepreneur Muhammad Yunus founded the Grameen Bank microfinance organization/community development bank. The institution makes small loans without requiring collateral, to enable people too poor to acquire ordinary bank loans to borrow money and become small-scale entrepreneurs. Yunus was awarded the Nobel Peace Prize for the work in 2006.

448 ENTERTAINER

JOHN LENNON

Liverpool, England
1940–1980

John Lennon was a founding member of iconic British rock band the Beatles, who led the "British invasion" of the U.S. music and cultural scene in the 1960s. He was often provocatively outspoken, saying in 1966 about the Beatles, "We're more popular than Jesus now." He shared writing credits with Paul McCartney on almost 200 Beatles songs, and alongside his wife, Japanese-American artist Yoko Ono, was a major figure of the counterculture and prominent critic of the war in Vietnam. After the band split in 1970, he recorded his most famous solo song, "Imagine," in 1971. In 1980 he was murdered in New York City.

BELOW: Lennon and Yoko Ono promoted peace. In 1969 they erected huge posters declaring "WAR IS OVER IF YOU WANT IT" in twelve cities.

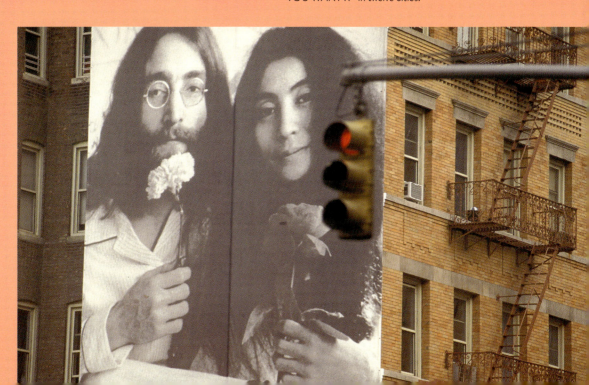

449 ATHLETE

MUHAMMAD ALI

Louisville, Kentucky
1942–2016

A sporting icon and outspoken activist.

American boxer Muhammad Ali was one of the most charismatic sporting figures of the twentieth century, famous for his poetic trash-talking, with his claims that he could "float like a butterfly and sting like a bee" and that he was "the Greatest." He was the first to win the world heavyweight championship three separate times. Born Cassius Clay, he won a gold medal in the 1960 Rome Olympics as a light heavyweight and, after turning professional, defeated Sonny Liston in 1964 to become world heavyweight champion. By this time he had become a Muslim, and renounced his birth name as a "slave name," changing it to Muhammad Ali. He was stripped of his titles after refusing to be drafted into the U.S. Army in 1967 because of his opposition to the Vietnam War, but he returned in triumph to boxing. His iconic fights included his 1974 knockout victory over George Foreman in Zaire, and his 1975 victory over Joe Frazier in the Philippines. After retiring in 1981, Ali devoted his time to political activism and philanthropy, and in 1984 announced that he had been diagnosed with Parkinson's syndrome, attributed by some to head injuries he received as a boxer.

RIGHT: On May 25, 1965, Cassius Clay—in his first fight as Mohammad Ali—defeated Sonny Liston. He knocked him down during the first round of their match and so retained his title as heavyweight champion.

KNOWN FOR

- Being the first boxer to win the world heavyweight title three separate times
- Declaring himself a conscientious objector and refusing to serve in the US Army in the Vietnam War
- Anti-Vietnam War and Black Power campaigner

450 ARTIST

ISABEL ALLENDE

Lima, Peru
1942–

Isabel Allende scored a major hit with her first novel, *The House of the Spirits* (1982), which was named Book of the Year in Chile and has been translated into more than twenty languages. A writer in the magical realism genre, she has published more than twenty novels, with worldwide sales of over 77 million books. Born to Chilean parents in Peru, Allende was a journalist in Chile but fled after her father's cousin, President Salvador Allende, was assassinated in 1973. Since the late 1980s she has lived in the United States, and she was awarded the Presidential Medal of Freedom in 2015.

BELOW: Before turning to novel writing, Allende cofounded the feminist magazine *Paula* in 1967 and wrote the column "Civilize Your Troglodyte."

451 SCIENTIST

STEPHEN HAWKING

Oxford, England
1942–2018

British theoretical physicist Stephen Hawking achieved fame as author of the popular science bestseller *A Brief History of Time* (1988). From the age of twenty-one he lived with amyotrophic lateral sclerosis (ALS), also known as Lou Gehrig's disease, which gradually paralyzed him and, after losing his power of speech, he communicated through a speech-generating mechanism from his wheelchair. Hawking was an expert on black holes and predicted that they emit radiation—an initially controversial position that eventually became widely accepted, and the emissions were called "Hawking radiation."

ABOVE: Hawking was Lucasian Professor of Mathematics at the University of Cambridge from 1978 to 2009.

452 ACTIVIST

CHICO MENDES

Xapuri, State of Acre, Brazil
1944–1988

Rubber tapper, environmental activist, and trade union leader Chico Mendes worked tirelessly to defend the Amazon rainforest and the rights of its Indigenous peoples, but was murdered by ranchers in 1988. He began work as a rubber tapper aged nine alongside his father. Initially denied an education, he was taught to read by activist rubber tapper Euclides Fernando Tavora, and then became a literacy teacher and union organizer himself. In 1987 Mendes was awarded the Global 500 Award of the United Nations Environment program for his environmental activism.

ABOVE: Mendes's urgent message lives on. The Chico Mendes Institute for Biodiversity Conservation was established in 2007.

453 ARTIST

BOB MARLEY

Nine Miles, St. Ann, Jamaica
1945–1981

Reggae pioneer Bob Marley became an international superstar in the 1970s, bringing Jamaican music and culture, and the Afrocentric Rastafari religious movement he followed to worldwide attention. He combined elements of reggae, ska, rocksteady, and rock music to create a global phenomenon. Marley's greatest hits album *Legend* (1984), released after his death aged thirty-six from skin cancer, is the best-selling reggae album of all time, and through his career and since he sold an estimated 75 million records.

ABOVE: Marley's first hit was "Simmer Down," with the Wailers in 1963. Later triumphs included "No Woman No Cry" and "Redemption Song."

454 POLITICAL LEADER

AUNG SAN SUU KYI

Rangoon, Burma (now Yangon, Myanmar)
1945–

As leader of a nonviolent campaign against Myanmar's military rulers, Aung San Suu Kyi was held under house arrest for fifteen of the years between 1989 and 2010, and became a globally known political prisoner. She was released and won a seat in the national legislature in 2012 and then, in 2016, became effective head of state. She and the country faced international outrage at the apparent genocide of the Rohingya people in Rakhine State, Myanmar. After a coup ushering in a return to military rule in 2021, she was sentenced to more than twenty-five years in jail.

ABOVE: The UN, United States, and most European states condemned Aung San Suu Kyi's arrest, trial, and imprisonment. In late 2023 she was reportedly ill in captivity.

455 ACTIVIST

STEVE BIKO

King William's Town, South Africa
1946–1977

Victim of police violence who became an icon of Black struggle.

ABOVE: As a young man Biko studied at the University of Natal Medical School and cofounded and became first president of the Black South African Students' Organization (SASO).

Activist Steve Biko became an internationally revered icon of the Black struggle in apartheid South Africa when he died in police custody in 1977. Biko, a founder of the grassroots anti-apartheid Black Consciousness Movement, was arrested and incarcerated in Port Elizabeth on August 18, 1977, and turned up naked in Pretoria more than three weeks later on September 11. He died the following day of a brain hemorrhage. The police at first denied responsibility but, in 1997, five former policemen confessed to the Truth and Reconciliation Commission that they had killed him. The policemen applied without success for amnesty. Biko was celebrated in the 1977 book *Biko* by his friend, South African journalist Donald Woods, and in the celebrated 1980 anti-apartheid protest song "Biko" by rock star Peter Gabriel, as well as in the movie *Cry Freedom* (1987). Biko took up and popularized the American consciousness-raising slogan "Black is beautiful" and, in 1972, was behind the founding of the Black People's Convention to promote Black consciousness.

KNOWN FOR
- Being an icon of anti-apartheid struggle
- Promoting the Black Consciousness Movement

456 POLITICAL LEADER

DONALD TRUMP

Queens, New York
1946–

Donald Trump was a businessman and TV star before becoming the forty-fifth U.S. president (2017–2021). He was the first former president to be charged with a crime when he was indicted in New York on March 30, 2023, on state criminal charges relating to hush money paid to a former adult film star, and in June that year the first to be charged with a federal crime when he was indicted in Miami on charges relating to mishandling of classified documents. In August 2023 he was further indicted on charges related to efforts to overturn the result of the 2020 U.S. presidential election. None of these events appeared to dent his popularity among his supporters.

457 POLITICAL LEADER

GEORGE W. BUSH

New Haven, Connecticut
1946–

President George W. Bush (2001–2009) led the United States into the 2003 Iraq War in the wake of the terror attacks in New York City and Washington, D.C., on September 11, 2001. The eldest son of the forty-first U.S. president, George H. W. Bush (1989–1993), he was a businessman and governor of Texas (1995–2000) before becoming the forty-third president.

ABOVE: Bush's narrow victory over Al Gore in the 2000 presidential election was one of the closest in U.S. history.

458 ARTIST

STEVEN SPIELBERG

Cincinnati, Ohio
1946–

This "New Hollywood" director has a golden touch at the box office.

King of the blockbuster, Steven Spielberg made three iconic films—*Jaws* (1975), *E.T. the Extra-Terrestrial* (1982), and *Jurassic Park* (1993)—that were the highest-grossing films of all time on their release. A member of the "New Hollywood" generation that revitalized the U.S. movie industry in the 1960s to 1980s, and the most commercially successful movie director in history, Spielberg also made the acclaimed World War II Holocaust picture *Schindler's List* (1993), the celebrated five-film *Indiana Jones* series starring Harrison Ford as an intrepid archaeology professor (1981–2023), the alien-encounter picture *Close Encounters of the Third Kind* (1977), *The Color Purple* (1985), based on the novel by Alice Walker, and the highly praised semi-autobiographical picture *The Fablemans* (2022). During the 1990s he won three Academy Awards—Best Director and Best Picture for *Schindler's List,* and Best Director for the World War II epic *Saving Private Ryan* (1998).

> *"Steven's films are marked most importantly by a faith in our common humanity."*
>
> U.S. president Barack Obama on presenting Steven Spielberg with the Presidential Medal of Freedom, November 24, 2015

RIGHT: The director on set during filming of *Indiana Jones and the Last Crusade.* The highest-grossing film of 1989, the picture earned $474 million worldwide.

SALMAN RUSHDIE

Bombay (now Mumbai), India
1947–

Author of *The Satanic Verses* who faces death threats and violence.

Indian-born novelist Salman Rushdie was forced to go into hiding following the 1988 publication of his novel *The Satanic Verses*. The novel, which features a character based on the Prophet Muhammad and plot elements connected to his transcribing of the Quran, outraged some Muslims and, on February 14, 1989, he was condemned in a *fatwa* (legal opinion) by Iranian supreme leader Ayatollah Ruhollah Khomeini—a financial reward of $3 million was offered for Rushdie's execution. The author took refuge in protection by the British police. Although he gradually began to live a more normal life, the threat never entirely subsided and on August 12, 2022, he was stabbed on stage when he was due to deliver a lecture in Chautauqua, New York, and subsequently lost an eye. Rushdie was born in Bombay and educated in England. His first novel *Grimus* (1975) was followed by a major success with *Midnight's Children* (1981). Other novels include *Shame* (1983), *Quichotte* (2019), and *Victory City* (2023). He has also published a memoir, *Joseph Anton* (2012), so named from an alias he assumed when in hiding.

BELOW: Rushdie announced in June 2023 that he was writing a novel about the 2022 knife attack in New York that took his eye, saying, "It's something I need to get past in order to do anything else."

460 POLITICAL LEADER

MOHAMMED AL BIN MAKTOUM

Dubai, United Arab Emirates
1949–

Sheikh Mohammed ibn Rashid Al Maktoum, emir of Dubai and minister of defense, prime minister, and vice president of the United Arab Emirates since 2006, has overseen the growth of Dubai and the establishment of government-owned enterprises such as the Emirates airline and the construction of the Burj Khalifa, the world's tallest building.

461 POLITICAL LEADER

NARENDRA MODI

Vadnagar, India
1950–

Charismatic right-wing populist Indian politician Narendra Modi is leader of the pro-Hindu Bharatiya Janata Party (BJP), and has been prime minister of India since 2014. His administration took measures promoting Hindu culture and reforming the economy, seeking to improve transportation infrastructure and boost direct foreign investment in India. The revoking of Jammu and Kashmir's special status in 2019—bringing it under direct government control—was controversial, and agricultural reforms introduced in 2020 sparked mass protests; the reforms were repealed in 2021.

RIGHT: Modi is far more popular than his BJP party. He has an approval rating of 77 percent and is the most popular elected leader in the world.

SYLVIA RIVERA

Bronx, New York
1951–2002

Activist who campaigned on New York streets for the rights of drag queens and transgender people.

Latina drag queen/transgender woman Sylvia Rivera cofounded the Street Transvestite Action Revolutionaries group (STAR) to help homeless teenage drag queens, gay people, and transgender women, and campaigned for many years for transgender rights. A trans woman, Sylvia was originally named Ray Rivera. Born to a Venezuelan mother who took her own life when Rivera was just three years old, she was raised by her grandmother and ran away from home aged eleven, working as a child prostitute. When she met Marsha P. Johnson on the streets of New

> "Sylvia was the Rosa Parks of the modern transgender movement."
>
> Riki Wilchins, gender activist, writing in the *Village Voice* on Sylvia Rivera's death, 2002

York, they both identified as drag queens. Rivera may have taken part in the Stonewall riots of June 28, 1969, a confrontation between gay rights activists and police outside the Stonewall Inn, a bar in Greenwich Village. Rivera joined the Gay Liberation Front, but, like many people of color and transgender individuals, had to fight for acceptance among gay-rights campaigners. She and Johnson founded the STAR group in 1970, but Rivera withdrew from activism in 1973 after being booed when making a speech at a gay rights rally. Twenty years later Rivera was honored at a celebration to mark the twenty-fifth anniversary of the Stonewall riots. In 2001 she resurrected STAR, replacing the word "Transvestite" with "Transgender." The Sylvia Rivera Law Project was established in 2002 to meet the legal needs of transgender, gender-fluid, and gay individuals.

LEFT: Rivera (right) talks to fellow activists in New York City in 2002. In an essay that year she wrote, "I don't even like the label *transgender*. I'm tired of living with labels. I just want to be who I am. I am Sylvia Rivera."

KNOWN FOR
- Being a drag queen and prominent transgender activist
- Establishing the refuge STAR House in 1970–1971; it later inspired refuges such as Transy House in Brooklyn

463 POLITICAL LEADER

CYRIL RAMAPHOSA

Johannesberg, South Africa
1952–

Activist and politician Cyril Ramaphosa was the African National Congress (ANC) chief negotiator in the 1990s talks to end apartheid in South Africa. He was deputy president of the country under Jacob Zuma from 2014 to 2018, became president of the ANC in 2017, and president of South Africa in 2018.

ABOVE: Ramaphosa was chairperson of the African Union from 2020 to 2021.

POLITICAL LEADER

VLADIMIR PUTIN

Leningrad, Soviet Union (now St. Petersburg, Russia)
1952–

Russian president who continues to defy the West in Crimea, Syria, and Ukraine.

Politician and onetime intelligence officer, Vladimir Putin was president of Russia from 1999 to 2008, and 2012 onward. Imposing authoritarian rule, he made a series of moves that drew strong international condemnation—annexing Crimea in 2014, intervening in Syria in support of the regime of Bashar al-Assad and, in February 2022, invading Ukraine. In March 2023 the International Criminal Court issued a warrant for his arrest for war crimes over alleged abductions of children during the Ukraine war. Putin was a KGB intelligence officer before entering politics in 1991. He served under Boris Yeltsin (president of Russia 1991–1999), then was briefly prime minister before becoming acting president when Yeltsin resigned. He was elected president in 2000, reelected in 2004, then—subject to a two-term limit—became prime minister under President Dmitry Medvedev until 2012. He stood again as president in 2012 and was reelected in 2018; in 2021, amendments to the constitution established that he could be reelected twice more, potentially keeping him in power until 2036.

> "There is no such thing as a former KGB man."
>
> Vladimir Putin in response to prime minister Sergei Stepashin calling himself a former KGB officer, 2000

RIGHT: Putin is the longest-serving Russian president. His rule has been characterized by corruption and authoritarian government, with the brutal repression of his opponents.

465 ATHLETE/POLITICAL LEADER

IMRAN KHAN

Lahore, Pakistan
1952–

After leading the Pakistan cricket team in its victory in the 1992 Cricket World Cup in Australia and New Zealand—a triumphant end to a twenty-one-year top-flight cricket career—Imran Khan entered national politics as a populist critic of corruption and inequality. He founded his own political party, Pakistan Tehreek-e-Insaf (Pakistan Justice Movement), in 1996, and served as prime minster of Pakistan from 2018 to 2022. He was forced to stand down after losing a vote of no confidence on April 10, 2022. He was arrested and, in August 2023, convicted of corruption and sentenced to three years in jail, but the same month he was granted a retrial.

ABOVE: In his cricket years, Khan was a playboy and sex symbol. As a politician he has been criticized for lack of consistency and for being too willing to align with conservative religious elements.

466 MILITARY LEADER

AHMAD SHAH MASSOUD

Bazarak, Panjshir, Afghanistan
1953–2001

Ahmad Shah Massoud was a guerrilla commander during the Soviet occupation of Afghanistan from 1979 to 1989. With the establishment of the Islamic State of Afghanistan in 1992, he was minister of defense and commander of government military activities against militias and warlords. Following the rise of the Islamic fundamentalist Taliban in 1996, he became an armed opposition leader and was forced into exile. In 2001 he urged European leaders to put pressure on Pakistan on account of its support for the Taliban. He was assassinated on September 9, 2001, in a suicide bombing ordered by al-Qaeda leader Osama bin Laden.

467 POLITICAL LEADER

TONY BLAIR

Edinburgh, Scotland
1953–

Leader who inspired "New Labour."

Tony Blair oversaw the repackaging of the UK Labour Party as "New Labour" and, in 1997, led it to its largest general election victory in history, delivering a 179-seat majority in the House of Commons. At forty-three, Blair was the youngest prime minister since Robert Jenkinson in 1812. He went on to be the second longest-serving in modern history after Margaret Thatcher, and won three successive general elections in 1997, 2001, and 2005. The Good Friday (Belfast) Agreement of April 10, 1998, in the Northern Ireland peace process, was a major achievement, but the decision to back U.S. foreign policy in Afghanistan, and the 2003 invasion of Iraq, provoked fierce opposition.

ABOVE: Blair, seen here with ally Gordon Brown in 1990, became an MP in 1983. He stood down and was succeeded by Brown as prime minister in 2007.

468 POLITICAL LEADER

XI JINPING

Fuping county, Shaanxi province, China
1953–

Chinese leader Xi Jinping, in power from 2012, pursued authoritarian policies, with rises in surveillance and censorship, an anti-corruption campaign, the introduction of a cult of personality, and removal of term limits for his presidency. His foreign policy was increasingly hard-line, notably over the status of Taiwan and in relations with the United States, and he sought to boost Chinese influence in Africa and Eurasia through the Belt and Road Initiative infrastructure development project. The internment of Uyghur Muslims in Xinjiang—officially vocational educational and training centers—provoked international protest.

469 POLITICAL LEADER

SHINZO ABE

Tokyo, Japan
1954–2022

Politician who was the longest-serving prime minister in Japanese history.

Shinzo Abe was prime minister of Japan as president of the Liberal Democratic Party (LDP) from 2006 to 2007 and 2012 to 2020, a total of close to nine years. The grandson of Nobosuke Kishi, Japan's prime minister from 1957 to 1960, and son of Shintaro Abe, Japan's foreign minister from 1982 to 1986, Abe studied at Seikei University in Tokyo, and the University of Southern California in Los Angeles, before entering politics in 1993. He was chief cabinet secretary in 2005 for prime minister Junichiro Koizumi, whom he replaced the following year. However, he resigned after a year for health reasons and because the LDP lost control in elections on July 29, 2007. He returned in 2012 as the LDP won a landslide victory, and won further elections in 2014 and 2017. A conservative and nationalist, his economic policies—dubbed "Abenomics"—set out to sweep away stagnation in the Japanese economy through measures such as government spending on public works and boosting the money supply. He stood down for health reasons in 2020 and was replaced as prime minister by Yoshihide Suga on September 14, 2020. Then, on July 8, 2022, he was assassinated while campaigning by a man with a homemade gun reputedly angry at Abe's alleged links to a religious group.

ABOVE RIGHT: Politics was in Abe's blood. Both his grandfather and great-uncle served as prime minister.

KNOWN FOR
- Being the longest-serving Japanese prime minister
- Developing "Abenomics"—economic policies to revitalize the Japanese economy
- Being the youngest Japanese prime minister since World War II; he was fifty-two when elected

470 ARTIST

ANG LEE

Ping-t'ung County, Taiwan
1954–

Taiwanese film director Ang Lee was the first non-white film director to win the Best Director Academy Award, in 2006 for *Brokeback Mountain*. In 2013 he won a second award for *Life of Pi*, and earlier took Best Foreign Language Film in 2001 for *Crouching Tiger, Hidden Dragon*. Lee studied in Taiwan as well as at the University of Illinois, and at New York University, where he was a classmate of American director Spike Lee.

471 ENTERTAINER

OPRAH WINFREY

Kosciusko, Mississippi
1954–

African American television star, producer, and media proprietor Oprah Winfrey made her name with her talk show *The Oprah Winfrey Show*, which ran for twenty-five years (1986–2011) and was celebrated for its focus on self-help, spirituality, and literature. In 2008 she created her own cable channel, the Oprah Winfrey Network (OWN), which focuses on entertainment and lifestyle programming.

BELOW: Oprah is recognized as a powerful force in politics. Her endorsement of Barack Obama in the 2008 Democratic primaries was judged to be worth at least 1 million votes.

472 SCIENTIST

TIM BERNERS-LEE

London, England
1955–

Computer scientist Berners-Lee invented the World Wide Web and reshaped the way we connect with each other.

Tim Berners-Lee was working at the European Organization for Nuclear Research (CERN) in Geneva when he developed the World Wide Web in 1989. In a previous spell at CERN, in 1980, he had invented an early version of hypertext—a program he called "Enquire"—that used links within and between computer files. He then worked at a British company designing software before returning to CERN to work on its computer network, which enabled researchers to access and communicate between machines on the internet. In 1990–1991 Berners-Lee developed the software for a system using hypertext that enabled researchers to place information centrally on a web server and access it from any of a network of machines, each of which had a web client program or browser. He was familiar with computers as a child—his mathematician parents worked on the Ferranti Mark I, an early commercial computer.

> *"The Web was not a physical 'thing' that existed in a certain 'place.' It was a 'space' in which information could exist."*
> Tim Berners-Lee

RIGHT: The 2016 Turing Award that celebrates contributions to computer science honored Berners-Lee "for inventing the world wide web, the first web browser, and the fundamental protocols and algorithms allowing the web to scale."

473 INDUSTRIALIST

STEVE JOBS

San Francisco, California
1955–2011

This entrepreneur made computers user-friendly.

With an easy-to-use computer interface, iPod music players, MacBook laptops, iPhones, and iPads, computing pioneer and founder of Apple Steve Jobs transformed people's relationship with technology. Jobs briefly studied at Reed College in Portland, Oregon, traveled through India—becoming a Buddhist—and worked at Atari, the electronic games outfit, before cofounding Apple in 1976 with his business partner, Steve Wozniak. They released the Apple I and Apple II personal computers and then, in 1984, the Macintosh, the first mass-produced computer with a graphical user interface. Jobs left Apple in 1985, driven out in a power struggle, founded the NeXT computer company, and was behind the creation of Pixar, which produced the first 3D computer-animated feature, *Toy Story,* in 1995—and became hugely successful. He returned to Apple in 1997 and released the iMac in 1998, the iPod in 2001, the iTunes music store in 2003, the MacBook in 2006, the iPhone in 2007, the MacBook Air in 2008, and the iPad in 2010. Diagnosed with a pancreatic neuroendocrine tumor, he stepped down as Apple CEO in August 2011 and died on October 5 that year.

KNOWN FOR

- Launching the first computer to work straight from the box—the Apple II, in 1977
- As Apple CEO, focusing on product design and marketing
- Performing tests on all Apple products himself

ABOVE LEFT: Jobs focused on simplicity. "Simple can be harder than complex," he said. "You have to work hard to get your thinking clean."

474 INDUSTRIALIST

BILL GATES

Seattle, Washington
1955–

University dropout who led the personal computer revolution.

Bill Gates left Harvard University without graduating to cofound computer software company Microsoft with his friend Paul Allen on April 4, 1975. Operations took off in 1981 when they licensed their MS-DOS operating system to IBM to use in its newly developed personal computer. In 1985 Microsoft released the first iteration of its Windows operating system, which provided a graphical user interface for MS-DOS. Gates became a billionaire in 1986 and, in 1999 with his wife Melinda, founded the Bill and Melinda Gates Foundation to combat extreme poverty and advance health care globally. Gates remained chairman of Microsoft until 2014, and in 2020 left the organization to focus entirely on charitable work.

475 POLITICAL LEADER

PAUL KAGAME

Tambwe, Gitarama Province, Ruanda-Urundi (now Nyarutovu, Rwanda)
1957–

Paul Kagame was a commander in the Rwandan Patriotic Front, an armed group that defeated Hutu forces to end the 1994 Rwandan genocide in which 800,000 were killed. He became vice president and minister of defense under the new Rwandan government and, in 2000, was elected president. He has been praised for improving the economy and social conditions but criticized for suppression of opposition, interfering by sending Rwandan troops to fight in the civil war in the neighboring Democratic Republic of the Congo, and changing the constitution to allow him to carry on as president—potentially until 2034.

"I've been very lucky, and therefore I owe it to try and reduce the inequity in the world."

Bill Gates, in an interview for *Rolling Stone*, 2014

LEFT: Gates and fellow billionaire Warren Buffett founded the Giving Pledge in 2010, under which the super-rich promise to give at least half their wealth to philanthropic causes.

476 POLITICAL LEADER

OSAMA BIN LADEN

Riyadh, Saudi Arabia
1957–2011

The founder of al-Qaeda who plotted the 9/11 attacks against the United States.

From a base in Afghanistan, Osama bin Laden declared an Islamic holy war on the United States in 1996, and masterminded the terror attacks on New York and Washington, D.C. on September 11, 2001. In response, President George W. Bush unleashed "the War on Terror," and the United States invaded Afghanistan. Bin Laden was one of more than fifty children of a Saudi Arabian millionaire, Mohammed bin Laden, founder of a construction group. He studied in Jeddah, Saudi Arabia, then traveled to Pakistan and joined the Islamist rebel *mujahideen* in their fight against the Soviet Union in Afghanistan. With the militant Abdullah Azzam, he formed al-Qaeda (which means "the Base") in 1988, and the organization was used to train militants and plan attacks—including in 1998 the simultaneous bombing of the U.S. embassies in Nairobi, Kenya, and Dar es Salaam, Tanzania, that killed 224. An attack in 2000 on the USS *Cole*, which was docked in Aden, Yemen, killed seventeen. After the 1998 attacks, he was on the FBI's Ten Most Wanted Fugitives list and, in the wake of 9/11, the agency offered a $25 million bounty. U.S. special operations forces killed him at his compound in Abbottabad, Pakistan, on May 2, 2011.

ABOVE: Many in the Islamic world viewed bin Laden as a hero for taking on Western imperialism.

477 ENTERTAINER

MICHAEL JACKSON

Gary, Indiana
1958–2009

"I am the one"—this pop genius "moonwalked" to fame.

Michael Jackson first came to fame as the youngest of the Jackson 5—a group of singing brothers signed to Motown Records in 1969. His debut solo album, *Off the Wall* (1979), sold 20 million copies, followed by *Thriller* (1982), which sold 40 million. He first performed the "moonwalk" dance he made a trademark on a live performance of "Billie Jean," on a Motown television special. *Bad*, the follow-up album to *Thriller*, was released in 1987, and five of its singles became U.S. number ones. An eccentric lifestyle and accusations of child molestation dented his image in the 1990s and 2000s, leading to financial troubles. He married twice, once to Elvis Presley's daughter, Lisa Marie Presley, in 1994. He was preparing for a comeback tour when he died suddenly of cardiac arrest.

> "People ask me how I make music. I tell them I just step into it. It's like stepping into a river and joining the flow. Every moment in the river has its song. So I stay in the moment and listen."
>
> Michael Jackson, *Dancing the Dream*, 1992

RIGHT: Jackson brought joy to millions, but at a cost. Driven hard in the Jackson 5 by his father Joe, he later said "my childhood was taken away from me."

478 ACTIVIST

WINONA LaDUKE

Los Angeles, California
1959–

Native American environmentalist Winona LaDuke helped create the Indigenous Women's Network in 1985, and cofounded the environmentalist group Honor the Earth in 1993. The daughter of a Jewish mother and a Native American father of the Ojibwe people, she grew up mostly in Oregon, but settled on the Ojibwe White Earth Reservation in Minnesota in 1982. She founded the White Earth Land Recovery Project in 1989 to try to repurchase reservation land bought by non-Native Americans. LaDuke was Ralph Nader's running mate when he ran for president in the elections of 1996 and 2000 as the Green Party candidate.

ABOVE: LaDuke campaigned against a new section of Canadian multinational Enbridge's Line 3 oil pipeline in 2020–2021.

479 POLITICAL LEADER

BARACK OBAMA

Honolulu, Hawaii
1961–

Obama was the first African American U.S. president.

Campaigning for the presidency in 2008, Barack Obama promoted "Change we can believe in" in conjunction with the slogan "Yes, we can!" A superb orator, in his speeches he declared, "Yes we can . . . to opportunity and prosperity . . . yes we can . . . heal this nation . . . we can . . . repair this world." Obama's campaign ended with a historic moment of change, with his victory over John McCain delivering the first African American president in the White House. Obama was president from 2009 to 2017, winning reelection for a second term in 2012. Born the son of an American mother and a Kenyan father in Hawaii, he taught at the University of Chicago Law School from 1992 to 2004, then became U.S. senator for Illinois from 2005 to 2008. As president, he implemented an economic stimulus package, and reformed financial regulation and health care—issuing the controversial Affordable Care Act of 2010 that became known as "Obamacare." He oversaw the withdrawal of U.S. troops from Iraq in 2011, ordered the raid that found and killed Osama bin Laden, signed the 2015 Paris climate agreement, and normalized relations with Cuba in 2015–2017—in 2016 becoming the first U.S. president to visit Cuba since 1928.

RIGHT: Pundits say Obama's skills as an inspirational speaker place him in the company of the greatest presidential orators—JFK and FDR.

DIANA, PRINCESS OF WALES

Sandringham, England
1961–1997

Princess whose short life and sudden death left a major legacy.

Diana, Princess of Wales, was the first wife of the then-heir to the British throne, Prince Charles, and mother of Princes William and Harry. The couple's difficult relationship, 1992 separation, and 1996 divorce, together with her glamorous life and much-admired activism, made her a major international figure. Her sudden death in a Paris car crash on August 31, 1997, stunned the world, and sparked an outpouring of grief in the UK. A member of the British nobility, she was educated in Kent and Switzerland, and worked as a nanny and nursery helper in London before she became engaged to Prince Charles on February 6, 1981.

They were married at St. Paul's Cathedral, London, on July 29 that year. Prince William was born on June 21, 1982, and Prince Harry on September 15, 1984. Diana's activism in support of people with AIDS, the Red Cross and its campaigns against land mines, terminal illness hospices, and refuges for women who had experienced domestic abuse were a major part of her legacy.

BELOW: Diana was just nineteen and Prince Charles thirty-one when they were married. He said, "Diana will certainly help to keep me young."

"She was the People's Princess… and that is how she will stay, how she will remain in our hearts and our memories forever."

British prime minister Tony Blair's tribute to Diana, 1997

ATHLETE

MICHAEL JORDAN

Brooklyn, New York
1963–

"Air Jordan" leapt to basketball glory.

Probably the greatest player in the history of basketball, Michael Jordan was nicknamed "Air Jordan" for his amazing leaping ability, and enormously boosted the popularity of the NBA around the world, becoming the first NBA player billionaire on the strength of his product endorsements. With Jordan in his prime, the Chicago Bulls won the NBA Finals six times in 1991 to 1993 and 1996 to 1998. At the collegiate level, he starred for the University of North Carolina before being drafted by the Bulls in 1984. And with him in dominant form, the U.S. basketball team won Olympic gold at the 1984 and 1992 Olympics. Jordan retired from basketball in October 1993 and played minor league baseball, then returned to lead the Bulls to three more NBA titles, in 1996–1998. He was named the NBA's Most Valuable Player five times, in 1988, 1991, 1992, 1996, and 1998.

RIGHT: Jordan playing for the Chicago Bulls during the 1996 NBA eastern conference final. Famous around the world, he starred as himself in the 1996 movie *Space Jam*.

JEFF BEZOS

Albuquerque, New Mexico
1964–

Entrepreneur who revolutionized shopping with the launch of Amazon.

E-commerce magnate Jeff Bezos founded Amazon in 1994 as an online bookstore, and the company expanded to become the world's largest online sales outfit. Bezos graduated from Princeton University in 1986, and worked on Wall Street from 1986 to 1994, rising to become senior vice president at investment bank D. E. Shaw & Co, before founding Amazon with his then-wife MacKenzie Scott on July 5, 1994, in a garage he had rented in Bellevue, Washington. Amazon's first book sales were in July 1995. He expanded into online sales of music CDs, videos, and other goods in 1998, launched cloud-computing service Amazon Web Services in 2006, and the Kindle reading device for electronic books in 2007. In 2010 Amazon Studios began making its own films and television shows. In 2013 Bezos purchased the *Washington Post* newspaper for $250 million. He also established the Blue Origin aerospace and suborbital spaceflight company in 2000, and it developed the New Shepard reusable suborbital launch vehicle, capable of carrying passengers and payload into orbit and then landing again; the first crewed test took place on July 20, 2021, with Bezos and his brother Mark on board.

LEFT: Bezos named his online bookstore Amazon after the Amazon River partly because, at the time, web searches were alphabetical, so a company beginning with A would appear more quickly.

KNOWN FOR

- Being the founder and CEO of Amazon, the world's largest e-commerce company
- Being the founder of Blue Origin aerospace/spaceflight company
- Owning the *Washington Post*

483 ENTREPRENEUR

JACK MA

Hangzou, Zhejiang province, China
1964–

Chinese entrepreneur Jack Ma founded the Alibaba Group of online businesses. Ma worked as a tourist guide, teacher, and for an IT outfit established by the Chinese government before founding Alibaba in 1999, initially offering business-to-business sales, then moving into online payments with Alipay, and a consumer-to-consumer marketplace (comparable to eBay) with Taobao, both in 2003. In 2014 Taobao added a search engine and online mall to its offerings. Ma established the philanthropic Jack Ma Foundation in 2014.

ABOVE: Ma won international recognition for his efforts to aid the fight against COVID-19. His philanthropy is focused on education, public health, and the environment.

484 ARTIST

J. K. ROWLING

Bristol, England
1965–

J. K. Rowling created the boy wizard Harry Potter and his friends Ron Weasley and Hermione Granger in a phenomenally successful series of books. Published from 1997 to 2007, the books describe their adventures at Hogwarts School of Witchcraft and Wizardry, and were made into an iconic and hugely successful film franchise from 2001 to 2011 starring Daniel Radcliffe, Rupert Grint, and Emma Watson. After studying at Exeter University, Rowling worked at Amnesty International and as a language teacher before settling in Edinburgh and writing the Harry Potter series.

485 POLITICAL LEADER

BASHAR AL-ASSAD

Damascus, Syria
1965–

Bashar al-Assad succeeded his father Hafez al-Assad as president of Syria in 2000, maintaining his authoritarian control and, in 2011, repressing a revolt that developed into a seemingly endless civil war that had killed around 600,000 people by May 2023. He studied medicine at Damascus University, and was a doctor in the Syrian army, before his older brother Bassel's 1994 death in a car accident elevated him to the position of his father's heir. The 2011 protests in Syria, which followed the pro-democracy movements in North Africa and the Middle East dubbed "the Arab Spring," were brutally repressed and quickly spiraled into a years-long conflict, with the government supported by Russia, Iran, and Lebanese Hezbollah militants, and the rebels backed at times by Saudia Arabia, Turkey, and a U.S.-led coalition. The Assad government attracted fierce international condemnation for its use of chemical weapons and barrel bombs, and his supposed election victories in 2000, 2007, 2014, and 2021 were regarded as shams.

486 POLITICAL LEADER

GEORGE WEAH

Monrovia, Liberia
1966–

This former soccer star became Liberian president.

George Weah had a stellar career as a professional soccer player, playing as a striker for major clubs including AC Milan, Paris St. Germain, Manchester City, and Chelsea, before entering politics. In four years at Milan, he helped the Italian team win the Serie A league title twice, while he also played for his country in the African Cup of Nations in 1996 and 2002, and was named African Footballer of the Year in 1989, 1994, and 1995. Turning to politics in 2005, Weah ran for president for the Congress for Democratic Change, and for vice president in 2011. He was elected to the Liberian Senate in 2014, and then in 2017 was elected president, defeating Joseph Boakai. As president, Weah reduced his own salary by 25 percent in the light of difficulties with the economy, made official visits to Senegal and France, and declared a national emergency, creating a task force backed with a substantial emergency fund to combat sexual violence in the country.

RIGHT: The former soccer player said, "My government will be open. Anyone found guilty of corruption will be dealt with . . . If you are corrupt you will have to hang your boots."

487 ENTREPRENEUR

JERRY YANG

Taipei, Taiwan
1968–

Taiwanese computer programmer/entrepreneur Jerry Yang was co-creator of Yahoo! Inc. Yang and David Filo were graduate students at Stanford University when they created an index of web pages, "Jerry and David's Guide to the World Wide Web," in 1994 and, after being renamed Yahoo! and incorporated in 1995, it became a popular online directory/search engine in the early years of the Internet, and expanded rapidly.

488 SCIENTIST

LINUS TORVALDS

Helsinki, Finland
1969–

Finnish computer scientist Linus Torvalds originated the Linux kernel (the program at the heart of a computer's operating system, or OS). Torvalds developed Linux in 1991, made it freely available on the Internet, and released the source code so users could modify it. Google's mobile OS Android and the Chrome computer OS are based on the Linux kernel.

489 ENTREPRENEUR

ELON MUSK

Pretoria, South Africa
1971–

Future travel is backed by this entrepreneur-investor.

South African–born entrepreneur and investor Elon Musk founded spacecraft, launch vehicle, and satellite manufacturer SpaceX, and invested in and became CEO of electric vehicle and clean energy outfit Tesla. He was also cofounder of the PayPal electronic payment firm, and acquired and became CEO of social media company Twitter, which he rebranded as X. In addition, he founded the Boring Company, a tunnel and infrastructure building outfit, and cofounded the artificial intelligence research body OpenAI and neurotechnology company Neuralink. Born in South Africa, Musk moved to Canada aged eighteen, where he studied economics and physics. After moving to Stanford University, he dropped out and cofounded Zip2, a company licensing online city guide software to the press, sold to Compaq in 1999 for $307 million. He then cofounded an online bank, X.com, that in 2000 became part of the electronics payments company PayPal, sold to eBay for $1.5 billion in 2002. The same year Musk became a U.S. citizen, and founded Space Exploration Technologies (SpaceX).

ABOVE AND BELOW: A showman as well as an entrepreneur. SpaceX's partly reusable launch vehicle Falcon Heavy carried Musk's Tesla car and a dummy named Starman on its inaugural flight on February 6, 2018.

KNOWN FOR

- Quitting Stanford University after two days
- Creating a $100 million reward for improvements in carbon capture technology
- Being the world's wealthiest individual in 2023, with $220 billion

490 ENTREPRENEUR

LARRY PAGE

East Lansing, Michigan
1973–

Google founder and onetime CEO made Internet searches faster.

American entrepreneur and computer scientist Larry Page cofounded Google with Sergey Brin and Scott Hassan in 1998, initially as a search engine. The company grew rapidly and made many acquisitions and offered a range of services including email (Gmail), navigation (Google Maps), web browsing (Chrome), video sharing (YouTube), and the Android mobile operating system. Page studied at the University of Michigan and Stanford University. He was Google CEO from 1997 to 2001 and 2011 to 2015 and, in 2023, was a board member and controlling shareholder at Google's parent company, Alphabet Inc., and was reputedly worth $95.8 billion.

491 ENTREPRENEUR

SERGEY BRIN

Moscow, Soviet Union
1973–

Russian-born American business magnate Sergey Brin, who cofounded Google with Larry Page and Scott Hassan, was born in Moscow and emigrated with his parents from Russia in 1979. He lived in Vienna and Paris before immigrating to the United States after his father was appointed to a mathematics professorship at the University of Maryland. Brin studied at Maryland, and then received a master's degree in computer science and embarked on a PhD at Stanford University, where he met Page. Like Page, in 2023 Brin was a board member at Alphabet Inc.; at the time he was reputedly worth $89 billion.

BELOW: Page (left) and Brin take questions at a media event in 2008. They were joint recipients in 2004 of the Marconi Prize, awarded annually for advances in communication.

POLITICAL LEADER

JACINDA ARDERN

Hamilton, New Zealand
1980–

Ardern was New Zealand's youngest prime minister in more than 150 years.

Jacinda Ardern became prime minister of New Zealand on October 26, 2017, aged thirty-seven, making her the world's youngest female head of government, and the country's youngest prime minister since Edward Stafford in 1856. She had become leader of the Labour Party only two months before. Ardern introduced strict gun laws in the aftermath of the March 15, 2019, mosque shootings in Christchurch, in which fifty-one were killed, and closed the country's borders to non-citizens and non-residents to combat the COVID-19 pandemic. Then, in the 2020 general election, she won a landslide victory to create the first majority government in New Zealand since the introduction of proportional representation in 1996. However, in January 2023 she resigned as Labour Party leader and as prime minister saying, "I know what this job takes, and I know that I no longer have enough in the tank to do it justice."

"It takes courage and strength to be empathetic and I'm very proudly an empathetic and compassionate leader."

Jacinda Ardern, interview with BBC, 2018

LEFT: Adern (right) with New Zealand climate change minister James Shaw in October 2022. Before becoming a politician, Ardern worked for New Zealand prime minister Helen Clark and British prime minister Tony Blair.

493 ATHLETE

SERENA WILLIAMS

Saginaw, Michigan
1981–

This powerful tennis star set records—with and without her older sister.

Serena Williams won twenty-three Grand Slam singles titles, more than any other female player in the "open era" (from 1968 on). She outscored her rival and older sister Venus Williams, who won seven Grand Slam singles titles. Although they are rivals and have played one another in nine major finals, they also support one another and together won fourteen Grand Slam doubles titles. From an early age the sisters were coached by their parents, mother Oracene Price and, especially, their father Richard Williams. Serena and Venus have each won four Olympic gold medals—three in doubles and one in singles.

ABOVE: Serena is arguably the greatest women's tennis player in history. Her first Grand Slam was the U.S. Open in 1999.

494 ACTIVIST

ALICIA GARZA

Los Angeles, California
1981–

Police killings energize activist to cofound Black Lives Matter movement.

With fellow activists Opal Tometi and Patrisse Cullors, Garza launched the Black Lives Matter movement in 2013 in response to killings of Black people by police. She inspired the #BlackLivesMatter hashtag when, after the July 2013 acquittal of George Zimmerman of the murder of Trayvon Martin, she wrote in a Facebook post: "I continue to be surprised at how little Black lives matter . . . Our lives matter." Cullors shared this post with the now-famous hashtag. The movement became well known after street protests in 2014 following the deaths of Michael Brown and Eric Garner, and now has an international reach.

ABOVE: In 2020 Garza also cofounded Supermajority, a membership organization "dedicated to making women the most revered and respected voting bloc in the country."

495 POLITICAL LEADER

KIM JONG UN

Pyongyang, North Korea
c. 1982–

"Respected Comrade" who succeeded his father as leader of North Korea.

Kim Jong Un became supreme leader of North Korea in 2011, and leader of the Korean Workers' Party in 2012. He is the son of Kim Jong Il, leader from 1994 to 2011, and grandson of Kim Il Sung, the country's founder and first supreme leader from 1948 to 1994. Like his grandfather and father before him, Kim maintains a cult of personality, and rules the country as a totalitarian dictatorship. State media refer to him as "Respected Comrade" and "Marshal Kim Jong Un." He reputedly ordered purges of officials, and some reports claimed that he was behind the 2017 assassination of Kim Jong Nam, his older half-brother and at one time presumed heir to the leadership. Kim Jong Un revived his grandfather's 1960s *byungjin* policy, focused on developing the military and the economy in tandem, and boosted the North Korean nuclear weapons program, leading to tensions with South Korea and the United States. In 2018 he engaged in summits with South Korean president Moon Jae-in and U.S. president Donald Trump.

BELOW: Kim Jong Un in April 2019 in Vladivostok, Russia, where he held his first summit with Russian leader Vladimir Putin. Kim supported Russia's 2022 invasion of Ukraine.

496 ENTREPRENEUR

MARK ZUCKERBERG

White Plains, New York
1984–

American media magnate and philanthropist Mark Zuckerberg was a student at Harvard University when he cofounded the website Facebook in February 2004. Initially launched to college campuses, it grew swiftly and expanded worldwide; by 2012, the site had 1 billion users. Zuckerberg is CEO of Meta Platforms, which owns Instagram, WhatsApp, and Messenger as well as Facebook. His philanthropic outlets include the Chan Zuckerberg Initiative, founded by Zuckerberg with his wife Priscilla Chan in 2015, which engages with immigration reform and criminal justice among other issues.

ABOVE: In 2010, Zuckerberg was *TIME* magazine's Person of the Year. In 2013 he cofounded the pro-immigration and criminal justice reform group FWD.us.

497 ATHLETE

USAIN BOLT

Montego Bay, Jamaica
1986–

Jamaican sprinter Usain Bolt won eight Olympic gold medals. He is the only sprinter to win the 100-meter and 200-meter golds at three successive Olympics—in 2008 (Beijing), 2012 (London), and 2016 (Rio de Janeiro)—and twice won gold in the 4 x 100-meter relay, in 2012 and 2016. In addition, he won eleven World Championships, and was the first athlete to win four World Championship 200-meter titles. He set new world records of 9.58 seconds for the 100 meters and 19.19 seconds for the 200 meters at the 2009 World Championships in Berlin. He often posed before or after races in a trademark "Lightning Bolt" pose, with his right arm across his chest and left arm raised and pointing.

ABOVE: Bolt adopts his "Lightning Bolt" celebratory pose on taking the gold medal in the 200 meters at the 2016 Rio de Janeiro Olympics.

498   ENTERTAINER

TAYLOR SWIFT

West Reading, Pennsylvania
1989–

With sales of more than 114 million records worldwide, singer-songwriter Taylor Swift is one of the most successful recording artists in history. She signed a deal with Sony/ATV Music Publishing aged just fourteen, and with her debut album *Taylor Swift*, released when she was sixteen, became the first female country artist to write a platinum-certified album.

LEFT: In July 2023 Swift became the first woman (and the third artist after Prince and Herb Alpert) to have four albums in the U.S. Top Ten at the same time. She also beat Barbra Streisand's record of the most number-one albums (twelve) by a female artist.

499   ACTIVIST

MALALA YOUSAFZAI

Mingora, Pakistan
1997–

Malala Yousafzai won global attention through her public attacks on moves by the "Pakistani Taliban" (*Tehrik-e-Taliban Pakistan*, or TTP) to destroy or close girls' schools. She survived a TTP assassination attempt aged fifteen, addressed the United Nations on her sixteenth birthday, and in 2014 won the Nobel Peace Prize jointly with Indian social reformer Kailash Satyarthi.

500 ACTIVIST

GRETA THUNBERG

Stockholm, Sweden
2003–

Swedish environmental activist who delivered the "Greta effect."

Greta Thunberg rose to prominence as a teenage activist in 2018, holding a protest for three weeks on Fridays outside the Swedish Parliament holding a sign saying *Skolstrejk för klimatet* (School Strike for Climate), and this inspired global school climate protests in 2018 named "Fridays for Future." Thunberg became a powerful climate change activist, addressing the 2019 UN Climate Change Conference and the 2019 UN Climate Action Summit in New York (to which she traveled by yacht to avoid the emissions associated with flying), as well as the European Parliament and the World Economic Forum. Her inspirational effect on climate activism was described in the press as "the Greta effect." She has been diagnosed with the autism spectrum disorder Asperger syndrome, and raised awareness of the condition. She said, "I have Aspergers and that means I'm sometimes a bit different from the norm. And . . . being different is a superpower."

> *"Entire ecosystems are collapsing. We are in the beginning of a mass extinction, and all you can talk about is money and fairy tales of eternal economic growth. How dare you!"*
>
> Greta Thunberg, address to the UN Climate Action Summit, 2019

LEFT AND RIGHT: Over the course of a few months in 2018, Greta went from demonstrating quietly to being an important spokesperson for the environmental movement.

INDEX

A

Abe, Shinzo 367
abolitionists *see also* slavery
    Abraham Lincoln 229
    Alexander Hamilton 205
    Benjamin Franklin 191
    Elizabeth Cady Stanton 232
    Frederick Douglass 234
    Harriet Tubman 237
    Henry David Thoreau 233
    John Brown 237
    John Newton 196
    Josiah Wedgwood 199
    Olaudah Equiano 204
    Sojourner Truth 223
    Vicente Guerrero 218, 219
    William Wilberforce 210
Aboriginal Australians 212, 215, 217, 347
Abraham 14
Achaemenian Empire 16, 31, 32, 36, 49
Achebe, Chinua 336
actors
    Charlie Chaplin 288
    Eva Perón 321
    Hattie McDaniel 295
    Ira Aldridge 228
    Lucius Ambivius Turpio 56
    Marilyn Monroe 333
    Molière 182
    Ronald Reagan 311
    Sidney Poitier 334
adventurers *see* explorers, of
Aeschylus 35
Afghanistan 195, 222, 252, 292, 309, 365
Afonso I of Kongo 147
African Methodist Episcopal Church (AME) 210, 211
Afrocentrism 326
Afsharid dynasty 189
Agrippa 63
Ahmad Baba 171

Akbar 167
Akhenaten 19, 22
al-Qaeda 372
Alaric 85
Aldridge, Ira 228
Alexander the Great 46, 48, 49
Alexander VI (pope) 140
Alfred the Great 100
Ali, Muhammad 352
Ali, Sonni 143
Ali Yasi Dan Tsamiya 125
Allen, Richard 210, 211
Allende, Isabel 352
Amenhotep III 18
American Red Cross 238
Amina 166
Anaximander 25
Andersen, Hans Christian 227
Anderson, Elizabeth Garrett 248
Annan, Kofi 348
Anthony (saint) 82
Archimedes 52
architects
    Agrippa 63
    Frank Lloyd Wright 266
    I. M. Pei 316
    Imhotep 12
    Leonardo Da Vinci 147
    Michelangelo 151
    Mimar Sinan 156, 157
    Pakal the Great 92
    Raphael 155
    Roxelana 163
Ardern, Jacinda 384
Aristarchus of Samos 52
Aristophanes 44
Aristotle 46, 47
Ark of the Covenant 25
Armstrong, Neil 341
Asante Empire 186, 249
Asantewaa, Yaa 249
Ashoka 51
Assad, Bashar al- 380
astronomers

Abu Rayhan al-Biruni 103
Anaximander 25
Aristarchus of Samos 52
Avicenna 104
Galileo Galilei 173
Gan De 49
Leonhard Euler 192
Nicolaus Copernicus 151
Ptolemy 76
Sima Qian 56
Zu Chongzi 86
Atahualpa 162
Atatürk 285
athletes 315, 322, 352, 377, 380, 385, 388
Attila the Hun 85
Augustus Caesar 62
Aung San Suu Kyi 355
Aurangzeb 180, 181
Austen, Jane 215
Australia
    British penal colonies 201
    exploration of 176, 180, 185, 197
    prime ministers 254
    rights of indigenous peoples 212, 215, 217, 347
Avicenna 104
Aztec Empire 147

B

Babur 152
Babylon, Mesopotamia 16, 26
Bach, Johann Sebastian 188
Bacon, Francis 173
Baldwin, James 328
Barnard, Christiaan 324
Barton, Clara 238
Barton, Edmund 254
Bassi, Ghana 104
Battle of the Little Bighorn 243
Beauvoir, Simone de 308
Beethoven, Ludwig van 214
Begum, Fatma 292
Bell, Alexander Graham 253

Benin, West Africa 140, 258
Bennelong, Woollarawarre 212
Berners-Lee, Tim 369
Bezos, Jeff 378
Bhumibol Adulyadej 333
Biko, Steve 356
bin Laden, Osama 372
Biruni, Abu Rayḥan al- 103
Bismarck, Otto von 232
Black empowerment
    Alicia Garza 386
    Blanche Kelso Bruce 251
    James Baldwin 328
    Malcolm X 330
    Marcus Garvey 288
    Martin Luther King 336
    Muhammad Ali 352
    Thurgood Marshall 309
Blair, Tony 366
Boccaccio, Giovanni 124
Bolívar, Simón 220
Bologne, Joseph 203
Bolt, Usain 388
Bonaparte, Napoleon 212
Borgia, Rodrigo 140
Boudicca 71
Bourke, Sir Richard 217
Bridgetower, George 218
Brin, Sergey 383
British monarchy 131, 156, 157, 165, 235, 331, 376
Brooks, Gwendolyn 316
Bruce, Blanche Kelso 250, 251
Buddhism 38, 51, 90, 98, 132, 345
Buffett, Warren 339
Buganda 121
Bungaree 215
Buonarroti, Michelangelo 151
Bush, George W. 357

C

Caesar, Augustus 62
Caesar, Julius 59
Cai Lun 75
Caligula 70
Calvin, John 163
Cao Cao 80
Capac, Manco 114
Carnegie, Andrew 246
Carolingian Renaissance 97
Carson, Rachel 307
Carter, Howard 22
Carter, Jimmy 327
Carver, George Washington 263
Castro, Fidel 330
Catherine the Great 199
Catholicism 121, 146, 148, 155, 251
Cervantes, Miguel de 171
Chanel, Gabrielle Bonheur "Coco" 287
Changamire 186
Chaplin, Charlie 288
Charlemagne 97
Charles, Ray 341
Charles V 159
Chaucer, Geoffrey 127
Chevalier De Saint-Georges 203
Chilembwe, John 271
China 53, 264, 294, 306, 366
Chopin, Frédéric 230
Christianity 14, 16, 21, 65, 66, 69, 82, 85
Chumo the Holy 64
Church of England 156, 157, 196
Churchill, Winston 277
Cicero, Marcus Tullius 58
civil rights campaigners
    Dolores Huerta 341
    James Baldwin 328
    Malcolm X 330
    Martin Luther King Jr. 268, 336, 337
    Rosa Parks 314
    W. E. B. Du Bois 268
Cleopatra 61
Cold War 338, 343
Columbus, Christopher 145, 146
composers
    Banjo Paterson 262
    Duke Ellington 298
    Frédéric Chopin 230
    Johann Sebastian Bach 188
    Joseph Bologne 203
    Ludwig van Beethoven 214
    Rabindranath Tagore 261
    Ray Charles 341
    St. Hildegard of Bingen 108
    Wolfgang Amadeus Mozart 206
Confucius 30
Constantine the Great 82
Cook, James 197
Copernicus, Nicolaus 151
Cortés, Hernán 156
Crazy Horse 250
Cuba 330, 336
Curie, Marie 267
Cyrus the Great 31

D

Dae-Jung, Kim 326
Dalai Lama 345
Dampier, William 185
Dante (Dante Alighieri) 121
Darius the Great 32
Darwin, Charles 228
David (king of Israel) 25
da Vinci, Leonardo 147
de Gaulle, Charles 290
Demosthenes 47
Deng Xiaoping 306
Descartes, René 179
Diana, Princess of Wales 376
Dickens, Charles 231
Diop, Cheikh Anta 326
Disney, Walt 304
Dost Mohammad Shah 222
Dostoevsky, Fyodor 238
Douglass, Frederick 234
Doyle, Arthur Conan 261
Du Bois, W. E. B. 268
Durrani, Ahmad Shah 195

Durrani Empire 195, 222
d'Youville, Marie-Marguerite 190

E

Earhart, Amelia 296
Edison, Thomas 254
Einstein, Albert 281
Eisenhower, Dwight D. 290
El Cid 106
Eliot, George 236
Elizabeth I 165
Elizabeth II 331
Ellington, Edward Kennedy "Duke" 298
Enheduanna 13
Enlightenment 196
environmental campaigners 350, 354, 374, 390
Equiano, Olaudah 204
Eratosthenes 53
Erikson, Leif 102, 145
Ethiopia 113, 290
Euclid 50
Euler, Leonhard 192
Euripides 40
Evans, Mary Ann 236
Ewuare the Great 140
explorers, of
   Africa 44, 123, 139
   Asia 119, 123, 129
   Australia 176, 180, 215
   Europe 123
   India 148
   New Zealand 180, 197
   North America 102, 145, 152
   North Pole 274
   Northwest Passage 274
   South America 145, 156, 159
   South Pole 274
   Strait of Magellan 152–153
Ezana of Axum 85

F

female leaders
   Amina 166
   Aung San Suu Kyi 355
   Boudicca 71
   Cleopatra 61
   Ellen Johnson Sirleaf 349
   Indira Gandhi 316
   Jacinda Ardern 384
   Margaret Thatcher 329
   Njinga 176
   Patsy Mink 335
   Ranavalona 218
   Roxelana 163
   Seondeok of Silla 92
   Theodora of Byzantium 87
   Yaa Asantewaa 249
Ferdowsi 101
Florey, Howard 298
Ford, Henry 262
France 183, 206, 212, 290
Francis of Assisi (saint) 115
Francis (pope) 347
Franciscan monastic order 115
Franklin, Benjamin 191
Franklin, Rosalind 323
Freud, Sigmund 257

G

Gabon 168
Galen 78
Galilei, Galileo 173
Gama, Vasco da 148
Gan De 49
Gandhi, Indira 316
Gandhi, Mohandas 268
Garibaldi, Giuseppe 227
Garvey, Marcus 288
Garza, Alicia 386
Gates, Bill 371
Gautama, Siddharta 38
Genghis Khan 114
German reunification 338
Geronimo 242
Ghana 104, 186, 310
Ghana Empire 94
Ginsburg, Ruth Bader 344
Gist, George 217
Goethe, Johann Wolfgang von 204, 205
Gonçalves, Antão 139
Gongsun Long 49
Gorbachev, Mikhail 343
Grant, Ulysses S. 240
Greece 36, 37, 40, 48
Gregory I (pope) 91
Gregory IX (pope) 111
Gregory VII (pope) 105
Grey Nuns 190
Guan Yu 80
Guerrero, Vicente 218, 219
Guevara, Che 336
Gutenberg, Johannes 135
Guy-Blaché, Alice 275
Gyatso, Tenzin 345

H

Hamilton, Alexander 205
Hammurabi 16
Hannibal 55
Hannibal, Abram 190
Hanno of Carthage 44
Hatshepsut 18
Hawking, Stephen 354
Hawkins, John 164
Hemingway, Ernest 300
Henry V 131
Henry VIII 156, 157
Heraclitus 34
Herodotus 40
Hideyoshi, Toyotomi 166
Hildegard of Bingen (saint) 108
Hill, Octavia 249
Hippocrates of Cos 42, 43
Hitler, Adolf 288
Homer 24
Huerta, Dolores 341
Hugo, Victor 226
Hyeokgeose of Silla 62

I

Ibn Battuta 123
Ibn Khaldun 125
Ibn Rashid Al Maktoum, Sheikh Mohammed 361
Ibn Saud 282
Idrisi, Muhammad al- 108
Ieyasu, Tokugawa 168
Imhotep 12
Inca Empire 114, 139, 143, 162
Innocent III (pope) 112
Innocent VIII (pope) 142

inventors
    Alexander Graham Bell 253
    Alfred Nobel 244
    Archimedes 52
    Benjamin Franklin 191
    Guglielmo Marconi 276
    James Watt 201
    Jang Yeong-sil 133
    Konosuke Matsushita 296
    Nikola Tesla 258
    Thomas Edison 254
Iran 16, 31, 101, 189, 305
Iraq 305, 348, 357, 366, 374
    see also Mesopotamia
Isabella of Castile 146
Islam 14, 16, 21, 90, 125, 330
Israelites 21, 23
Italy 55, 59, 85, 141, 227
Itzcoatl 130
Ivan III 142

J
Jackson, Michael 373
Jahan, Shah 177
Janszoon, Willem 176
Japan
    attempts to invade Korea 169
    modernization 255
    national unification 166, 168
    prime ministers 367
    religions 90, 98
    restoration of imperial rule 247
Jefferson, Thomas 202
Jerusalem 23, 25, 26, 107, 113
Jesus of Nazareth 66
Joan of Arc 136, 137
Jobs, Steve 370
John of Patmos 68
Johnson Sirleaf, Ellen 349
Jordan, Michael 377
Joyce, James 285
Judaism 14, 16, 21, 25
Julian of Norwich 128
Julius II (pope) 144
Jung, Carl 276

K
Kafka, Franz 287
Kagame, Paul 371
Kahlo, Frida 306
K'ak Tiliw Chan Yopaat 94
Kano 109, 125
Kant, Immanuel 196
Kato Kimera 121
Kaya Magan Cissé 94
Keller, Helen 283
Kemal, Mustafa 285
Kennedy, John F. 317
Khan, Abdur Rahman 252
Khan, Amanullah 292
Khan, Imran 365
Khan, Mohammad Daoud 309
Khomeini, Ruhollah 305, 360
Khwārizmī Muhammad ibn Mūsā al- 98
Kim il-Sung 312
Kim Jong Un 387
King, Martin Luther, Jr. 268, 336, 337
Kohl, Helmut 338
Korea see also North Korea; South Korea
    Independence Movement 305
    invasion attempts 166, 169
    kingdoms of 62, 64, 67
    rulers of 92, 126, 132
Kublai Khan 117
Kukai 98

L
LaDuke, Winona 374
Lalibela, Gebre Mesqel 113
Lao Tzu 33
Laozi 33
Lavoisier, Antoine 202
Lee, Ang 368
Lee, Stan 324
Leeuwenhoek, Antonie van 183
Leibniz, Gottfried Wilhelm von 184
Lenin, Vladimir 270
Lennon, John 351
Leo I (pope) 86
Leo III (pope) 99
Leonardo da Vinci 147
Liberia 380
Lincoln, Abraham 229
Linnaeus, Carl 192
Louis XIV 183
Louverture, Toussaint 203
Lovelace, Ada 233
Lu Xun 283
Lucretius 60
Lukeni lua Nimi 129
Luther, Martin 155
Luxemburg, Rosa 272, 273

M
Ma, Jack 379
Maathai, Wangari 350
Mabo, Eddie 347
MacDonald, Ramsay 265
Machiavelli, Niccolò 148, 149
MacKillop, Mary 251
Magellan, Ferdinand 152–153
Mahal, Mumtaz 178
Maktoum, Mohammed al Bin 361
Malawi 271
Malaysia 329
Malcolm X 330
Mali Empire 118, 122, 143
Mandela, Nelson 319
Manden Charter 118
Mani 81
Manichaeism 81
Mao Zedong 294
Marco Polo 119
Marconi, Guglielmo 276
Marcus Aurelius 78
Marie Antoinette 206
Marie de France 110
Marley, Bob 355
Marshall, Thurgood 309
Martin de Porres (saint) 176
Marx, Karl 235
Mary (mother of Jesus) 65
Massoud, Ahmad Shah 365
Matamba 177
Matathir bin Mohamad 329
mathematicians
    Abu Rayhan al-Biruni 103
    Alan Turing 313

Archimedes 52
Eratosthenes 53
Euclid 50
Galileo Galilei 173
Gottfried Wilhelm von
  Leibniz 184
Isaac Newton 184
Leonhard Euler 192
Nicolaus Copernicus 151
Pythagoras 29
René Descartes 179
Zhang Heng 76
Zu Chongzi 86
Matsushita, Konosuke 296
McDaniel, Hattie 295
Medici, Alessandro de' 164
medicine
  Avicenna 104
  Christiaan Barnard 324
  Elizabeth Garrett Anderson 248
  Florence Nightingale 237
  Galen 78
  Hippocrates of Cos 42
  Imhotep 12
  Rosalind Franklin 323
Mehmed the Conqueror 141
Meiji, Emperor 255
Mendeleev, Dmitri 245
Mendes, Chico 354
Mendoza, Pedro de 159
Mesopotamia 13, 14, 26, 79 *see also* Iraq
Mexico 92, 130, 156, 168, 218
Michelangelo (Michelangelo Buonarroti) 151
microbiology 183, 239
microscopes 183
military leaders
  Agrippa 63
  Alaric 85
  Alexander the Great 48
  Alfred the Great 100
  El Cid 106
  Giuseppe Garibaldi 227
  Hannibal 55
  Henry V 131
  Horatio Nelson 208

Joan of Arc 136, 137
Julius Caesar 59
Mithridates the Great 56
Napoleon Bonaparte 212
Otto von Bismarck 232
Pontiac 194
Septimius Severus 79
Spartacus 57
Sunzi 33
Ulysses S. Grant 240
William the Conqueror 106
Milk, Harvey 339
Mink, Patsy 335
Mithridates the Great 56
Modi, Narendra 361
Mohism 42
Molière 182
Mongol Empire 114
Monroe, Marilyn 333
Montesquieu 190
Montezuma II 147
Moses 21
Mother Teresa 310
Mozart, Wolfgang Amadeus 206
Mozi 42
Mughal Empire 152, 167, 177, 178, 180, 181
Muhammad (prophet) 90
Murdoch, Rupert 344
Musa, Mansa 122
Musk, Elon 382
Mutapa Empire 186
Mutota, Nyatsimba, Prince 135

N
Nadir Shah 189
Nandi Bhebhe 211
Nasser, Gamal Abdel 320
Ndongo 177
Nebuchadnezzar II 26
Nefertiti 19
Nelson, Horatio 208
Neo-Babylonian Chaldean empire 26
Nero 72
Newton, Isaac 184
Newton, John 196
Nietzsche, Friedrich 252

Nightingale, Florence 237
Njinga of Ndongo and Matamba 177
Nkrumah, Kwame 310
Nobel, Alfred 244
Nobel Prize 244, 267, 277, 301, 326, 345, 350, 389
Nogbaisi, Ovonramwen 258
Noguchi, Hideyo 278
North Korea 312, 326, 378
Nyere, Julius 323

O
Obama, Barack 374
Obasango, Olesegun 348
Onjo of Baekje 67
Osei Tutu 186
Ottoman Empire 141, 158, 163, 285
Ovid 64
Owens, Jesse 315

P
Pachacuti Inca Yupanqui 139
Page, Larry 383
painters
  Frida Kahlo 306
  Jacques Louis David 41
  Leonardo Da Vinci 147
  Michelangelo 151
  Pablo Picasso 284
  Rabindranath Tagore 261
  Raphael 155
  Rembrandt Van Rijn 180, 181
  Sequoyah 217
  Vincent van Gogh 256
Pakal the Great 92
Pakistan 365
Pankhurst, Emmeline 259
paper, invention of 75
Parks, Rosa 314
Pasteur, Louis 239
Paterson, Banjo 262
Paul III (pope) 148
Paul (saint) 67
Pei, I. M. 316
penal colonies 201
Pepi II Neferkare 14
Pericles 36

periodic table 245
Perón, Eva 321
Peter (saint) 69
Peter the Great 187
Phillip, Arthur 201
philosophers
   Adam Smith 195
   Anaximander 25
   Avicenna 104
   Francis Bacon 173
   Friedrich Nietzsche 252
   Gongsun Long 49
   Gottfried Wilhelm von Leibniz 184
   Heraclitus 34
   Jean-Jacques Rousseau 193
   Laozi 33
   Lucretius 60
   Marcus Aurelius 78
   Marcus Tullius Cicero 58
   Mary Wollstonecraft 209
   Montesquieu 190
   Mozi 42
   Plato 45
   Plutarch 73
   René Descartes 179
   Seneca the Younger 68
   Siddharta Gautama 38
   Simone de Beauvoir 308
   Socrates 41
physicists
   Albert Einstein 281
   Anaximander 25
   Cheikh Anta Diop 326
   Chien-Shiung Wu 312
   Ernest Rutherford 271
   Galileo Galilei 173
   Isaac Newton 184
   Marie Curie 267
   Stephen Hawking 354
Picasso, Pablo 284
Pindar 35
Pius II (pope) 132, 133
Pius XI (pope) 258
Plato 45, 47
playwrights
   Aeschylus 35
   Aristophanes 44
   Aristotle 46, 47
   Euripides 40
   James Baldwin 328
   John of Patmos 68
   Molière 182
   Sophocles 37
   Terence 56
   William Shakespeare 174, 175
Plutarch 73
Poca Hontas 179
poets
   Banjo Paterson 262
   Ferdowsi 101
   Geoffrey Chaucer 127
   Giovanni Boccaccio 124
   Gwendolyn Brooks 316
   Homer 24
   James Baldwin 328
   Kukai 98
   Lu Xun 283
   Lucretius 60
   Marie de France 110
   Ovid 64
   Rabindranath Tagore 261
   Rumi 116
   Sappho 27
   Solon 27
   St. Hildegard of Bingen 108
   Victor Hugo 226
   Virgil 60
   William Shakespeare 174, 175
   Yeshaq I 132
   Zhang Xu 94
Poitier, Sidney 334
Polo, Marco 119
Pontiac 194
popes
   Alexander VI 140
   Francis 347
   Gregory I 91
   Gregory IX 111
   Gregory VII 105
   Innocent III 112
   Innocent VIII 142
   Julius II 144
   Leo I 86
   Leo III 99
   Paul III 148
   Pius II 132, 133
   Pius XI 258
   Sixtus IV 139
   Urban II 106
   Urban VIII 175
Poquelin, Jean-Baptiste 182
Portugal 148
Powell, Colin 348
Presley, Elvis 346
Prophet Muhammad 90
Protestant Reformation 134, 148, 155, 159, 163
Proust, Marcel 273
Ptolemy 76
Putin, Vladimir 364
Pythagoras 29

Q

Qian, Sima 56
Queen of Sheba 25
Quin Shin Huang 53
Quiriguá 94

R

Ramaphosa, Cyril 363
Ramses II 22
Ranavalona 218
Raphael 155
Reagan, Ronald 311
Red Cloud 240
Reformation 134, 148, 155, 159, 163
Rembrandt Van Rijn 180, 181
Richard I 112
Rivera, Sylvia 362, 363
Robinson, Jackie 322
Roman emperors 62, 72, 73, 79, 82
Roosevelt, Franklin D. 286
Roosevelt, Theodore "Teddy" 260
Ross, John 222
Rousseau, Jean-Jacques 193
Rowling, J. K. 379
Roxelana 163
Rumi, Jalal al-Din al 116
Rushdie, Salman 360
Rutherford, Ernest 271
Rwanda 371
Ryōma, Sakamoto 247

S

Saladin 110
Sappho 27
Sargon 13
Satyarthi, Kailash 389
Saud, Abdulaziz bin Abdul
    Rahman al 282
Saudi Arabia 282
Sejong the Great 132, 133
Selassie, Haile 290
Seneca the Younger 68
Seondeok of Silla 92
Sequoyah 217
Severus, Septimius 79
Shakespeare, William 174, 175
Shawnee people 212
Sheba, Queen of 25
Shona kingdom of Mutapa 135
Sinan, Mimar 156, 157
Sitting Bull 243
Sixtus IV (pope) 139
slavery *see also* abolitionists
    Abram Hannibal 190
    Ahmad Baba 171
    Frederick Douglass 234
    Gaspar Yanga 168
    George Washington Carver 263
    Harriet Tubman 237
    Israelites in Egypt 21
    John Hawkins 164
    John Newton 196
    Miguel de Cervantes 171
    Olaudah Equiano 204
    Sojourner Truth 223
    Spartacus 57
    Toussaint Louverture 203
Smith, Adam 195
Sobekneferu 16
Sobhuza II 301
Socrates 41
Solomon 23, 25
Solon 27
Songhai Empire 143, 171
Sophocles 37
South Korea 312, 326, 387
Spartacus 57
Spartacus League 272, 273

Spielberg, Steven 358
St. Anthony 82
St. Francis of Assisi 115
St. Hildegard of Bingen 108
St. Marie-Marguerite
    d'Youville 190
St. Martin de Porres 176
St. Mary of the Cross 251
St. Paul 67
St. Peter 69
St. Teresa of Calcutta 310
Stalin, Joseph 278
Stanton, Elizabeth Cady 232
Stopes, Marie 282
Suez Crisis 320
Suleiman 158
Sun Tzu 33
Sun Yat-sen 264
Sundiata Keita 118
Sunni Muslim Ayyubid
    Empire 110
Sunzi 33
Swaziland 301
Swift, Taylor 389
syllabaries 217
Syria 380

T

Tacitus 74
Tagore, Rabindranath 261
Taishi, Shotoku 90
Tambo, Oliver 315
Taoism 33
Tasman, Abel 180
Tecumseh 212
Ten Commandments 21
Tenochtitlan, Mexico 130
Terence 56
Tesla, Nikola 258
Thailand 333
Thatcher, Margaret 329
Theodora of Byzantium 87
Thoreau, Henry David 233
Thunberg, Greta 390
Timur the Lame 126
Timurid Empire 126
Tolkien, J. R. R. 293

Tolstoy, Leo 241
Torvalds, Linus 381
Trajan 73
Trump, Donald 357
Truth, Sojourner 223
Tsaraki 109
tsars 142, 187
Tubman, Harriet 237
Turing, Alan 313
Tutankhamun 22
Tutu, Desmond 342
Twain, Mark 247

U

United Nations 348
Urban II (pope) 106
Urban VIII (pope) 175
U.S. presidents
    Abraham Lincoln 229
    Barack Obama 374
    Donald Trump 357
    Dwight D. Eisenhower 290
    Franklin D. Roosevelt 286
    George W. Bush 357
    George Washington 200
    Jimmy Carter 327
    John F. Kennedy 317
    Ronald Reagan 311
    Theodore "Teddy" Roosevelt
        260
    Thomas Jefferson 202

V

van Gogh, Vincent 256
Vázquez de Ayllón, Lucas 152
Victoria 235
Virgil 60

W

Washington, George 200
Watt, James 201
Weah, George 380
Wedgwood, Josiah 199
Wilberforce, William 210
William the Conqueror 106
Williams, Serena 385

Winfrey, Oprah 368
Wollstonecraft, Mary 209
Wright, Frank Lloyd 266
writers
    Arthur Conan Doyle 261
    Charles Dickens 231
    Chinua Achebe 336
    Dante Alighieri 121
    Ernest Hemingway 300
    Franz Kafka 287
    Fyodor Dostoevsky 238
    Giovanni Boccaccio 124
    Hans Christian Andersen 227
    Henry David Thoreau 233
    Herodotus 40
    Isabel Allende 352
    J. K. Rowling 379
    J. R. R. Tolkien 293
    James Baldwin 328
    James Joyce 285
    Jane Austen 215
    Johannn Wolfgang von Goethe 204, 205
    Leo Tolstoy 241
    Marcel Proust 273
    Marco Polo 119
    Mark Twain 247
    Mary Wollstonecraft 209
    Miguel de Cervantes 171
    Molière 182
    Niccolò Machiavelli 148
    Plutarch 73
    Qiao 80
    Salman Rushdie 360
    Seneca the Younger 68
    Simone de Beauvoir 308
    Tacitus 74
    Victor Hugo 226
    Wole Soyinka 345
Wu, Chien-Shiung 312

X

Xerxes 36
Xi Jinping 366

Y

Yaji I 125
Yang, Jerry 381
Yaqubi, al- 100
Yaupanqui, Topa Inca 143
Yeshaq I 132
Yi Song-gye 126
Yi Sun-sin 169
Yousafzai, Malala 389
Yu Gwan-sun 305
Yuan Dynasty 117
Yuan Longping 336
Yunus, Muhammad 351

Z

Zhang Heng 76
Zhang Xu 94
Zheng He 129
Zimbabwe 186
Zoroaster 16
Zu Chongzi 86
Zuckerberg, Mark 388
Zulu Empire 211, 221
Zulu, Shaka 221

PICTURE CREDITS

The publisher would like to thank the following for permission to reproduce copyright material:

AKG Images: 75.

Alamy: A.J.D. Foto Ltd: 100; Agefotostock: 13; Album: 249, 285 (bottom); CBW: 131, 239; Chronicle: 60 (left); CSU Archives/Everett Collection: 377; GL Archive: 168; Granger - Historical Picture Archive: 86, 127, 166; Dennis Hallinan: 95; Peter Horree: 163 (left); imageBROKER: 84, 113; JJs: 346; Craig Lovell/ Eagle Visions Photography: 219; PCN Photography: 356; Pictorial Press Ltd: 209; Edward Roth: 2, 332; Russotwins: 179; Science History Images: 130, 278, 308; TCD/Prod.DB: 275; ZUMA Press: 333.

Art in Flanders/KMSKA/Hugo Maertens: 140.

Art Institute of Chicago: 132, 167, 228 (top), 228 (bottom), 235.

© José Luiz Bernardes Ribeiro, CC BY-SA: 54.

Bayerische Staatsgemäldesammlungen Neue Pinakothek München, CC BY-SA: 204.

Biblioteca comunale di Trento: 105, 142 (left).

Bibliothèque nationale de France: 26, 52, 103, 107, 109, 110, 114, 119, 122, 226, 236.

British Library: 221; Harley 3011 f. 69v: 91 (right).

Brooklyn Museum, CC BY: 14, 162.

Cleveland Museum of Art: 138

ETH Bibliothek, Zurich: 276.

Folger Shakespeare Library, CC BY-SA: 152-153.

Getty Images: Apic: 262; Scott Barbour: 342; Georges Bendrihem: 345 (left); Bettmann: 280, 284, 285 (top), 309, 314, 320, 322, 323, 324, 352; Bloomberg: 383; CBS Photo Archive: 307; China News Service: 379; Murray Close: 359; CNN: 372; DEA Picture Library: 44, 61; DEA/A. de Gregorio: 111; DEA/G. Nimatallah: 78; DEA/M. Seemuller: 220; Dinodia Photo: 178; Fine Art: 8, 191, 238; Fine Art Photographic: 230; Getty Images for Supermajority: 388; Steve Granitz: 373; Lynn Grieveson: 384; Gijsbert Hanekroot: 355 (left); Heritage Images: 28, 58 (right), 108, 134, 141, 146, 156, 159, 172, 174, 182, 189, 241, 279; Chris Hondros: 349; Derek Hudson: 329; Evan Hurd Photography: 325; Anwar Hussein: 331; Interim Archives: 317; Keystone France: 269, 321; Brooks Kraft: 318-319; Leemage: 1, 22, 77, 213; David Lefranc: 351; Karjean Levine: 369; Haywood Magee: 293; Laurent Maous: 316; Eamonn McCabe/ Popperfoto: 360; Aurelien Meunier: 381; Mirrorpix: 354 (left); Ed Oudenaarden: 302-303; Mariette Pathy Allen: 362; Photo 12: 195; Photo Josse/Leemage: 144; Pictures from History: 81, 133, 222 (bottom); Print Collector: 60 (right); Jo Raedle: 378; Roger Ressmeyer: 339; John Shearer/TAS23: 391; Gregory Smith: 326; Wendy Stone: 350; Justin Sullivan: 367; Topical Press Agency: 264; Ullstein Bild: 17, 57, 124, 272, 292, 334, 353; Underwood Archives: 310 (top); Universal History Archive: 88-89, 106 (left), 137, 245, 270; Universal Images Group: 53, 123, 214, 233 (left); Kerem Yucel: 374

J. Paul Getty Museum: Digital image courtesy of Getty's Open Content Program: 3, 50, 62, 143, 231.

Heritage Auctions: 301.

iStock: Clu: 79; Fbxx: 51; Jpa1999: 55; Nastasic: 25.

LACMA: 39, 101, 158, 181 (bottom).

Library of Congress, Washington DC: 194, 215, 224-225, 229, 237 (left), 243, 244, 247, 251, 252 (left), 253, 257, 259, 261 (left), 261 (right), 265, 266, 268, 277, 286, 288, 291, 299, 300, 304, 327, 330, 335.

Macesito, CC BY-SA: 226.

The MacKinney Collection of Medieval Medical Illustrations: 43.

Metropolitan Museum of Art: 12, 15, 18 (left), 18 (right), 20, 33, 41, 47, 67, 68, 70, 82, 91 (left), 115, 116, 117, 126, 145, 150, 155, 160-161, 170, 177, 181 (top), 200, 203, 205, 206, 255.

Museum of New Zealand, Te Papa Tongarewa: 197.

NASA: 340.

Nationaal Archief/Fotocollectie Anefo: 338.

National Archives and Records Administration: 310 (bottom), 311, 343.

National Archives of Malawi, CC BY-SA: 271.

National Gallery of Art, Washington: 24, 64, 65, 66, 69, 120, 223, 256.

National Gallery of Victoria, Melbourne: 298.

National Library of Norway: 227, 274.

National Museum in Warsaw: 27 (top).

National Museum of African Art, Smithsonian Institution: 118.

National Palace Museum, CC BY: 30.

National Portrait Gallery, Smithsonian Institution: 202, 210, 216, 222 (top), 232, 233 (right), 234, 240 (top), 240 (bottom), 242, 246, 260, 263, 283, 306.

Nationalmuseum/Anna Danielsson, CC BY-SA: 148 (bottom); Cecilia Heisser: 154.

Philadelphia Museum of Art: 164.

Carlo Raso: 112 (bottom).

Rijksmuseum: 31, 34, 58 (left), 72, 163 (right), 165, 179 (right), 185, 192 (left), 193, 196, 207, 208, 211.

Shutterstock: 360b: 355 (right); Anastasios71: 45; Vangelis Aragiannis: 36; ArTono: 173 Astarik: 129; Beibaoke: 80; BGStock72: 63; Josh Bodden: 23; ChameleonsEye: 357; Chrisdorney: 128; Hung Chung Chih: 294; Conde: 10-11; Gil Corzo: 367; Curioso: 48; Rob Crandall: 344; Kobby Dagan: 390 (left); EtaCarinae89: 125; Everett Collection: 183, 184, 187, 190, 234, 254, 289 (top), 297, 368; David Fowler: 366; FrentaN: 83; Eddy Galeotti: 148 (top); Gilmanshin: 7, 59; Vladimir Goncharenko: 99; Lukasz Janyst: 151; JDMatt: 169; Jdwfoto: 375; Jimmie48 Photography: 385; Karasev Viktor: 142:R; Alexander Khitrov: 389; Jerome Labouyrie: 336; Chris Lawrence Travel: 71; Frederic Legrand - Comeo: 382 (inset); Viacheslav Lopatin: 96; Meunierd: 106 (right); Alexandros Michailidis: 363; Dima Moroz: 27 (bottom); Morphart Creation: 21, 40 (top), 175; Liv Oeian: 392 (inset); Sanga Park: 305; PavleMarjanovic: 83; Photocosmos1: 392-393; Celso Pupo: 390 (right); Pvince73: 312 (left); Lev Radin: 371; Anthony Ricci: 345 (right); Marko Rupena: 364; RuslanKphoto: 157; Salvacampillo: 365; Mark Sawyer: 382; Renata Sedmakova: 74; Skunk Taxi: 188; Spatuletail: 37, 87; Stocklight: 348; IR Stone: 46; Repina Valeriya: 40 (bottom) T van de Brink: 32; Wjarek: 73, 112 (top); World of Stamps: 76; Vladamir Wrangel: 19; Yangchao: 306; YashSD: 361; Leonard Zhukovsky: 102.

Shutterstock Editorial: 313.

Miranda Smith, Miranda Productions, Inc., CC BY-SA: 354 (right).

Smithsonian Institution: 312 (right).

SMK Open: 198.

State Library of New South Wales/Mitchell Library: 217.

State Library of South Australia: 250.

Thielska Galleriet/Tord Lund: 252 (right).

UCLA Library Special Collections/Los Angeles Times Photographic Collection, CC BY-SA: 287, 295, 315.

Unsplash/Agatha Depine: 347; Provincial Archives of Alberta: 376; Unseen Histories/National Archives and Records Administration: 337.

Allen Warren, CC BY-SA: 328.

Wellcome Collection: 179 (left), 192 (right), 201, 237 (right), 248; CC BY-SA: 267.

Yale University Library/Cushing/Whitney Medical Library: 104.

Front cover images (left to right, from top row): Franklin D. Roosevelt, Library of Congress; Confucius, National Palace Museum; Ruth Bader Ginsburg, Shutterstock/Rob Crandall; Sitting Bull, Library of Congress; Queen Elizabeth I, Rijksmuseum; Frida Kahlo, National Portrait Gallery, Smithsonian Institution; Barack Obama, Shutterstock/jdwfoto; Charles Darwin, Art Institute of Chicago; Dalai Lama, Shutterstock/Anthony Ricci; Winston Churchill, Library of Congress; George Washington, Metropolitan Museum of Art; Jane Austen, Library of Congress; Martin Luther King, Jr., Unseen Histories/National Archives and Records Administration; Diana, Princess of Wales, Provincial Archives of Alberta; Vincent van Gogh, National Gallery of Art, Washington; Ernest Hemingway, Library of Congress; Amelia Earhart, Shutterstock/Everett Collection; Julius Caesar, Shutterstock/Gilmanshin; Mark Twain, Library of Congress; William Shakespeare, Getty/Heritage

Back cover images (left to right): Plato, Shutterstock/Anastasios71; Sojourner Truth, National Gallery of Art, Washington; King Louis XIV, Shutterstock/Everett Collection; Mother Teresa, National Archives and Records Administration; Oprah Winfrey, Shutterstock/ Everett Collection.

All reasonable efforts have been made to trace copyright holders and to obtain their permission for the use of copyright material. The publisher apologizes for any errors or omissions in the list above and will gratefully incorporate any corrections in future reprints if notified.